MUSLIM KINGSHIP IN INDIA

MUSLIM KINGSHIP IN INDIA

Edited by
Nagendra Kr. Singh

ANMOL PUBLICATIONS PVT. LTD.
NEW DELHI - 110 002 (INDIA)

ANMOL PUBLICATIONS PVT. LTD.
4374/4B, Ansari Road, Daryaganj
New Delhi - 110 002

Muslim Kingship in India

First Edition, 1999
ISBN 81-261-0436-8

PRINTED IN INDIA

Published by J.L. Kumar for Anmol Publications Pvt. Ltd., New Delhi - 110 002 and Printed at Mehra Offset Press, Delhi.

Contents

Contents

Preface

The title "Muslim Kingship in India", is a mythico-historical study of pre- and post- Muslim conquest. The coverage of this study is a unified India under the Muslim rule and present India, Pakistan and Bangladesh is a part of it. This title has been studied in two parts--Muslim kingship before the Muslim conquest and Muslim kingship after the Muslim conquest. I have not included Akbar as a Muslim king in this study for avoiding controversies. After the introduction of new religion--*Din-i-Ilahi*--his acceptance as a Muslim king became controversial subject.

The Muslim king can't be regarded in the domain of law as an omnipotent sovereign answering the Austinian definition. A Muslim sovereign is bound by the sacred law of Islam. The Islamic code stands supreme. The Muslim Kings have usually refrained themselves from asserting their authority so as to mould the sacred law. The *Ulema* and *Mujtahids* have always exercised a tremendous influence over the people, and have served as checks on the royal prerogative.

Acknowledgment of God's authority and His right to issue commands is embedded in our constitution. The sovereignty of law in Islam is unchangeable. The end of law in every legal system is to promote the welfare of men, but the conception of the Muslim law goes further. The welfare of men is not merely in respect of life on this earth, but also of future life, so that imperishability of human life is another postulate underlying the Islamic conception of the law. The Muslim law is fundamentally democratic and opposed in essence to absolutism. It is presumed that every Muslim in *Dar-ul-Islam* knows the laws of the land.

Let us now consider what the *Holy Qur'an* tells us about the institution of Kingship. 'Allah bestows sovereignty on whom He pleases and takes away sovereignty from which He pleases' (3:26). Allah produced not only prophets, but also kings among the *Bani Israil* and the grant of kingdom to them is described as one of Allah's favours to them. The Holy Book has narrated the stories of some of these kings:

(i.) ***Talut*** - who was chosen by Allah for appointment as a king over *Bani Israil*, because he was gifted with knowledge and strength.

(ii.) **David** - whom Allah granted kingdom and gifted him with wisdom and power. He was granted not only wisdom but also sound judgement in speech and decision.

The Holy *Qur'an* also referred some kings who were unbelievers. The Holy *Qur'an* does not specifically abolish the institution of kingship. There is no trace in the Holy Book of any divine right to rule of any individual or family or class or race without reference to the will of the people.

As regards the qualifications of the head of the Islamic State, we would point out that the believers from one single brotherhood, all are equal in the sight of Allah. The most honoured is the one who is the most pious. Allah's promise of granting power and authority in the land is for those who believe and work righteous deeds, and this authority is to be granted to them not for their personal aggrandizement or for selfish ends, but for establishing Islam in the land, for suppressing wrong and oppression, and for securing peace and prosperity.

Apart from the perfect faith and high morals, the king must possess wisdom, knowledge of sound judgement and good physical strength. It is not Islam and its doctrines which have devastated in the western Asia and brought about the present sad state of things but it is tyranny of the Muslim princes or kings who have wilfully perverted the doctrine of the prophet-- and efficaciously distorting and crushing all liberal principles, they have prevented the dawn of the Muslim Renaissance.

The present title "Muslim Kingship in India" has been compiled in twelve chapters, which is broadly classified in two parts-Muslim Kingship before the Muslim conquest and Muslim kingship after the Muslim conquest in India. First chapter throws light on the theory of kingship in Islam. Historicity of the *Somari* dynasty is described in second chapter however third chapter gives analytical description of the rulers of Multan. Fourth chapter deal with the political scenario of Sindh in the time of Abbasid Caliphate. The *Habari* dynasty of Sindh has been discussed in fifth chapter, while sixth chapter throws light on the Muslim colonial centres in India.

Historicity of Muslim kingship after the Muslim invasion has been described in six following chapters in second part of the book: Muslim conquest of Delhi, the kingship of Timurlane, Humaun flight and restoration, the accession of Jahangir, Aurangzeb accessing to the throne and subjugation of Eastern India. Besides these chapters, we have enclosed comprehensive bibliography and Index for advance study. In this study, I have not included the reign of Akbar to avoid controversy, though he was prominent ruler of the Mughal dynasty.

I am thankful to all those scholars whose works have been utilised in compilation of this work. I am also thankful to Indian Muslim for my inclination of Islamic study.

Delhi Nagendra Kr. Singh

Chapter - 1

Kingship in Islam

It has been observed that politics and religion according to the Semitic conception were more or less identical and synonymous. The institution of *Khilafat* bears both a spiritual and temporal character. The Arabs in addressing the *Khalifah* used the word *Imam*[1] which signifies the leader of prayers in the mosque. Out of the Imamate the idea of sovereignty and kingship took its root. The later Muslim jurists who have philosophically dealt with the theory of sovereignty point out monarchy as a necessary institution, and further according to their view kingship was an indispensable condition precedent to civilization.

The *Umayyads* themselves recognised that a change had come in the nature of the Islamic Empire, in fact Muawiyah openly said that he was the first king of Islam. The democratic principles of Islam were trampled down, and instead absolute sovereignty came into existence.

The *Umayyad* dynasty was thrown over by the *Abbasides* (in A.D. 749) who ruled the Muslim Empire for the next five centuries. The Muslims of Spain who were originally under the Umayyads, passed under the rule of the fugitive prince Abdur Rahman, who declared himself Khalifah of Islam also. In the meanwhile, the Fatimids Khilafat as rival to the Abbasides had come into existence in Egypt, it was destroyed by Sultan Saladin.

In A.D.1258, the Abbaside Empire was shattered by the great conqueror Hulaku Khan, and the last of the Abbaside took refuge in Egypt, he continued to be recognised as the spiritual Imam and Khalifa in all its old glory, till Sultan Salim obtained in his favour renunciation of the office of Khilafat. Thereafter the Ottoman

Sultans were recognised as the lawful Khalifahs of Islam. The institution of Khilafat has ceased to exist since the deposition of the last Ottoman Khalifa Abdul Majid by the National Assembly of Angora.[2]

The traditional custom of electing a Khalifa was reduced to mere formality, nevertheless sometimes the ceremony was performed in all its old glory. Here is an interesting sketch depicted by Von Kremer:

> "The only and exclusive source of sovereignty and power was election by the assembled community of Muslims... the successor to the throne went to the chief mosque... ascended the pulpit and delivered his inaugural address which was followed by election and homage."

On such an occasion the Umayyad Caliphs appeared dressed completely in white. The Abbasides were clad in black.....on such occasions the Caliph was decked with the insignia of Sovereignty.[3] For deposing a Sovereign the people generally met in the chief mosque. Some man of position addressed the assembly when charges were formulated and made against the ruling Caliph and his deposition was declared in the interest of Islam.[4]

Later on election and homage were paid in a great State Assembly in the presence of State officials and judges. When the Umayyads succeeded in establishing an equally glorious dynasty in Spain, they transplanted at the Court of Cordova the characteristic principles of pomp and magnificence of Damascus. The spectacle at Cordova was equally majestic.

The Ottoman Sultans also preserved the idea of free election. Each new Sultan was solemnly elected by the Ulema and divines of Constantinople, and they acted in the capacity of representatives of the Muslims. Thus the theoretical position though it had been modified still maintains the broad characteristic of free election.[5] However, the succession to kingship was not altogether hereditary.

It is true that first Muslim King Muawiyah secured succession for his son, but out of the fourteen rulers of the Umayyad dynasty only four had their sons as successors, and all of them (even though it be nominally) were elected. The cases of a minor being elected are very rare, for instance when Muqtadir was to be being elected are very rare, for instance when Muqtadir was to be elected the *Kazi*, Musanna refused to elect and pay homage to him. He observed:

"I would not elect a boy to be a Khalifah."[6]

This firm attitude cost him his life.

As regards the Ottomans, kingship was not absolutely hereditary, the eldest son usually did not succeed. The Sultan's successor was the eldest and fittest member of the royal family. During the reign of the Umayyads the following were the chief offices:

1. The *Diwan-ul-Khiraj* the board of land tax which was in the nature of the Department of Finance.
2. The *Diwan-ul-Khitam*, the Board of the Signet, the ordi nances after being sealed were issued.
3. The *Diwan-ul-Rasail,* the Board of correspondence.
4. The *Diwan-ul-Mustaghillat,* The Board of Revenue.
5. The *Nasir-ul-Masalim,* the judiciary. Every province had a Governor, a Kazi and a police officer.

The Abbasides were the first to create the office of *Wizarat* (Prime Minister), it is admittedly of the Persian origin. When the *Buwayyid* Sultan had virtually taken the Khalifa under their tutelage the office of *Wizarat* came more into prominence. There were two kinds of *Wizarat*: (1) unlimited, (2) limited. The *Wazir* with unlimited powers was called the Grand Wazir. He practically exercised the prerogatives of the Sultan without preliminary sanction while it was necessary for the limited *Wazir* to obtain Sultan's sanction for his administrative acts.

The Governorship of the provinces was also divided into unlimited and limited ones like the *Wizarat*. They exercised only temporal powers. It should be noted that the Governors appointed by the *Khulfa-ur-Rashidun* occupied different position, they were the representatives of the Khalifa, in not merely administrative, military, financial and judicial matters but also in all spiritual and religious matters of Islam. During the reign of the Abbasides the following were the chief offices:

1. The *Diwan-ul-Khiraj*, the Board of Taxes.
2. The *Diwan-ul-Dhiyya,* the Board of the Crown lands.
3. The *Diwan-ul-Zamimah*, the Board of Accounts.

4. The *Diwan-ul-Jund Wal Shaqiriyya*h, the Military Board.
5. The *Diwan-ul-Barid*, the Post Office Board.
6. The *Diwan Zimam Wa Nafaqatt* the Board of General expenditure.
7. The *Nasir-ul-Masolim* the Board for the administration of Justice.

The recent Ottoman Sultans had a cabinet of ministers almost of modern type with the exception of the *Sheikh-ul-Islam* who occupied a unique position and shared in "the spiritual life" of the Khalifa. The following are the four chief offices as founded in the *Qanun Namah*, the fundamental laws of the Turks:[7]

1. The *Wazir*
2. The *Kazi Asker*, the Military judge
3. The *Dafader*, the Finance Minister
4. The *Nichandji,* the secretary

Fifty years after the dawn of Islam, kingship was established all over the Muslim world. It is true that some of the Muslim Kingship, the Umayyad dynasty like Yazid I, Walid II and Marwan III or of those of the Abbaside dynasty like Mustanjid and Muqtadir discredited Islam; but such reigns cannot cast a melancholy shadow on the splendour and glory of the reigns of Umar bin Abdul Aziz or Mansur or Harun and Mamun. The great potentates of the Umayyads and Abbasides and those of the Ottomans like Muhammad II and Salim compared favourably with the greatest of the ruling dynasties known to the world.

The Islamic culture was at once brilliant and varied. In philosophy, astronomy, medicine, surgery, mathematics, physics. Chemistry, architecture, manufacture and trade the Muslims were the pioneer. The works of Socrates, Plato and Aristotle were critically studied and new results were arrived at by Ibn Rushd (Avirtoes) Abu Ali Sina (Avicenna) and al-Farabi. Ibn Rushd was also an astronomer. Abul Hasan (Abhazen) was a great physicist Jabir (Geber) is recognised as the Patriarch of Chemistry. Amir Yaqub is credited with the invention of artillery.

The Muslim architecture is famous all over the world. The Arabs were great traders. The poetical works of Sadi, Jami, Umar Khayyam and Hafiz are appreciated throughout the world. The Muslim Jurisprudence was greatly developed by jurists like Imam

Jafar, Abu Hanifi'i, Shafi, Malik and Hanbal and their followers. The Umayyads of Spain were equally renowned for their rule.

The most autocratic of the Muslim King cannot be regarded in the domain of law as an omnipotent sovereign answering the Austinian definition. A Muslim sovereign is bound by the sacred law of Islam. [8] The Islamic code stands supreme. The Muslim kings have themselves usually refrained from asserting their authority so as to mould the sacred law. The Ulema and Mujtahids have always exercised a tremendous influence over the people, and have served as checks on the royal prerogatives. Acknowledgment of God's authority and His right to issue commands are embedded in Islamic constitution.[9]

The sovereignty of law in Islam is unchangeable. The end of law in every legal system is to promote the welfare of men, but the conception of the Muslim law goes further; the welfare of men is not merely in respect of life on this earth, but also of future life, so that imperishability of human life is another postulate underlying the Islamic conception of the law.

The Muslim law is "fundamentally democratic and opposed in essence to absolutism."[10] It is presumed that every Muslim in *Dar-ul-Islam* knows the laws of the land. To this extent the maxim "*Ignorantia juris non excusat*" applies to the Muslim law.[11] "When the law is promulgated in Dar-ul-Islam, the mission of the law-giver is complete, and a person who remains ignorant of the law, is due to his own negligence and not to the non-publicity of the law and hence his ignorance is not excusable"

The conception of the Muslim State is the institution of Khilafat as the supreme executive. This idea was translated into facts, it was realised only for a short period during the *Khilafat* of *Khulafa-ur rashidun* and then vanished from the angle of vision of the Muslims. Sir William Muir observed, "The Caliphate ended with the fall of Bagdad. The illusory resuscitation by the Mamluks was a lifeless show; the Osmani Caliphate a dream [12] and "that while the Umayyad Caliphate from first to last, was coordinate with the limits of Islam, this is no longer true of the Abbasides."[13]

In my opinion, the real Islamic institution of Khilafat—which is the admiration of the world and the pride of the Muslims—

perished with the first followers of Islam, it has ever since been a dream. But the Muslim ideals are imperishable they stand out to day in all their ancient splendour as testimony to the Golden age of Islam. They are our heritage not for adoration and worship, but to be followed by acts and precepts to achieve a new era for mankind.

Islam stands for the welfare of humanity. Vambery has well depicted the scene, "It is not", he says, "Islam and its doctrines which have devastated the western portion of Asia and brought about the present sad state of things, but it is the tyranny of the Muslim princes who have wilfully perverted the doctrines of the Prophet... and efficaciously distorting and crushing all liberal principles they have prevented the dawn of a Moslem Renaissance."[14]

References

1. Abu Bakr was called successor to the Prophet but `Umar respect fully declined to take this title, saying that he was unfit for this honour and he was content to be called Imam and also *Amir-ul-Muminin,*
2. March, 1924.
3. S. Khuda Buksh, *The Orient under the Caliphs,* p. 252.
4. *Ibid.,* p. 268,
5. The orthodox view that the Quraish are only eligible for the office of Khalifahhas never been accepted by the Muslim world. The Shia on the other hand confine eligibility for the office of Khalifa to the House of Ali only.
6. S. Khuda Buksh, *Op. Cit.*, p. 257.
7. Sir, E. Erasy, *History of the Ottoman Turks*, p. 158; " The dome of the State is supported by four pillars" .
8. J. Bryce admits this (*Studies in History and Jurisprudence,* p. 90), he says, "In all Muhammadan countries the monarch is legally, as well as practically, restrained by his inability to change the sacred Law."
9. The theory of some jurists is that the origin of law is to be found in a primordial covenant entered into between God and man.
10. A.H. Lybyer "the Turkish Parliament" *Proceedings of the American Political Science Association,* Vol. VII, p. 67.
11. Ignorance of fact is in some cases a ground for exemption under the Muslim law.
12. Sir William Muir, *The Caliphate,* p. 596.
13. Ibid., p. 132.
14. *Western Culture in Eastern Lands,* p. 357.

Part - I

Muslim Kingship before the Muslim Conquest

2. The Somrah Dynasty
3. The Rulers of Multan
4. Sindh in the Time of the Abbasid Caliphate
5. The Habari Dynasty of Sindh
6. Muslim Colonial Centres

Chapter - 2

The Somrah Dynasty

The few doubtful years of the eleventh King and the period of the last King are not included in the reckoning. If these few years be added, their period of rule is at least 375 years, and if the beginnings of their rule be traced to some time after Sultan Abdu-r-Rashid (i.e. 444 A.H.) the date of the end of their rule will be 819 A.H. But it has been mentioned that the end was reached during the time of Mohammad Shah Tughluq in 752 A.H. Hence the period of their rule seems to be 67 years ahead of the period mentioned.

The End of the Somrahs

During Muhammad Shah Tughluq's time began the conflict between the Sultan of Delhi and the Somrahs. In the last days of Muhammad Shah Tughluq' a Mughal named Taghi revolts in Gujarat and on the King approaching flees away to Thath and takes refuge with the Somrahs. The King goes on chasing him and reaches Thath. Here he encounters a united army of the Mughals and Somrahs. Suddenly the King goes off his head and dies there. The kingless army suffers severe hardships at the hands of the Mughals and Somrahs and finds a way out of this two-edged difficulty by electing Firuz Shah as their King and goes back to Delhi. This is an event of 752 A.H.[1]

But a few years after when Firuz Shah comes here in 762 A.H. he finds here the Kingdom of the Jams. Jam Unar and his nephew Banhabnah become rulers. Jam was the title of the Kings of the Samah dynasty. This shows that this is the period which marks the end of the Somrahs and the beginning of the Samahs. 752 A.H. is given as the date of the beginning of the Samahs in *Tuhfatu-l-aram* which shows that this revolution took place after the invasion of

Muhammad Shah Tughluq. According to Firishta, the Muslims had a large share in it.

It appears that, after the revolt of the Ismailis or Hindu-looking Somrahs, the Muslims in general, thought it advisable to destroy the Somrahs through a native tribe newly converted to Islam. A leader of the Samah tribe named Unar murdered the last ruler of the Somrahs named Hamir (Amir) whose verbal version is Armail and established his sway.

The list of Somrah Kings and the fixing of their period of rule from the critical point of view need a lot of research work. It behoves our Indian historians to exert themselves a little. For instance, when a year or two before 620 A.H. Sultan Jalalu-d-din Khwarazm Shah fled away from the Tartars to Sind, the Somrah King named Jalsi was fleeing away, and having loaded his goods in boats, took refuge in some island.[2] This name -- Jalsi is not found in the list. The Nawalkishore edition cannot be relied upon.

It is possible that Jalsi is the corrupted form of Chanesar the 14th number in our list. Likewise in 734 A.H. at the time of Ibn Batutah's arrival in Sind the King was Unar. This name, too, is not found in that list but it is possible that it is the same name which occurs as Umar in the 18th number.

Samah

The Samah who held possession over Sindh after the Somris had their capital at Thath, called Deybal by the Arabs. Persian historians write the plural of Samah as Samagan and English authors as Sammas, forming the plural by adding an s. Hence some people have been deceived into describing their name as 'Sammas.' They were Muslims by religion though it is a matter of dispute whether they were Muslims from the beginning or were converted later on.

Their capital was Thath. Jam was the official title and the name was a mixture of Indian and Arab elements. For example the name of a famous Samah King was Jam Nanda Nizamu-d-din. They were so powerful that they held out against the Sultan of Delhi for a long time. They ruled over Sindh for one hundred and seventy-five years from 752 A.H. to 927 A.H.

There is a lot of divergence among historians regarding the origin of this class too. Some historians of Sind have recognised them to be of Arab descent and hold that they were descended from Abu Jabal. Later Persian historians, Firishta and Abul Fazl's *Ain-e-Akbari*, have called them the descendants of the Persian King Jamshed simply on the score of their title, Jam. But this baseless theory is due to the resemblance between Jam and Jâm. European historians like Elliot,[3] the writers of the Encyclopaedia Britannica[4] and the Encyclopaedia of Islam[5] call them Rajputs converted to Islam.

But none save the last-mentioned have taken the trouble of backing their statements by arguments. The pith of the argument of the last-mentioned is only this much-that Jam was the title of the Rajput Rajas of Cutch and Nawanagar. The truth is that this theory is backed even by the statements of some old historians. It is written in Tarikh Masumi that Samahs came from Cutch to Sind.[6]

It appears from Chach-Namah that the Samahs were settled down in Sind even before Muhammad bin Qasim (96A.H.). When Muhammad bin Qasim reached their settlement they greeted him with songs and music and were highly pleased. Muhammad bin Qasim appointed Kharim son of Umar.[7] as their chief. Tarikh-i-Tahiri says that thus the country on the sea-coast came into the possession of the Samah whose progeny exists even now. Rai Bhara, Jam Sahta, Chhota and the Rajas of Cutch belong to this clan.[8]

We came across a sentence in Tarikh Baladhari, a book of 297 A.H. Its translation runs thus : "Then Daud bin Yazid bin Hatim was appointed Governor of Sind. With him had gone the father of Samah who holds Sind under his control now a days. He is a slave set free by the Kandah clan." [9]

Should it be understood that the descendants of this very Samah came to be known as the Samah clan and that quite possibly they might have settled down in Cutch and that they snatched away Sind from the Somrahs in 752 A.H.?

Samrah Kings

The Samrahs appeared on the scene at a later time, that is, when the Muslim Government was firmly established in Delhi.

the names and titles and dates of Samah Kings are more definitely known. According to Firishta the detail of these Kings is as follows: "During Shah Mohammad Tughluq's reign the efforts of Mussalmans made the Government of Sindh slip out of the hands of Somrahs into those of the Sammas. Many chiefs of this clan were Muslims and often they owed allegiance and paid tribute to the Sultans of Delhi. Sometimes they raised the standard of revolt.

The first person who became their king in Islamic times was Jam Afza Unar or Wanar.[10] He was very wise and ruled for three and a half years. After him ruled his brother Jam Juna who was a lover of justice. He was succeeded by his son Jam Mani who revolted against the Sultan of Delhi. In 762 A.H. Sultan Firuz Shah attacked him. At first he was unsuccessful. Then on coming back from Gujrat the Sultan attacked him. At last Jam Mani made peace.[11]

The account of this war and treaty has been detailed by the historian Siraj 'Afif who saw things with his own eyes. He has written the name of the then Jam as Unar and has mentioned his nephew Banhabnah as the joint ruler. The power of the Samahs can be estimated from the fact that he encountered Firuz Shah, the Sultan of Delhi, with forty thousand infantry and twenty thousand cavalry. Owing to lack of commissariat the Sultan was unsuccessful and, leaving Sindh, he went to Gujrat. Next year when he came back he again attacked the Jam who was constrained to make peace. This is an event of 762 A.H. (1361 A.D.).

Sayyid Jalalu-d-din Huseyn Bukhari, who was a pious and God-fearing man and whose name has occurred in the religious account of the Somrahs, lived in Uch. The Jam, after holding consultations, sent a messenger to him asking him to come and request the Sultan to forgive his fault. The Sayyid came, and the King received him with the fullest devotional favour. He gave hopes to both sides. Taking the Jam and the joint ruler Banhabnah with him he introduced them to Firuz Shah and the terms of armistice were laid down.[12]

Name of Samha Kings

Mir Masum and Firishta have written the names and the period of Samah Kings. There is a slight difference between the two regarding some early names. For example, the name of Kheyru-d-din is not mentioned in Firishta but instead Jam Mani is written.

It is possible that Mani and Kheyru-d-din denote one person. There is slight difference regarding some last names too.

No.	Name of Kings	Period of Rule
1.	Jam Unar or Wanar or Unar	3 years six months.
2.	Jam Juna, brother of Jam Unar bin Banhabnah	14 years. Contemporary of Alau-d-din Khilji.
3.	Jam Tamaji	15 years ---do.----
4.	Jam Kheyru-d-din	16 years ---do.----
5.	Jam Banhabnah	..
6.	Jam Tamaji	..
7.	Jam Salahu-d-din	11 years.
8.	Jam Nizamu-d-din bin Salahu-d-din	2 years and a few months.
9.	Jam Ali Sher bin Nizamu-d-din	6 years and a few months.
10.	Jam Karan bin Jam Tamaji Jam Unar's dynasty having had its day, another dynasty of the Sammas sat on the throne. The name of the first King of this dynasty was Fath Khan.	One day and a half.
11.	Fath Khan bin Sikandar	15 years.
12.	Jam Tughluq bin Sikandar, brother of Fath Khan	28 years.
13.	Jam Mubarak (a near relation of Jam Tughluq)	3 days.
14.	Jam Sikandar bin Jam Fath Khan bin Jam Sikandar	1 year six months.
15.	Jam Rai Waran. (he was a Muslim)	Came from Cutch in 858 A.H.
16.	Jam Sanjar (a chief of Samma clan)	8 years and a few months. the
17.	Jam Nanda Nizamu'd-din,	62 years.
18.	Jam Firoz bin Jam Nanda	Last king.

In 890 A.H. during the reign of Jam Nanda, Shah Beg Arghun came from Qandhar and invaded Sind; but success did not crown his efforts. After Jam Nanda there was warfare between Jam Nanda's son named Jam Firuz and another relation-claimant, Jam Salahu-d-din for the throne. Jam Salahu-d-din, was the paternal cousin of the

cousin of the wife (Begum) of Sultan Muzaffar, ruler of Gujarat. Sultan Muzaffar of Gujerat helped Jam Salahu'd-din. Jam Firuz sought help from Shah Beg Arghun who, taking opportunity by the forelock, conquered Sind in 927 A.H.and exterminated the Sammas for ever.[13]

The dates of the Kings mentioned above total 192 years but the period between 752 A.H. and 927 A.H. is only one hundred and seventy-five years. Perhaps the years of Jam Nanda's rule are given more than the actual period ruled by him. One cause why there are so many names is slet two persons of that dynasty ruled jointly, for which we have the testimony of Siraj 'Afif.[14]

Religion of the Sammas

The Sammas were Muslims but it is still a mystery as to when they embraced Islam and to what sect of Muslims they belonged, and no attempts have as yet been made to unveil it. Historians have ascertained the history of their religious changes by means of their Indian and Arab names.

For example, Firishta has taken the first four Kings whose names in serial order are Jam Unar, Jam Juna, Jam Mani and Jam Tamaji to be Hindus and is of opinion that the chain of Muslim Kings starts from Jam Salahu-d-din. He writes, "And from the names of the persons mentioned and from the name of Tamaji in particular, it appears that they wore the sacred thread (i.e. were Hindus).

But the truth is that one should not be misled by the character of their names. The first name is Jam Unar. We have already learnt from Ibn Batutah's statement that the Somrah at that time whose name was Unar, was not a Hindu and thought himself to be a Muslim. He was so much offended at Hindu suzerainty that he revolted against the Sultan of Delhi and adopted the royal title of Malik Firuz. The Jam whose period of rule has been specially commended in Tarikh-i-Tahiri was Jam Nanda and his father's name is mentioned as Banhabnah.[15]

Jam Rai Waran is an entirely Hindu name but when he came from Cutch and conquered Thath he proclaimed that he had come only to defend the territory of the Muslims.[16]

imitation of the Sultans of Delhi. The Jam who adopted the title of Kheyru-d-din had lived with his father for a pretty long time at the Court of Delhi.[17]

The last king, Jam Nanda, combines both Indian and Arab elements in his name. Nanda seems to be the tribal name and Nizamu-d-din the Arab royal title. The name of the Jam who fought against Sultan Firuz Shah has been mentioned by Shams Siraj as Rai Unar .[18] It is a Hindu name but circumstances indicate that he was not a Hindu but a Muslim by religion.

It is evident that if the opinion that they were Arabs is correct, they must have been Muslims from the very beginning. If they were Hindus, we guess that they did not become Muslims after climbing the throne but that they were Muslims long before gaining the throne and were Sunnis. Before describing the circumstances which lead us to think so, we want to describe the pious person and his chain (of followers) through whose efforts this clan entered the pale of Islam. Arnold has written merely by guess-work that this tribe became Muslim through Arab merchants.[19] But we personally think that the motive cause was Sufism instead of commerce.

References

1. *Tarikh-i-Firuz Shahi*--Ziya Barni, pp. 523-525 (Calcutta).
2. *Firishta*, vol. 2, p. 316 (Nawalkishore).
3. *Tarikh-i-Hind*, vol. I., p. 497.
4. The article on Sind, vol. 25, p. 143 (Eleventh Edition).
5. The article on Samma.
6. *Maisumi* (Elliot) p. 223.
7. *Chach Namah* (Elliot) p. 191.
8. Tabri (Elliot) p. 268.
9. Baladhari p. 445 (Leiden).
10. In the Nawalkishore Press edition of Firishta the name of this *Jam* is *Afza* but this is a mistake of the copyist or the MS. The correct word is *Unar* or *Wanar* Or *Oonar* as is found in Ibn Batutah and Siraj Afif.
11. *Tarikh-i-Firishta*, Vol. 2, p. 317 (Nawalkishore Press).
12. *Tarikh-i-Firuz* Shahi Shams Siraj Afif pp. 240.
13. Firishta, vol, 2, p, 320 (Nawlakishore).
14. *Tarikh-i-Firuz Shahi,* pp, 199 247 (Calcutta).
15. Tarikh-i-Tahiri (Elliot), p. 273.
16. Tarikh Maisumi (Elliot), p. 231.

15. Tarikh-i-Tahiri (Elliot), p. 273.
16. Tarikh Maisumi (Elliot), p. 231.
17. Ibid p. 225.
18. *Tarikh-i-Firuz Shahi* - Sham Siraj `Afif, p. 199 (Calcutta).
19. *The Preaching of Islam* (Urdu translation) p. 292 (1907 A.D.)

Chapter - 3

The Rulers of Multan

It has been mentioned above that Multan was annexed by the Arabs in the first century A.H. (7th century A.D.) and remained from that time to Mahmud's time under Arab rule. Every Arab traveller of the third and fourth centuries has mentioned it. Even at the time of Mahmud's invasion and afterwards there were Muslim settlements here. In the beginning, this town, like other towns of Sind, was within the ambit of the Omayyad dominions. After thirty or forty years the wheels of fortune took a new turn.

In 132 A.H. the 'Abbasids replaced the Omayyads and held in their hands the reins of the Islamic empire. The centre of government shifted from Damascus to Baghdad. Multan remained bound up with the 'Abbasid Government till Mu'tasam's time. Then it happened that whenever a king was powerful he kept intact his possession over distant towns. But if the king was weak, the governors of the towns became independent. Multan remained under the governors of Sind and Mansurah for some time; but later threw off the yoke of Sind and became a self-governing State. The date of this independence is probably the middle of the third century A.H.

Multan denotes not a single town but a whole province which was sometimes a State, nay, a kingdom. Mahalabi, Minister of Egypt, wrote in the fourth century A.H.: Its boundaries are wide. It extends up to Makran on the west and up to Mansurah (Sind) in the south.[37] The Kannauj, which lay near the river Sind, was included in Multan in 300 A.H.[38] According to census reports there were one lac and twenty villages within the orbit of the Islamic State of Multan.[39]

Persian historians were not familiar with the first and second dynasties. However, according to the statements of Arab travellers, they were pure Arabs. The Persian historian were familiar, because of Sultan Mahmud with the third dynasty. In this connection a few corrections can be made. The Arabic patronymic of him whom they called Abu'l-Futuh was Abu'l-fath and the name they wrote as Nasir was, according to the oldest authority of Gurdezi Nasar.

This verbal correction is important because Firishta and others described them to the Lodis and Pathans whereas the names Shaikh Hamid, Nasar, and, Daud are pure Arabic names and Nasar instead of 'Nasir,' is the purely Arabic origin. The patronymic Abu'l-Fath or Abu'l-Futuh is a particular feature among the Arabs. Particularly Abu'l-Futuh and the honorific title of 'Shaikh' are purely Arabic.

Among the Ismaili Batinis (Esoterics) the word 'Shaikh' was specially used in the sense of ' Amir' since it had more a religious than a political significance. Hasan bin Sabbah was known as Shaikhu'l-Jabal. Hence the story that they were Lodis and Pathans is a fiction. Even the existence of Islam among those people at that time can hardly be recognised. Three different line of rulers had emerged in Multan:

(a) Manbah bin-Asad was descended from the Qureysh family of Asmah bin -Lowa'i. This family is known as Banu Manbah. There are unmistakable signs its existence from 290 A.H. to 340 A.H. (from Ibn-Rasta to Istakhrii)

(b) Jalam bin Sheyban who, according to Beruni, is the first Qirmati or Ismaili to have possessed Multan, flourished between 340 or 367 A.H. and 375 A.H., that is between Istakhri or Ibn Hauqal, and Bashari. Bashari is the first Arab traveller who mentions the relation between Multan and the Fatimids of Egypt.

(c) Shaikh Hamid's son was Nasir and his son was Abu'l-Fath or Abu'l-Futuh Daud Qirmati. Shaikh Hamid was contemporaneous with Alaptagin and Sabuktagin, that is, his period and that of his son Nasar(if he ever was ruler) can be placed between 351 A.H. and 390 A.H. Sultan Mahmud's contemporary was Abu'l-Fath Daud. Hence the period of his rule extended from 390 A.H. to 396 A.H. (the date of the first conquest of Multan) or even to 401 (the second conquest of Multan and the capture of Daud).

On this ground, it can be said that Shaikh Hamid, Shaikh Nasar, and Abu'l Futuh Daud were Arabs by descent and were descended from Jalam bin Sheyban. A famous Indian author[1] has written an entirely baseless statement that Abu'l-Futuh Daud was the same person who is famously known in the History of Sind as Somrah and that Somrah was his Hindu and Abu'l-Fath his Islamic name. This error is due to his assumption that the same dynasty ruled both in Multan and Mansurah.

Since the ruler of the Multan line was Abu'l-Futuh and that of the Sind line was Somrah, he took the two names to be those of one person. This is entirely erroneous. From the preliminary sentences of the letters in Kitabu'd-Duruz written to "the Mowahhidin (Unitarians) of Multan and India in general and to Shaikh Ibn Somar Rajah Bal in particular" it cannot be proved that Ibn Somar was the ruler of Multan. Nor has any historian mentioned Somar's name in connection with the Multan rulers; nor is there any authority for believing that way.

The connection of the Somrahs was with Sind alone which was an independent State entirely separate from Multan. The unanimous verdict of Arab travellers goes to prove it. This much is proved from the letters that Abu'l-Fath Daud, ruler of Multan, and Somrah subscribed to the same faith and probably, after the downfall and incarceration of Abu'l-Fath, Somrah became the spiritual head (Shaikh and Imam) of the Carmathians of Sind.

One thing can be said concerning all this. It was a rule with the Ismailis that, for the convenience of preaching their faith among many peoples, to declare hereditary nearness with those peoples in order to draw them closer. Thus Shaikh Hamid and others might have declared themselves Pathans in order to draw the Pathans closer to themselves. They were not in any way connected with the Hindus; nor were Hindi words used with their names.

Mixture of Indo-Islamic Culture

In Multan there was a delightful mixture of Arab and Indian cultures. The town was beautiful, though small. There were sepa-ate markets for every profession and calling. There was a rampart wall all round the town. Outside Multan, at the place where there were military barracks for the Amir's army, there were tall buildings. Beruni has said that in the town there was a mosque built by Muhammad bin Qasim (probably between 340 A.H. and 375). Jalam bin Sheyban, the Ismaili Qirmati closed it down as an Umayyad relic. He demolished the famous idol-house dedicated to the sun-god and built a Jami Mosque on its site. When Sultan Mahmud conquered Multan (in 396 A.H. or 403 A.H.) he opened the former mosque and left the second dilapidated. At the time when Beruni wrote his book (in 424 A.H.) it had become levelled to the ground and henna trees were standing there.

Istakhri (340 A.H.) has written that 'the Amir of Multan goes on an elephant to the Jami' mosque to say his Friday prayers. The Arab Amirs had come to like immensely this elegant conveyance of the Hindu Rajas'. Again, he says that the inhabitants of Multan put on pyjamas and the majority of the people speak Persian and Sindhi. In fine, the Hindus and the Muslims had become similar in matters of dress and religion.

Regarding the manner of dress and the language spoken, Ibn-Hauqal (367 A.H.) makes the following statement: "The Hindus and the Muslims here dress alike. There is the custom of growing long hair in Multan. In Mansurah, Multan and their suburbs, Arabic and Sindhi are spoken. The inhabitants of Makran speak Persian and Makrani. `Kurtas' (loose and long garments) are worn, but the merchants, like the people of `Iraq and Persia, use shirts and sheets"[2].

Bashari came here in 375 A.H. He has drawn a fine picture of the culture and manners prevailing here. He says:

> "Multan is smaller than Manusurah but is more populous. Fruits, though not many, are cheap .... And, as in *Seyraf* (the port of `Iraq), so also here there are many-storied buildings of the `*Sal*' wood. No corruption, no liquor-drinking. Those who are found guilty of this offence are killed or punished severely."

In their transactions of sale and purchase they do not lie; nor do they weigh less than what ought to be weighed. They treat travellers courteously. The majority of the inhabitants are Arabs. They drink canal water. There is fertility and opulence. Trade is in a flourishing condition. Sufficient luxury. The Government is just and impartial. In the bazar will be found no woman who is embellished. Nobody will talk to a woman openly on the road or street. The water is fine; life is lived happily; there is mirth and courtesy here. Persian is understood. Trade is fairly lucrative. The people are healthy, but the town is dirty. Houses are narrow. The air is warm and dry. The people are wheat-coloured and dark.[3] The coinage of Multan has been fashioned after the Fatimid coinage but mostly *Qanhriyyat* are current.[4]

Mansurah

To the Arabs the largest town of Sind was Brahmanabad whose original Indian name, as is mentioned by Beruni, was Bahamnawa. The Persians called it Brahmanabad and this name became current among the Muslims. Later on, military and political necessities compelled the Arabs to build their own towns of which Mahfuzah Beyda and Mansurah became very famous.

In the last days of the Umayyads when Arab power wavered and the Sindhis began to drive them towards the coast, the Arab Governor at that time, Hikam bin Awanah Kalbi mustered all the Arabs at one place and built a town named Mahfuzah on the other side of the river.

Amru who was a brave man and a politician and the son of Muhammad bin Qasim was also with Hikam. He performed all the duties of Hikam. He built Mansurah on the sea-coast at a distance of two farsakhs from Brahmanabad [5].

In the days of the Abbasids, that is, during the period of Mu'tasim Bi'llah (mid third century A.H.), when a member of the Barmakid family 'Imran bin Musa bin Yahya bin Khalid was appointed Governor of Sind, he built a town named Beyda. But fate had ordained fame and immortality for Mansurah.

The founder of Mansurah

Why was this town so called? Some wrongly thought that it was built during the time of the Khalifah Mansur the 'Abbasid and hence became known as Mansurah. This is entirely wrong as this town was already built in the time of the Umayyads. Likewise, Mas'udi has ascribed it to Mansur bin Jamhur[6] who had become the ruler of Sind when the Umayyad power was on the wane and the 'Subside empire was being established. But this is not correct.

One should not be misled by names. Its founder, as is stated by our oldest authority Baladhari (d.279) was 'Amru,, son of Muhammad bin Qasim. Hence Mansurah (Victorious) like Mahfuzah (Safe and Secure), was a name of good omen.

The Date of its Foundation.

Hikam, during whose time 'Amru built this town, was sent by Khalid bin 'Abdullah Qasri the Amir of 'Iraq. Khalid became Amir of 'Iraq in 105 A.H. and was dismissed in 120 A.H. Hikam was the second Governor of Sind sent by Khalid, so his period probably dates from 110 A.H. On this hypothesis, the date of the foundation of Mansurah should fall somewhere between 110 A.H. and 120 A.H.

First of all Ibn Khardadhbah (250 A.H.) mentions it as situated on the banks of the river Sind.[7] Again, Baladhari (279 A.H.) says, " It was built a little away from the river.[8] " Ibn Hauqal and Istakhri have both written that it was built on the banks of the river Mahra at such a place that the river, branching, turned it into an island."

Some Arab geographers have given its latitude as 93^0 from the west and 12^0 from the south.[9] Luckily I have before me the map of Sind prepared by Ibn Hauqal in his own time. It shows that at a little distance from the place where the river Sind, after traversing the Punjab, flows into the Indian Ocean, there is a new branch of the river which, turning at a little distance, rejoins the river.

Due to the area of land covered by this branch, on the banks of the river a small plot of land is formed into an island. The town was built here and, surrounded by water on all sides, was guarded against the sudden attacks of invaders. It was just like Seringapatam which has been formed by the turns and twists of the Kaveri in Mysore. There is a similar town in Trichinopoly too (within the boundaries of Madras). According to the ancient military science, such places were very strategic.

Abu'l -Fazl has, in his '*Ain-i-Akbari*,' solved the intricacies and unravelled the skein of knots. He says that the old name of

Bhikar, a famous town of Sind, was Mansurah.[10] The truth is that the whole geographical account of Mansurah exactly applies to it. Abu'l-Fazl says,. ''Here all the six rivers unite into one, and, then, divided into two, flow below it, one to the south and the other to the north.'' The name of Bhikar is very familiar in Indian histories and is known even to this day.

Mansurah was safe on account of its situation and it lay on the river-bank and near the sea. It was suitable for the incoming and outgoing of traffic from Arabia and 'Iraq as, in times of danger, they could edge away. Hence very soon it became the Arab capital in Sind.

In the 3rd century A.H., we hear its name mentioned as a capital. Baladhari (d. 279 A.H.) says in the description of Mansurah, ''This is the town where Hukm now a days stays."[11] All the later Arab travellers mention it in that capacity and at last it became the ''*Daru'l-Amarah,*'' or capital of the Qureyshite Arab Kingdom.

References

1. The late Maulvi `Abdul Halim Sharar wrote it on pages 9 and 12 of the second volume of his *History of Sindh.* Perhaps the Maulana was misled by Elliot's remarks (Vide Vol. 1, p. 491).
2. *Safarnamah-i-Ibn Hauqal p.* 232 (Leiden).
3. *Ahsanu't-taqasim* by Bashshari p. 48 (Leiden).
4. *Ibid*, p. 482. Qanahri seems to be some ordinary coin. Elliot `has written `Qandhariyat' and he suggests that these coins were minted in Qandhar. This isbaseless and is a mere invention.
5. *Futuh`u'l-buldan* by Baladhari p. 444 (Leiden).
6. *Maajmu-udh dhahab* Vol. I p. 379.
7. *Al-Masalik wa-l-Mamalik* by Ibn Khardhadhbah p. 174.
8. Ibid., p. 444 (Leiden).
9. *Mu'jmu'l-buldan* by Yaqut, word Mansurah.
10. *A`in-i-Akbari* vol. 2, p. 160 (Nawalkishore Press).
11. *Futuh`u' l-buldan* by Baladhari p. 444.

Chapter - 4

Sindh in the Time of the Abbasid Caliphate

The province of Sindh remained bound up with the centre at Baghdad till the days of Caliph Al-Ma'mun (218 A.H.). But, even in the last days of the 'Abbasids, Arab Amirs began to dream of independence. Fadl bin Mahan a slave of the Samaides conquered a town of Sandan and got the 'sanad' or authority for Amirship direct from Al-Ma'mun. He built a mosque[1] in which Friday prayers were said and the Khutbah was read in the name of the Khalifah.

After him, his brother Muhammad bin Fadl bin Mahan became the ruler and his period corresponds to that of Al-Mu'tasam bil'llah (227 A.H.). He attacked the Medes with a fleet of seventy ships. During his absence his brother, Mahan conquered and possessed the State, and perhaps these family feuds explain why the Kingdom slipped out of Muslim hands.[2] During the time of Al-Mu'tasam bi'llah, Muhammad bin Khalil proclaimed his independence in Qandabil but an officer of Mu'tasam named Imran Barmaki Governor of Sind, captured the chiefs of that place and sent them to Qasdar (Qazdar).[3]

During the time of 'Imran Barmaki exactly the same family feuds ensued between two Arab tribes Yamani (Qahtani) and the Hijazi (Nazari) as had put an end to the Umayyad supremacy. 'Imran sided with the Yamanis. At that time the leader of the Hijazis was a Qureysh chief 'Umar bin 'Abdul 'Aziz Habari who taking opportunity by the forelock, murdered 'Imran.[4]

The Habari Qureysh Dynasty of Sind

During the Prophet's time there was a certain person named Habar bin Aswad of the Banu Asad who was a sworn enemy of Islam and the Prophet. At last he embraced Islam in 8 A.H. at the time of the conquest of Mecca. One of his descendants had come to Sind with Hikam bin 'Uwanah Kalbi Governor of Sind. The grandson of this man was 'Umar bin 'Abdul 'Aziz Habari[5]. His genealogy is:

> "Umar, son of Abdul Aziz, son of Mundhir son of Zubeyr, son of 'Abdur Rahman, son of Habar son of Aswad."

During the Umayyad and the 'Abbasid periods this family had a share in influencing the trend of State affairs.[6] Becoming the leader of the Hijazis he killed Imran. The natural consequence was that Umar bin Abdul 'Aziz Habari assumed the rulership of Hijazi Arabs in Sind.

During the reign of the Khalifah Al-Mutawakkil when Harun bin Khalid, the Governor of Sind died, 'Umar bin 'Abdul 'Aziz sent a petition to the Khalifah's court requesting him to hand over to him the province of Sind in 240 A.H. The Khalifah granted his petition. Ya'qubi (d.278 A.H.), who wrote his book in 259 A.H.:

> "Harun bin Khalid, the Governor of Sind, died in 240 A.H."

Umar bin Abdul Aziz Sami, who descended from Samah bin Luwa'i and who had established his rule over Sind, wrote that he was administering the country quite well. Al-Mutawakkil granted his request and during the period of Al-Mutawakkil's caliphate he remained the permanent ruler.[7]

Ya'qubi's statement, describing 'Umar bin 'Abdul 'Aziz as a descendant of Samah bin Luwa'i, is not correct. Umar bin 'Abdul 'Aziz descended from Habar bin Aswad, who descended from Ka'b bin Luwa'i(v.Ibn Khaldun vol. 6, p.327, Egypt). Probably Ya'qubi has confused them with the Amirs of Multan who were Samaids.

However, even after the rule of 'Umar bin 'Abdul'Aziz Habari the 'Abbasid connection remained intact. In Al-Mu'tamad's reign (256-279 A.H.) the name of Sind appears in connection with the Baghdad administration, since it was during this period that, together with Turkistan, Sajistan and Kirman, the province of Sind was also entrusted to Ya'qub bin Leys, the founder of the Safari family of Khurasan.[8]

In 261 A.H., Al-Mu'tamad handed over to his ambitious brother Al-Mowaffaq the province of Sind together with the other Eastern countries. At the same time on the Arab and 'Iraqi coast of the Persian Gulf, the Qaramitah raised the standard of revolt while in the west rose the movement of the Ismaili Fatimids which in the end travelled up to Egypt.

Probably this is the time when the former nominal relation of Sind with Baghdad was snapped away. Baladhari, who died in 279 A.H. writes:

> "Samah son of Abu's-Samah who was a freedman of the Banu Kandah and who had come to Sind with an 'Abbasid Governor of the early 3rd century named 'Umar bin Hafs bin Hazar, has forcibly become an independent ruler of Sind."[9]

But it appears that the descendants of 'Umar bin 'Abdul 'Aziz had little peace of mind. 'Umar bin, 'Abdul 'Aziz Habari himself lived in Baniah a town in Sind.[10] But his descendants, having gained permanent possession of Lower Sind, made Mansurah their capital.

In 270 A.H., Abdullah, son of 'Umar bin 'Abdul 'Aziz Habari was the ruler of Mansurah. It was in his time that the Hindu Raja of Alra (Alwar in Sind) asked him for a Muslim preacher and scholar to acquaint him with Islam.[11] When Mas'udi came here in 303 A.H. he found 'Umar, son of 'Abdullah, ruling at Mansurah. He found there many Arab chiefs, Sayyids and members of the 'Alwai family too. The names of the King and the Wazir were 'Umar bin 'Abdullah and Riyah and the Qadi was of the family called Al-Abi'sh Shawarib respectively. The exact words of Mas'udi are:[12]

> "At the time I reached Mansurah, Abu'l-Mundhir 'Umar bin 'Abdullah was the ruler. It was there that I saw his minister Riyah, both his sons, Muhammad and 'Ali, and also an Arab chief who was one of the rulers of that place and who was named Hamzah."[13]

I also saw many descendants of Hazrat 'Ali bin Abi Talib who come from the lineage of 'Umar bin 'Ali and of Muhammad bin 'Ali. The family of the rulers of Mansurah, and that of the Qadis (this family being known as Al Abi'sh-Shawarib) had between them ties of relationship. The rulers of Mansurah are the descendants of Habar bin Aswad who are known as Banu Umar bin Abdul Aziz.

After Mas'udi came Ibn Hauqal in 367 A.H. The same family was ruling up to that time. Though there was no political or administrative tie yet the religious tie existed even now. They mentioned in the Khutbah the name of the 'Abbasid Khalifah. The exact words (of Ibn Hauqal) are:[14]

> "The ruler of the country is a Qureyshite who is said to come of the lineage of Habar bin Aswad. His ancestors ruled here and now he is the ruler. In the Khutbah was read the name of the 'Abbasid Khalifah."

When Maqdisi came here in 375 A.H., he found the same family at the head of the Government. But the influence of the Shi'a Daylami which ruled over Persia was extending through Baluchistan to Sind. But the Khalifah of Baghdad still continued to have hold of the magination of the people. Bashari says:[15]

> "Mansurah is ruled over by a Sultan of the Qureysh family. But in the Khutbah is recited the name of the 'Abbasid Caliph, and sometimes the name of 'Adadu'd-daulah (Deylami). When I was in Shiraz, an ambassador from this place had gone to the son of 'Adadu'd-daulah."

Ibn Hauqal says that Mansurah was one mile long, one mile broad, and was surrounded by rivers on all sides. The inhabitants were Muslims. Bashari says:

> "Mansurah is the central town of Sind and the capital. It is like Damascus. The houses are made of wood and clay. The Jami`mosque is made of bricks and stone and is large. Like the mosque of `Umar, it is supported by pillars of the '*Sal*' wood. It is situated in the centre of the market. There are four gates to town-Babu'l-Bahr (The River gate) Bab Turan, Bab Sandan Bab Multan." [16]

There were various towns of Sind within the radius of this Arab Kingdom. Bashshari says that Mansurah was the capital of Sind and among the towns were Deybal, Zandrij, Kadar, Mayal Batli. Istakhri mentions other towns too-such as Baniah, Sadusan Alwar, Saubarah Saymur, Masudi says:

> " There are three hundred thousand villages and hamlets etc., within the ambit of the Mansurah Kingdom."

It can give an idea of how large the Kingdom as Mas'udi again says:

> "There are fields and trees every where, and the population is interspersed.[17]

From this one can guess the prosperity and population of Mansurah. Masudi says:

> "The inhabitants of Mansurah are constantly at war with the Medes, a clan in Sind. The King has eighty military elephants. The rule is that there is a force of infantry five hundred strong for each military elephant. Of these, two elephants are very famous and brave fighters. The name of one was Munsir Qals and that of the other was Haydarah and they were tamed."[18]

Mas'udi has, in a way, told us the whole military strength of Mansurah. If there were five hundred fighters for elephant, there would be an army forty thousand strong for eighty elephants.

Literary and Religious Condition of Mansurah

The best account is given by Bashari in his Safar Namah. He says, "The inhabitants are good-natured and courteous. Islam is in a flourishing condition. There is plenty of learning and there are lots of scholars. They are of quick intelligence and sharp wit. They do pious deeds and spend sums in charity.[19]

> "The non-Muslim subjects *(Ahl-e-dhimmah)* worship idols. There are no preachers among Muslims. Most of the Muslims are '*Ahl Hadith*'. It saw here, Qazi Abu Muhammad of Mansurah who was a Daudi and an Imam of his faith. He had a circle of pupils. He is an author. He published many good books........In the large towns are found Hanafi theologians too. But there are no Malikis or Hanbalis or Mutazalis here. Their ways are ways of virtue. They are virtuous and chaste."[20]

The existence of *Ahl-i-Hadith* at such an early date is very surprising. Daudi does not signify Daudi Bohras but the followers of Imam Daud Zahiri who were a kind of *Ahl-i-Hadith.* Masudi says, "There is a separate language in Sind apart from the languages of India. Bashari says about Deybal, the port of Mansurah,

> "Only merchants live here. The languages spoken are Sindhi and Arabic."[21]

It can be guessed that Arabic had a powerful and lasting influence upon the language of Sind, as can be found even today. Arabic words are mixed up in the Sindhi language as in Urdu, most lasting influence is found in the fact that even today the Sindhi script is Arabic exactly as it was before.

Extinction of Mansurah

Nothing clear is known about the extinction of the Arab Kingdom of Mansurah. It is certain that it existed till Bashari's time (375 A.H.). Fifteen years later began Mahmud's invasions. In 416 A.H. Sultan Mahmud's famous invasion of Somnath took place, and on his way back he took the route to Sind from Gujarat. He pressed on from Sind on the banks of the river Sind to Multan and from Multan to Ghazni.

Historians have explained that he passed through Mansurah.[22] But Ibn Athir in his *Tarikhe Kamil* has an important sentence in his narrative of the events of that year.[23] ''And the Sultan intended to go to Mansurah. The Governor of Mansurah had turned an apostate. When he learnt the news of the Sultan's approach, he went out of the town, and, together with his men, hid himself in bushes. Sultan Mahmud gave chase to him. Many were killed; many drowned themselves in the river; a few were spared. The Sultan pressed on to Ghazni through Bhatiya.[24]

The question is, ''What is meant by turning an apostate''? If the ruler of Mansurah was not declared an apostate merely to justify Mahmud's incursion, it will mean that the ruler of Mansurah had like the ruler of Multan, perhaps become an Ismaili Qirmiti. We have the evidence of Bashari, who came 41 years before.

He testifies that the people of Mansurah were Sunnis, nay, Ahl Hadith (followers of Tradition). However that may be, it is proved that the Habari kingdom was annihilated in 416 A.H. at the hands of Sultan Mahmud. The famous research scholar Ibn Khaldun says on one occasion, while describing the family of 'Umar-bin-Abdul Aziz:

> ''One of the descendants of Habar bIn Aswad was `Umar bin`Abdul `Aziz who, in the turmoil following the murder of Al-Mutawakkil, brought Sind under his dominion. His descendants ruled over Sind one after another until they were blotted out by Sultan Mahmud. They had their capital at Mansurah.''[25]

Considering the stress that Bashari, who was a theologian, lays in 375 A.H. upon the people of Mansurah being conscientious Sunnis (Ahl sunnah) it seems difficult to believe that in 416 A.H.

they became Qaramitah. It is proved from Ibn Khaldun's statement that Sultan Mahmud snatched away the kingdom of Sind from the hands of the Habari Amir. It appears from Ibn Athir's statement that the Sultan learnt about the Amir from whose hands he snatched away the kingdom that he had turned an apostate that is , he had become a Ismaili Qirmati.

It has been mentioned above that unless the people of Mansurah were declared Qirmati Ismailis simply to give the Sultan a pretext for invading Mansurah, we can infer from Ibn Athir's statement that the Qirmatis had swamped the Sunni Habari dynasty after 375 A.H. or it may be inferred that after Multan had slipped out of their hands, they established their rule over Sind, and Sultan Mahmud blotted out this Qirmati kingdom in 416 A.H.

The Letter of the Druses

The Druse letter from which a quotation has been given is very important in this connection. It is written in the Druse letter sent by the religious leaders (Imams) of the Duruz of Syria, ''Addressed to the Muwahhidin (Believers in the Unity) of Multan and India in general and to Shaikh Ibn Somar in particular.''

In this letter Ibn Somar Rajah Bal was the legitimate heir of Bhotawra and Haudal Hila. The names of many other scions of the family are mentioned, some of which are Arabic and some Indian. He tries to excite their sense of shame thus:

''O revered Rajah Bal ! exalt thy family.''

Bring back the Mowahhidin and younger Daud within the pale of true faith.

Masud who has recently set him free from slavery and imprisonment has done so because he wants thee to perform thy duty against his nephew 'Abdullah and against all the inhabitants of Multan for which thou hast been appointed, so that the believers in (holiness) Taqdis[26] and 'Tauhid' (Unity of God) may be distinguished from the rebels and those who are steeped in darkness.[27]

Very important conclusions can be inferred from this letter:

(1) The Somars, who were inhabitants of Sind and later on founded the Somarid dynasty, were Ismailis.

(2) Their names were both of a Hindu and an Arabic character. This shows that the family was Indo-Arabic or compound-

ed of Arab and Indian elements.

(3) The rulers of Multan, Abu'l-Fath Daud, etc., and the Somaris of Sind were followers of the same faith.

(4) Somar was probably the Sheykh or Imam of the Ismailis. The Ismailis used Sheykh to denote their religious leader.

(5) It appears that Abu'l-Fath Daud left behind him a son known by the name of Daud Asghar or the younger Daud and set free by Sultan Mas'ud on his recanting the Isma ili faith.

(6) 'Abdullah Abu'l-Fath was the maternal grandson of Daud Akbar or the elder Daud, and nephew (sister's son) of Daud Asghar whom the people of Multan wanted to make their Amir.

(7) This letter was designed to make Ibn Somar Rajah Bal incite his clan to fight against Sultan Mas'ud, 'Abdullah and the people of Multan, and restore the lost power of the Qirmati Isma'ilis. In Multan attempts at restoration of the lost power were made, but they were fruitless.

(8) The last important thing which is inferred from this letter is the powerful personality of Somar, that he was a powerful and influential person. If Somar's son was the contemporary of Sultan Mas'ud, it should be said that Somar was the contemporary of Sultan Mahmud (d.421 A.H.)

(9) It was the Somaris who, twenty years after the date of this letter, during the weak Government of Sultan 'Abdur Rashid bin Mahmud Ghaznawi (d.444 A.H.) became rulers of Sind instead of the Ghaznawis.

Relic of the Habari Dynasty

Though the material relics of the Habari Kings have been lost for ever, yet a spiritual relic remains extant for ever and that is the family which migrated from this place to Multan and lived under the sheltering care of the Ghaznawis; Shaikh-ul-Islam Zakariya of Multan was born in 578 A.H., and died according to Firishta, in 666 A.H., and, according to Akhbaru'l-Akhyar in 661 A.H.

Shaikh Abdul Haqq of Delhi has described him as Asadi[28] that is, as belonging to the tribe of Habar. Shaikh 'Aini'd-din of Bijapur links him up in descent with Hazrat Habar bin Aswad bin Muttalib bin Asad[29]. Pirzada Muhammad Huseyn Sahib in his Urdu translation of Ibn Batutah, has quoted an Arabic excerpt from an old book

'Khulasatu'l-A'arifin found in the collection owned by the present descendants of the Shaikh.

This excerpt is quoted from the sayings of Sayyid Jalil Bukhari. The genealogical table given in the book also proves it. There are two histories connected with the coming of the Sheykhu'l-Islam's family to India. One is that he came to India in the first century A.H. with the Arab conquerors of Sind, as is found in Ibn Batutah.

The second is that he came to India from Arabia in the fifth century A.H. The two do not clash. This family arrived in Sind in the 2nd century A.H., and after the extinction of Mansurah went to Multan and settled down there under the protecting care of the Ghaznawi Kingdom. But the statement of his coming here via Khwarazm, as found in Firishta, is not correct.

A more important statement is by the author of Tarikh-i-Tahiri that Sheykh Bahau'd-din was a Sindhi and an inhabitant of the later Muhammad Tur built in the Sukkur district by the Samah tribe after the destruction of the earlier Muhammad Tur.[30]

Sind Under the Ghaznawis

That Sind was in the hands of the Ghaznawis till 444 A.H. is proved by the fact that tributes from Sind were sent till the time of Abdu'r-Rashid Ghaznawi (444 A.H.). After him the Ghaznawi Kingdom was embroiled in anarchy and turmoil, but nominally the Ghaznawis continued to be rulers of the Punjab and Sind.

In 578, the Ghorites began to muster strength and power in Sind. Nasiru'd-din Qabachah, a general of Shihabu'd-din, established his dominion over Sind, and Iltamish over Delhi. At last Iltumish defeated Qabachah and expelled him out of Sind. From that time Sind was really independent, though it was nominally bound up with Delhi. In the time of Muhammad Shah Tughluq (752 A.H.) Sind slipped out of the hands of one local ruling tribe into the hands of another local ruling tribe.

In 792 A.H., Sultan Firoz Shah peacefully brought it into his possession and entrusted it to local rulers in whose hands it continued to remain till 927 A.H. when Arghun, a Tartar Amir, conquered it. At last at the end of 1000 A.H. it came into the possession of Akbar the Great.

We are not concerned with the history mentioned above. We have to consider only two self-ruling tribes of early history - Somari and Samah. The local tribe which possessed Sind during the days of Ghaznawi was known as Somari.

The other local tribe which came to the head of the Government of Sind in 752 A.H., during the days of Muhammad Shah Tughluq, and which continued till 927 A.H. (1521 A.D.) was Samah. There is a lot of divergence among historians regarding the origin of the two tribes. Ths nationality and religion of the Somaris in particular are very debatable points.

From the reference to the letter of the Druzes which has occurred above it is clearly proved that is 422 A.H. (the period of Sultan Masud) Sheykh Ibn Somar Raja Bal was the ruler; he was an Ismaili; and the Imam of the Duruz tried to shame him into re-establishing the Isma'ili supremacy over Multan and Sind. No wonder that, on the breakdown of the Ghaznawi power, the Somaris established their rule over Sind in the time of Sultan Abdu-r-Rashid (444 A.H.).

This Kingdom of theirs lasted somehow from 444 A.H. to a few years after 734. In this connection Ibn Batutah's evidence is of the utmost importance. He came to India through Sind in 734 A.H., when the Somari tribe was ruling over Sind, and it owed allegiance to the Emperors of Delhi. Ibn Batutah, who had seen them, says, "Then I arrived at Janani.[31] which is a large and handsome town on the banks of the river Sind and which has lovely bazars.

The inhabitants are called Samirah who settled down here, as historians have written, at a time when Sind was conquered during the time of Hajjaj. The Samirah do not dine with anybody; nor can anybody see them dining. Nor do they intermarry with others. The name of their ruler (Amir) at this time is Wanar, whom I will describe later on.

Further he describes Siyustan and Sihwan (Siwan is now in Karachi district):

> "In this town live the Samirite Amir, Wanar, described above, and Amir Qeysar Rumi, and both are under the supremacy of the Sultan (of Delhi). Both had eighteen thousand horsemen."

There was a Hindu here named Ratan and he was a financial expert. He went to the Sultan's Court with some nobles.

The King liked him, gave him the title of the Rajah of Sind, invested him with the insignia of a Rajah and sent him to Siyustan which he gave him as a jagir when he arrived there. Wanar and Qeysar were highly offended at the supremacy of a disbeliever (Kafir) over them. They took counsel together and killed him ...and robbed the treasury.

All the people elected Wanar to be their King, giving him the title of Malik Firuz. Then Wanar, thinking that he was away from his tribe, was frightened and went away to his tribe...The soldiers made Qeysar their King...when the Viceroy of Multan learnt this news, he sent an army for chastisement and punished him severely. Ibn Batutah arrived at that time and put up at a Madrasah. He could not sleep on account of the stinking smell emanating from dead bodies.

1. The Samiris link up the settlement of their ancestors with the arrival of Hajjaj bin Yusuf Thaqfi.
2. They were not Hindus by religion. Nor did they like Hindu domination. There are some things which mark them off from Muslims in general.
3. At that time Sind was under the domination of the Sultan of Delhi. A Resident of the Sultan used to live with the Samiris.
4. In administrative affairs Sind was immediately under Multan and under Delhi through the medium of Multan.

Religion of the Somaris

Their faith in Ismailism is proved by the Druze letter but a few more points emerge from Ibn Batutah's statements. It appears obviously from Ibn Batutah's statement that the Somaris came with the Arab conquerors of India. It is evident that they were not Rajputs; but this also is evident, that they had adopted some particular non-Islamic customs with regard to eating, drinking and marriage.

Nevertheless, they did not call themselvesHindus but thought themselves to be Muwahhids (believers in the Unity of God) and Muslims. They adopted the Islamic title of Malik Firuz and considered it an insult and a degradation to be ruled over by a Kafir. So decidedly they were not Hindus. Such a motley religion was that of the Qirmitis and the Isma'ilis who made a juxtaposition of Islam with local customs and beliefs.

In India, they described Hazrat 'Ali as the incarnation of Vishnu and they included other such things in their code of belief. This facilitated the propaganda for their religion in every land. It is proved from histories that in early times propagandists came to Sind from Qil'ah ul-maut of the Isma'ili.[32] This custom of juxtaposing doctrines was found among them. They also adopted Hindu names and even today such instances can be found among the Khojas of Bombay.

In this connection is found a strange incident connected with the life of Makhdum Jahanhan Sayyid Jalalu'd-din Bukhari who was a disciple of the disciple of Sheykhu'l-Islam Zakariya of Multan. The description of Sayyid Jalalu'd-din Bukhari will come later. He lived in the town of Auj in Sind and numbers of people rallied to him. It is written that the ruler of Auj who was a Somra once came to him. There was a crowd of dervishes. 'Somra' turned one of them out of the mosque without Hazrat's permission. Instantly the Hazrat remarked:

> "Magar divana shudai" (Perhaps thou hast gone off thy head).

At that very time he became insane. The whole town was filled with the news of this event. At last his mother came and entreated Hazrat. The fault was forgiven. He recovered his senses, came to the mosque and kissed Hazrat's feet, recognised him as his spiritual leader and was among the chosen ones. May it be inferred from this incident that he recanted the Isma'ili faith and became a Sunni.

The Isma'ili Fatimid Kingdom of Egypt was put an end to by Sultan Salahu'd-din. After that Hasan bin Sabbah's Isma'ili (Nazari)Kingdom of Qila'ah-ulmaut existed from 483 A.H.(1090 A.D.) to 654 (1256) when Hulaku's sword shattered it into smithereens. The effect of the destruction of the real centre upon the Ismailites of Sind is evident. Hence it is quite possible that the Somris or some of them took to the Sunni faith through the initiation of Jalal Bukhari.

In order to solve the problem of the nationality of Somras, we should study the accounts given by ancient historians. You have heard the earliest statement of Ibn Batutah that they described their ancestors as having settled down in Sind at the time of the conquest of Sind by Hajjaj bin Yusuf. Then we havc the statement of Mir Mohammad Ma'sum author of Tarikh Ma'sumi, in the second chapter of which he says.[33] Sultan Mahmud conquered Multan and Sind. During the time of Sultan 'Abdu'r-Rashid (441-444 A.H) when the Kingdom was weakened by his levity, they threw the Ghaznawi yoke off their neck and the Somra tribe assembled at Thari and elected one named Somrah to be their King.

In the neighbourhood there was a powerful Zamindar (land-holder) named Sa'd with whom he came in contact and whose daughter he married. The fruit of the union was a son who was named Bhonkar who succeeded his father after the latter's death.[34] (MirMa'sum goes on to describe his descendants, some of whom bore Arabic names like Khafif and 'Umar and some of whom bore Hindu names like Duda).

The author of *Tarikh-i-Tahiri* has mostly written stories and fictions. He begins his book with 'Umar Somrah or the age of Somrah and with the love affairs of a Hindu lady. In this connection he says:

> "It was a Hindu tribe. It followed the Hindu religion. It ruled from 700 A.H. to 843 A.H. They had their place near Alwar and Muhammad Tur was their capital."[35]

In the *Beglar-namah* only this much is found that after the Islamic conquest of Sind the Arab tribe of Tamim ruled over it. After some time the Somars possessed it and remained in possession of it for four hundred years. The name of their capital was Mahatam Tur.

How amazing is the fact that the name of their capital, like the names of their persons, was Indo-Arabic. Sometimes it is Muhammad Tur and sometimes Mahatam Tur. It is said that Mahatam is the inversion of Muhammad. It is just possible that it may be so. It was situated between Joparkar and Dangabazar in the district of Deyrag which lay where modern Chachgam and Badban stand.

The author of *Tuhfatu'l-Karam* has quoted the following from *Muntakhabu't-tawarikh* (not that by Badauni) written by Muhammad Yusuf. "When Sultan Abdur Rashid bin Sultan Mahmud became the ruler of Ghazni the people of Sind found him a weak King. In 445 A.H. (1053 A.D.) the Somrahs assembled in Thari, elected as their King one named Somrah to whom was born a son named Bhangar from the daughter of Sa'd a zamindar (landholder).

Bhangar ruled for five years and died 461 A.H.[36] Again the same author says:

> "the Somrahs are descended from the Arabs of Samara who came to Sind in the 2nd century A.H. with the tribe of Tamim. Tamim was appointed Governor of Sind during the Abbasid regime."

Again he says:

> "Dalva Rai was the Rajah of Sind. He was merciless to his brother 'Chhota Irani' who went to the Khalifah of Baghdad who ordered seventy Arabs and Sayyids of Somrah to go with him. Sayyid settled down in Sind and Dalva Rai gave him his daughter's hand."[37]

The author of Tarikh-i-Tahiri[38] has explained the cause of the quarrel between Dalva Rai and his younger brother. The younger brother had leanings towards Islam from his very boyhood. He had read the Qur'an and had become a Muslim at heart. He went secretly for pilgrimage (to Mecca). On his way he married in a strange manner a girl named Fatimah. On his return journey when he reached Sayustan in Sind he died and was buried there. His grave attracted numbers of people.

All these quotations indicate that this tribe was of a mixed Indo-Arab descent. Those who describe it as Arab mention one aspect; those who call it Hindu point out another aspect. Somar, as is apparent from the Druze letter and Persian histories, was the founder of this Kingdom.

Hence the tribe came to be known as Somari Samarah etc. It has nothing to do with Samarra a town of 'Iraq. That town was originally Sarra man ra'a which in course of time, became known as Samarah among the masses. The 'Abbasid Khalifah Mu'tasam bi'llah (227 A.H.) had built it.

European historians have described them as Rajputs converted to Islam. The writer of the article on Sind in the

Encyclopaedia Britannica has written the same thing.[39] Elliot also attempted to prove it but none of them have backed their statement by arguments. It appears from the remarks of Persian historians that they were not pure Hindus. How, then, could they be pure Rajputs.

Maulvi 'Abdul Halim Sharar has written a strange thing - that they were Jews converted to Islam. Maulvi Sahib had this suspicion because a sect of Jews was Samari which was ascribed to the mountain of Shamrun in Syria. Another cause of this suspicion was a sentence of Bashshari which the late Maulvi Sahib has twisted to suit his purpose.

The fact is that in the description of sects and communities in his preface he has shown the particular importance of the numeral (4) and written, " The non-Muslims from whom poll-tax (*Jizya*) is levied (*ahludh-dhimmah*) are divided into four classes:

> "Jews, Christians, Fire-worshippers (*Majuss*) and the Sabaeans. Then there is the objection that Samrahs too are *ahlu'dh-dhimmah* and thus there are five classes instead of four. The objection is met by the statement that the Samrahs are a sect of the Jews. They also recognise Moses as their prophet."

These are the words in the original MS. In a marginal note the Editor has quoted words from another MS. in which the objection has been met. "The idol-worshippers of Sind too live in an Islamic country. Thus *ahlu'dh-dhimmah* should be divided into five" Bashshari says in answer:

> "The idol-worshippers of Sind are not *ahlu'dh-dhimmah* since they do not pay the Jizya (poll-tax)[40]. Hence *ahlu'dh-dhimmah* are only four classes."

The late Maulvi Sharar having seen 'Sind' below 'Samrah' linked them together and put forth a baseless theory. Bashshari's *Ahsanu't-taqasim* still exists, which everybody can consult for himself and arrive at the real fact.[41] That this name is found among Shia Ismailis is strange. Perhaps it is Unar as found in Siraj ' Afif Its pronounciations are Oonar or Wanar or 'Unar as is found in Ibn Batutah and some Persian histories of Sind.

References

1. A Jami mosque is one in which Muslims congregated for Friday prayers (Translator).
2. Baladhari, p. 446.
3. *Ibid* p. 445.
4. Baladhari, p. 446.
5. *Ibid.*
6. Ibn Khaldun, Vol. 2, p. 327.
7. *Tarikh Ya`qubi*, Vol. 2, p. 599 (Leiden).
8. *Tarikh Ibn Khaldun*, Vol. 3, p. 343 (Egypt).
9. Baladhari, p. 445.
10. *Ibn Hauqal - Dkrhu's-Sind.*
11. *Aja'ibul-Hind by Buzurg Shahryar*, p. 3 (Leiden).
12. *Muruju'dh-dhahab* by Mas'udi, vol. I, p. 377.
13. Dr. Bird, quoted by Elliot (vol. 1, p. 488) has quite misunderstood the sentence when he says, "The descendants of Hamzah Saiyyad ush-Shohada settled down hers."He was misguided by the word Hamzah. This Hamzah is not the uncle of the Prophet but some Arabhief of that name. Mas'udi is mentioning Hamzah and not his descendants. Hazrat Hamzah (uncle of the Prophet) had no male children 'nor did his progency multiply.
14. Safarnamah Ibn Hauqal, *Dhikru's-Sind.*
15. *Ahsanu't-taqasim* by Bashshari, p. 485.
16. *Ahsanu'ittaqasinm* p, 479.
17. *Muruju'dh-dhahab* vol. 1, p. 378.
18. *Ibid.*
19. *Muruju'dh-dhahab*, vol, 1, p 379; Ahsanu't-taqasim, p. 479.
20. *Ahsanu't-taqasim*, p. 481.
21. *Muruju'dh-dhahab*, vol, i, p. 281.
22. *Zeynu'l-Akhbar* by Gurdezi, p. 87 (Berlin).
23. *Kamil Ibn Athir*, Vol. 9, p. 243 (Leiden).
24. Elliot has, with reference to Ibn Athir, written, "Sultan Mahmoud appointed a Mussalman as king of Mansoora." But in Ibn Athir is found not this sentence but the statement, I have given above. He made the mistake because he relied on some European translation.
25. *Tarikh Ibn Khaldun*, vol, 2, p. 327 (Egypt).
26. The Ismailis iterate and reiterate `Tauhid' and Taqdis, as they deem it a heresy to believe in attributes of God-head as the Sunnis do. They believed in the negation of qualities which, according to their faith, meant Tauhid and Taqdis. This was the doctrine of the Mu`-tazilahs too, and hence they called themselves *Ahl `adl wa tauhid.*
27. Elliot, *op. cit.*, Vol. 1, p. 491.
28. *Akhbaru'-l-Akhyar*, p. 26 (Hashim Press, Meerut).

29. Firishta, vol, 2 p. 404 (Nawalkishore Press).
30. *Tarikh-i-Tahiri*-Elliot p. 256.
31. There is no trace of this town. It seems that it was destroyed by the river. A bu'l-Fazl also does not mention it.
32. *The Preaching of Islam* by Dr. Arnold, p. 293.
33. Firishta, Vol. 2, p. 416 (Nawal Kishore Press).
34. *Tarikh Ma`sumi* - from Elliot vol. I, p. 215.
35. *Tarikh-i-Tahiri,* Elliot, pp. 260 and 484.
36. *Tuhfat-ul-karam,* Elliot, Vol, I, p. 844.
37. *Ibid.,* p. 848.
38. *Tarikh-i-Tahiri*, Elliot p. 258.
39. Eleventh edition, vol 25, p. 143.
40. *Ahsanu't-taqasim* by Bashshari, p. 42 (London).

Chapter - 5

The Habari Dynasty of Sindh

The Kingdom of the Habari dynasty ruled over Sind, was stamped out, a few people of that family migrated to Multan. Among them was the blessed man of immortal fame known as Shaikhu'l-Islam Bahaud-din Zakariya. He flourished from 578 A.H. to 666 A.H. He had visited the great Islamic countries and it was due to his efforts that Multan became a centre of learning and spirituality.

Sayyid Jalal Bukhari, a famous Sufi, came from Bukhara to Multan and became Shaikh Bahu'd-din's disciple. The name of Makhdum-i-Jahanyan Sayyid Jalalu'd-din Huseyn Bukhari, grandson of Sayyid Jalal Bukhari, has occurred above twice (born 707 A.H. died 800 A.H.).

It was a custom with the great Sufis of those times to send their able and seasoned disciples far and wide to guide people and serve their spiritual needs. Shaikhu'l-Islam Zakariya Multani thus sent Sayyid Jalal Bukhari I to Uch, a town in Sind. Those were the last days of Somra rule in Sind. You have heard how the Somra Governor of Uch came to have faith in him and how he became his Murid.

It is evident from *Tarikh-i-Tahiri* that Shaikh ul-Islam Makhdum Zakariya Multani had relations not only with Sind but with the Sammas (Tahiri has written Somrah instead of Samma but it should be Samma in view of the period he mentions) and perhaps the secret of sending one of his greatest disciples to this district lay here. The following is a summary of the passages of *Tarikh-i-Tahiri*. From 700 A.H. (1300 A.D.) to 813 A.H. (1439 A.D.) for a period of 143 years a Hindu clan named Somrah (Samma) ruled over Sind. The capital was Muhammad Tur.

Not only I but many others have seen its ruins in the district of Virak. After its destruction, many inhabitants migrated and settled down in the district of *Sokura* (*Sukkur*) which was populated during the time of the Jams of Samma. They populated a village here and named it Muhammad Tur. Shaikhu'sh-Shuyukh Makhdum Bahau'd-din (Zakariya), Mulla Khalifah Sindhi, who is very famous in India, eminent people and big Zamindars live in this village.[1]

The other incident has been mentioned above--how the Somrah Governor of Uch received bey'at at the hands of Jalalu'd-din Huseyn Bukhari (707-800 A.H.), grandson of Sayyid Jalalu'd-din Bukhari, who was given the spiritual leadership of Sind by his spiritual teacher Makhdum Shaikh Bahau'd-din. According to Firishta:

> ''He went to the mosque, kissed the feet of the Sayyid, apologised to the dervishes, became a Murid (a disciple), and became one of the chosen ones.[2]

Sayyid Bukhari always used to preach in Sind. Great and eminent people were moved by his utterances.[3]

From the biography of the Sayyid (peace be on him) it transpires that the incident of the Somrah Governor's discipleship dates back to 750 A.H. or near about. A few years after, the Sammas replaced the Somrahs and took the reins of Government. It is just possible that the Sammas, the next ruling people, too were devotionally inclined toward the Sayyid.

When Muhammad Shah Tughluq invaded Thath, the capital of the Sammas, in 752 A.H. He died suddenly and when Firuz Shah Tughluq invaded it the first time, he was unsuccessful and went to Gujerat. This the people ascribed to the blessings of the 'Shaikh' and they made a sentence in Sindhi.

Barkat Shaikh Thiya, ek mooa, ek taha.[4] That is, it was due to the blessings of the Shaikh that the one died and the other fled away unsuccessful. In this sentence 'Shaikh' refers either to Shaikh Bahau'd-din Zakariya Multani or Sayyid Jalal Bukhari.

Next year when Firuz Shah, after returning from Gujerat, invaded Thath for the second time, Jam Unar and Banhabnah saw no other way save sending a messenger to Jalalu'd-din Huseyn Bukhari at Uch requesting him to take the trouble of coming and getting an armistice arranged. The Sayyid (peace be on him) came and arranged a treaty which contained suitable conditions. He told the Sultan that there was a very pious lady in Thath whose blessings saved the country from being conquered. She had died the day before yesterday.[5]

All these events clearly indicate that the Jams of Sama had a deep feeling of devotion to Shaikh Bahu'd-din Zakariya and Sayyid Jalalu'd-din Huseyn. They point out not only that they were Muslims but also that they were Sunnis.

It appears that this Suharwardy family was for them the light of guidance. These events are connected not with the last days of the Sammas but with their early period. This is evidence for my claim that the Sammas became Muslims from very early times.

It becomes all the more clear if we link up this point with the Sammas to the head of Government. The words of Firishta are:

> "During the last days of Shah Muhammad Tughluq, on account of the efforts and help of Muslims, the Kingdom slipped away from the hands of the Somrah class into those of the Samma class, and the majority of their officers were endowed with the wealth of Islam (i.e., were Muslims)."[6]

If the *Sammas* were not Muslims, why this Muslim sympathy? Besides Multan and Mansurah there were small Arab States and settlements whose traces are found till the end of the 4th century A.H., that is, till the time before Mahmud Ghaznawi. Some were conquered and annexed by Sabuktagin, father of Sultan Mahmud, and most of them by Sultan Mahmud.[7] Of these towns, the names of the following are found with special reference in the accounts of Arab travellers of the fourth century.

Deybal or Thath

It was a famous port, and, as I have mentioned above, the Arabs called it Deybal and Persian historians called it Thath. This town was the capital of the Sammas and it was attacked by Firuz Shah, Sultan of Delhi, without success. At last through the mediation of Hazrat Shaikh Jalalu'd-din, successor of a disciple of Hazrat Shaikhu'l-Islam Zakariya Multani, a treaty was arrived at.[8]

Eminent 'Ulama and traditionists flourished here and they have been described by 'Allamah Sam'ani (d.562 A.H.) and Kitabu'i-Ansab.[9] By virtue of its being a port, it was the centre for Arab merchants. Its population can be estimated from the fact that in 280 A.H., during the time of the 'Abbasid Khalifah Mu'tamad an earthquake took place, resulting in the destruction of many buildings.

The number of people who were crushed to death under the ruined buildings in this catastrophe numbered one hundred and fifty thousand.[10] Bashshari (375 A.H.) has written:

> "Round about there are a hundred villages. The Hindus form the majority of the population. All are traders and merchants. The languages spoken by them are Sindhi and Arabic. The revenue is very large."

Baladhari described it as situated between Multan, Kashmir, and Kabul a fact which may not be very correct. But names resembling it are found in Sind. Dr. Arnold, when writing *The Preaching of Islam* could not locate it.[11]

But we personally guess that the origin of this name is Asiwan which may be called Siwan too. Towns of this name are found between Delhi and Sind. This name occurs in Persian historians.[13] Ibn Batutah has also mentioned Sihwan and now it exists in the Karachi district.

Some have supposed Sayustan and Siwan to be one and the same. However, in the beginning of the 3rd century A.H. (during the reign of Mu'tasam, d.227) there was a population of Muslim merchants.[14]

Tanbali

There was a place named Tanbali in Sind. In 375 A.H. there were some Muslims settled here.[15]

Buqan

Baladhari has mentioned a place in Sindh known as Buqan (or Bukan) and has written that in his time all the inhabitants were Muslims.[16]

Qazdar

Some have written it as Qazdad. Its name is found among the conquests of Sabuktagin.[17] It was situated near the Indo-Afghan frontier. There was a population here of Khariji Muslims and they ruled over it. Perhaps in the middle of the 4th century A.H., when a Mu'tazali theologian controvertialist named Abu'l-Hasan 'Ali bin Latif arrived here, he found here a population of the Kharijis who ruled over it. He says that perfect peace reigns over the land.

There is no theft committed and people do not lock their houses. Should a traveller leave his belongings in the mosque, nobody will touch them. Here he met a Muslim tailor. There was a mosque too in the town.[18] Bashshari[19] describes it as situated on the coast inside the length of Makran at a distance of 12 manzils[20] from Tez the harbour of Baluchistan.

Another Arab geographer says that "it is at a distance of 20 manzils from Multan.[21] Ibn Hauqal says:

> "Qazdar is a city connected with which are many villages and hamlets. The name of the ruler is Mu'in bin Ahmad but the Khutbah is read in the name of the Khalifah of Baghdad. His palace stood in Bakaznan Bashshari Maqdisi, who came in 375 to this part of the country."

Again he says:

> "Qazdar is the capital of Turan. It stands in a desert."

Between the two parts into which it is divided there is a valley in which there is no bridge. In one part is the King's palace and the fort too stands here. The name of the other part is Budin. Here there are houses of merchants. It is very clean. The city is small but useful. People come here from Khurasan, Persia, Kirman and towns of India. But the water here is not good.....The water of the canal is drunk.[22]

In short, it was a small Islamic State. Amir Sabuktagin, Sultan Mahmud's father, thought it advisable to conquer the frontier States before marching upon India. Some time between 375 A.H. and 387 A.H., the date of Sabuktagin's death, he conquered this city and made the Muslim ruler of it pay tribute.[23]

Tooran

At the time of Ibn Hauqal it was an independent State.In Western Sind is Turan ruled over by Abu'l-Qasim who was an inhabitant of Basrah. He is a ruler, judge and general in one, though he does not know the difference between 3 and 10.

Vaihind

It is a famous and ancient town of India. It is mentioned in connection with the Ghaznawi conquests. Mahmud conquered it in 393 A.H. after his conquest of Peshawar.[24] In this town too there was a Muslim population in the pre-Mahmud days. Beruni has written its description in the Qanun Mas'udi.

It is the capital of Qandahar and it lies in the Sind valley.[25] Mr. Vincent A. Smith in The Early History of India locates the capital named Ohind near the river Sind and writes that after the Muslim conquest of Kabul in 256 A.H. the capital shifted to Ohind which was situated near river Sind and was the capital of the Hindu ruling dynasty.[26]

At the end of the 4th century (in 375 A.H., that is, fifteen or sixteen years before Mahmud's invasion) Bashshari says:''I made inquiries from one of the pupils of Abu'l-Heysham Neyshapuri and from a scholar of Shiraz who had toured the country pretty well. On inquiry I found Vaihind was the name of the capital and that the towns under its control were Wadhan' Batir, Nawj Lawar' Saman Kuj, etc[27] In the territory of Waihind there was a fairly large Muslim population and there was established a State of theirs. The Hindus had their own Raja and the Muslims their own ruler. The Hindus formed the majority of the population.[28]

Qannauj

Apart from the famous Kannauj of Hindustan, there was another Qannauj on the border of Sind and Punjab, often mentioned by Arab travellers. There was a Muslim population here too. After 300 A.H. this city came into Muslim possession. When Mas'udi saw it in 303 A.H. he found it annexed to Multan and under the Islamic Government.[29]

Bashshari came here seventy or seventy-five years later. At that time it was an autonomous State. He says that it is a large town and has rampart-walls all around it. Meat is sold in picmy. There are many gardens. The water is good. Trade is extensive. The inhabitants are handsome. There is a jami mosque inside the rampart-walls.

The Muslims live on wheat. Respectable people and eminent scholars live here.[30]

Further on he says that, though the Muslims form the majority of the population, the Hindus have their own ruler. Arab travellers and geographers were familiar even with the Kannauj in Oudh. Mahlabi, Vizier of Egypt, (about 386 A.H.) describes in his geography Kitab al-'Azizi ''Kannauj is among the most distant cities of India.

It lies west of Multan. Between Multan and Kannauj, there is a distance of 282 farsangs.[31] It is the capital and the largest city of India. The reports about Kannauj are very much exaggerated and overdone. It is said there are three hundred shops of jewellers only; that the Raja has two and a half thousand elephant. There are gold mines too. Idrisi, who wrote his geography in Sicily in 548 A.H., says:

> ''It is a very handsome city. It is the emporium of trade. The Raja is also called by the name of the town Khannuj.''

Idrisi describes the extent of Kannauj going right up to the Punjab and even to Kashmir. The geographer of Morocco Ibn Said Maghribi (585 A.H.) says:

> ''This city lies on both sides of the Ganges.''[32]

Neyrun

Among the coastal towns of India was one named Neyrun some have wrongly read it as Beyrun and described Abu Reyhan Beruni as a native of that place.[33] It lay between Deybal and Mansurah, and was at a distance of 15 farsangs from Mansurah. Mahlabi writes in the fourth century in his geography:

> ''The inhabitants of this place are Muslims.[34]

Elphinstone says in his 'History of India' that Neyrun was the old name of the modern town of Hyderabad in Sind.[35]

It lies on the border of Sind. At the time of Ibn Hauqal the Arab ruler of this place was A'isa bin Ma'dan. The seat of his Government was 'Kanir' which was half the size of Multan.

Mushki

Near it was another Arab State whose name was Mushki and whose ruler at the time of Ibn Hauqal was Maza'hir bin Raja. It was so large a State that its whole extent was traversed in 3days. In the Khutbah the name of the Khalifah of Baghdad was mentioned. We are tired of roaming the desert of Sind. Let us for a moment refresh ourselves by seeing the image of Paradise.

Kashmir

This is the land of which it can be aptly said that it was conquered not by the swords and stratagems of Muslim kings but by the spiritual efficiency of Muslim saints and theologians. Arab geographers and tourists came near it but did not go inside the country. They have described the difficulties which assailed the tourists. They called the whole territory from the sea to the chain of Kashmir mountains by the name of Sind.

After the Arabs, Sultan Mahmud assailed the rocks but in vain. But at the same time we find Muslim merchants and traders going to and coming from Kashmir. In 424 A.H., three years after the death of Sultan Mahmud, Sultan Mas'ud Ghaznawi invaded it. The inhabitants, including the Muslim merchants there, shut themselves in the fort.[36]

In the foregoing pages, we have tried to show pictures of the mutual relations which existed between Arabia and India, Islam and India, before the advent of Muslim conquerors through the Khyber. It will give an idea of the places where Muslims were settled before the Muslim conquests, and will serve to show how deep and many-sided were the relations between them and the Hindus, and how old is the connection of Islam with India. We have not read the story of Alexander and Darius which is nothing for us, but the romance of love and fidelity.

Soparah

A famous old town of Gujerat has been mentioned by the Arabs as Sobarah Istakhri (340 A.H.) mentions it among the famous towns of India and, later on, the travellers Bashshari of Jerusalem mentions it as situated near Khambayat. According to him there is a distance of four manzils between Khambayat and Soparah. He says:

> ''Soparah is at the distance of one farsang (8 miles) from the sea.''[37]

The archaeological researches into the antiquities of Gujerat carried on during recent years point out a town with the name of

Sobara. This is the very town which has been described by Arab travellers in their times.

In the Sunday issue of the Bombay Chronicle dated February 2,1930 (pp.31, 32) an article appeared concerning the archaeological research of Soparah. Its pith is as follows:

> "It appears from archaeological researches that traces of this city are found during the time of the famous Raja Ashoka of Magadh."

A commemorative edict of Raja Asoka has been found by our archaeologists. Siparah is still an obscure station in the B.B.C.I. Railway which has been so named because near it lies a town of that name. The late Bhagwan Lal Indarji had discovered this commemorative edict. Now this place lies in the Bombay Presidency three or four miles north of Bassein situated on the sea-coast and thirty miles off Bombay city.

In 250 B.C., it was one of the famous and flourishing cities of India. That is why it was one of the few lucky towns selected for the commemorative edict. The edict of Sopara was taken away and is now lying in the Prince of Wales Museum (Western India).

There are ten lines, four of which have been defaced. Its script is the parent of Devanagri and other Hindi scripts and the European research scholar Buchner has expressed his opinion that it came by the Commercial route from Iraq to India seven or eight centuries before Christ (vide the book).

Dr. Bhandarkar says that Sopara was a famous port the district of Thana in the Bombay Presidency. Its name in Mahabharat is Soorpapka and Ptolemy has in his geography written its name as Sopara. It was a sacred place and the capital of Aparanta.

The modern village of Soparah lies where the famous ancient city existed. It lies on the left side of a gulf which seems to turn and twist between the Railway bridge on the Bassein Gulf and the river Witarna.

In ancient Sopara there still remain traces of old buildings and houses. There is also a Ram Kund (a pond dedicated to the memory of Ram) which is a proof of its being a place of pilgrimage. When in 1881 A.D., this commemorative edict was discovered there were hardly six hundred homes here, and there were nearly two thousand people, Brahmans, Indian Christians and Muslims. Among the Muslims there were Arabs and Persians who settled down here seven centuries before the virtue of commercial relations. This will show that Muslims were settled down here as in other coastal towns of Gujerat. If the edict of Asoka and Ptolemy's geography point out the trace of this town two hundred years before Christ, the statements of Muslim Arab travellers point to its existence a thousand years after Christ.

Jat Physicians in Arabia

Mention has been made in these pages of the Jats having settled down in 'Iraq and Arabia but only their military qualities have been described. But we get to know a meritorious achievement of the Jats. Imam Bukhari (d. 256 A.H.) has written an event of the period of the Sahabis in his book Kitabu'l-Adab-ul-Mufrad that once when the mother of believers Hazrat 'Ayesha fell ill, her nephews sent for a Jat physician for her treatment.[39]

Royal Shoes of Sindh

We have mentioned the shoes of Khambayat. These shoes went from Mansurah (Sindh) to Baghdad, the 'Abbasid capital in 'Iraq. Very recently a short book of Imam Ahmad bin Hanbal (d. 242 A.H.) named Al-Wara has been published in Egypt with the help of a seven century old MS. found in Algeria. It is proved that the shoes of Sind were so handsome and showy that serious-minded people did not like to wear them and they were deemed fit to be worn only by princes.

References

1. *Tarikh-i-Tahiri* (Elliot), p, 257.
2. Firishta, Vol. 2, p. 416 (Nawalkishore).
3. *Ibid.*
4. *Tarikh-i-Firuz Shahi-Shams Siraj `Afif*, p. 231 (Calcutta).
5. *Tarikh-i-Firuz Shahi*, p. 241 (Calcutta).
6. *Firishta,* Vol. II, p. 317 (Nawalkishore).
7. *A`in-i-Akbari,* (Sindh).
8. *Tarikh-i-firuz Shashi-Shams Siraj `Afif,* (Calcutta), p. 241.
9. *Kitabu'l-ansab*, Photographed edition, word 'Deybal'.

10. *Tarikh-i-Khalifa,* by Suyuti (edited in Calcutta), p. 380.
11. *Da'wat-i-Islam* (The Urdu translation of *The Preaching of Islam*), P. 291.
12. *Makatub-i-Shibali* (letters of Shibli), Vol. 2, p. 17.
13. *Khaza'inu'l-Futuh* by Amir Khusru.
14. *Baladhari,* p. 446.
15. *Bashashri*, p. 480.
16. Baladhari, p. 345.
17. *Tabaqat-i-Nasiri,* p.7 (Calcutta).
18. *Ma`jamu'l-buldan* by Yaqut, Vol. 7, p. 78 (Egypt).
19. *Ahsanu't-taqasim*, p. 358.
20. *Manzil* Means a halting place (Translator).
21. *Taqwimu'I-buldan* by Abul'I-Fida, p. 349.
22. *Ahsanu't-taqasim* by Bashshari, p. 478 (Leiden).
23. *Tarikh-i-Firishta* (Nawalkishore) Vol. I, p. 19.
24. *Zyanu'I-Akhbar* by Gurdezi, (edited in Berlin), p. 66.
25. *Taqwimu'I-buldan* by Abu'I-fida, p. 357, (Paris-1840 A.D.).
26. *The Early History of India*, Vol. I, p. 345.
27. Ahsanu't-taqasim, p.477.
28. *Ibid*, p. 485 with marginal notes.
29. Mas'udi, Vol, I. p. 372 (Paris).
30. Bashshari, Vol I. p. 485.
31. A farsang covered 3 miles according to the old reckoning. According to modern reckoning it equals nearly 8 miles (Translator).
32. *Taqwimu'l-buldan* by Abu'l-Fida, p. 360. (Paris).
33. *Taqwimu'l-buldan* by Abul'l-Fida, p. 349 wit reference to Ibn Sa`id Maghribi and *Tarikhu't-Atibba* by Ibn Abi Useybi'a, Vol 2, p. 20. (Egypt).
34. *Tawimu'l-buldan* by Abul'l-Fida, p. 349.
35. *History of Indian by* Elphinstone, Vol, 2 p. 493 dated 1867 A.D. (Aligarh).
36. Firishta, Vol, I, p. 41 (Nawalkishore).
37. Each farsang was three miles on the old reckoning. The old mile equalled four thousand years, each year equalling sixth the dis tance between the little finger and the thumb. A farsang--nearly 8 miles of our days (Translator).
38. As I could not get the required issue, I have translated the Urdu rendering of the article (Translator).
39. *Al-adabul'-mufrad* by Imam Bukhari the chapter on *Bey'u'l-Khadim*, p. 35, (Egypt).

10. Tarikh-i-[illegible], by [illegible] (edited in [illegible]) p. 186.
11. [illegible] (The [illegible] translation of The [illegible]) [illegible] p. 291.
12. [illegible] Vol. 2, p. 15.
13. [illegible] by [illegible]
14. [illegible] p. 196.
15. [illegible] p. 130.
16. [illegible] p. 110.
17. [illegible] p. 7 ([illegible])
18. [illegible] Vol. 7, p. 78 ([illegible])
19. [illegible] p. 338.
20. [illegible] (a halting place) ([illegible])
21. [illegible] p. 149.
22. [illegible] p. 428 ([illegible])
23. [illegible] Vol. 1, p. 19.
24. [illegible] (edited in [illegible]), p. 60.
25. [illegible] p. 337 ([illegible])
26. [illegible] Vol. 1, p. 313.
27. [illegible] p. 77.
28. [illegible] p. 16 [illegible]
29. [illegible] Vol. 1, p. 72 ([illegible])
30. [illegible] Vol. 1, p. 183.
31. [illegible] according to [illegible]. According to [illegible] Bombay [illegible]
32. [illegible] p. 108 [illegible]
33. [illegible] p. [illegible] according to [illegible] and [illegible] Vol. 2, p. 70. [illegible]
34. [illegible] p. 380.
35. [illegible] Vol. [illegible] ([illegible] 1400 A.D. [illegible])
36. [illegible] Vol. 1, p. 14 [illegible]
37. [illegible] the [illegible] [illegible]
38. [illegible]
39. [illegible]

Chapter - 6

Muslim Colonial Centres

The histories of India included in the curricula of our schools and colleges are taught with a definite motive and the authors who write such books in English look upon things from a definite angle of vision. The history of Ancient India as found in these books is a piece of the history of Alexander and his successors. This invasion revolutionised India; it gave India an opulence of learning; and India attained a status in the world of history.

To discover every route of Alexander's invasion and journey, to correct corrupted Greek names, and to arrange topsy-turvy statements, -- this is the history of ancient India. When these historians come to Islam and India, they deseribe in a few lines the savage Arabs and terrible attacks of (God forbid) a ferocious Prophet and his successors. After a page or two they reach Ghazni direct from Arabia. Here they find Mahmud's army ready to launch a crusade upon India and, taking this army, they reach Punjab, Sind and Gujarat. After marauding expeditions, loot and plunder, they take this army back. After a hundred and fifty years, they bring Shihabu'd-din Ghori upon the soil of India and then they plunge into what is known as the Mediaeval History of India.

The question arises, if it was possible for the borders of Greece to have touched those of Indian in spite of long distances which separate them, is it not possible that on the ground of geographical propinquity the borders of India touched Afghanistan on the one hand and Makran and Sind on the other hand. Did not relations of war or peace exist between these countries? Did not these relations exist before the frontier tribes embraced Islam? Is it not necessary to join together the broken links and to make inquiry and research into this matter?

From a study of these books it is patent that, until the time of Mahmud of Ghazni, not a single Muslim mlechch had set his feet upon the sacred soil of India; that there existed no relation of any sort between the Hindus and the Muslims. But the readers of my previous articles much have formed a clear idea of the various, many-sided relations that existed between the two peoples.

There were always continuous, unbroken relations of war and peace between India and the countries on the other side of the Khyber, before the advent of Islam. Whenever the King of Kabul became powerful he annexed the territories right up to Vihindawar and Peshawar ; and when opportunity presented itself, Rai Lohawar extended the boundaries of his dominions up to Kabul and Kandahar.

The same thing happened to the territories round about Sind. Sometimes the Shah of Persia annexed the territories from Makran to the river Sindh and sometimes the Raja of Sind, having annexed Baluchistan and Makran, made his kingdom touch the frontiers of Iran. This seesaw of political changes went on till the seventh century A.D.

When the tide of Islamic conquest rushed to these places and the different tribes and communities took to Islam, the first Islamic kingdom on this part of the globe was the Samaniyah (Samanid) kingdom with its capital at Bukhara. But even then the eyes of the conquerors were not upon the lands beyond Kabul. Then came the Safariyah (Safarid) kingdom which was short-lived.

Even then the eyes of the conquerors were not cast upon the lands beyond Kabul and Kandahar. The 'Abbasid Caliphate entrusted the nominal rule of Sind to this kingdom. Alptagin, a Turkish officer of the Samanid kingdom, directed his attention away from the domain of that kingdom in order to escape invasions and chastisement by his lord. He made that distant country the pivot of his efforts and established a self-governing principality in Ghazni. This is an event of the mid-fourth century A.H.

Sultan Mahmud of Ghazni is the second or third ruler of that dynasty. During his thirty years' reign he humbled, by his terrible invasions, the Muslim and non-Muslim powers on all sides of Ghazni, added them to his small hereditary principality and laid the foundations of a mighty empire. He crushed the Islamic kingdom of

Eelkhan in Kashghar on the one side, the kingdom of Al-i-Zayar in Tabristan, the country of the Ghoris who had not yet taken to Islam and had not yet been subjugated by any power, on the eastern side. Later on, he vanquished the Arab Amirs of Multan and Sind on the eastern side, and some Rajas of Lahore and India, and established the Ghaznavid kingdom. Of these, all the powers, except those in India and Ghor, were purely Muslim powers.

The above details indicate that the Muslim invasions through the mountain passes of Afghanistan, upon the Inidan Rajas were not actuated merely by religious rancour, but formed only a link in the chain of the national wars which were waged for centuries. All this relates to northern Inida, but the state of southern India was different.

Mahmud of Ghazni invaded Gujarat in 416 A.H. (1064 A.D.), Shihabu'd-din Ghori in 574 A.H. (1178 A.D.), and Qutabu'd-din Eybak in 592 A.H. (1196 A.D.), but they came like the cloud and went away like the whirlwind.

After a hundred years Raja Baghela and his MinisterMadho were estranged one from the other, and it was the invitation of the latter which made 'Alau'd-din Khilji the ruler of Gujarat in 697 A.H. (1297 A.D.) Alau'd-din Khilji annexed the territories on the sea-coast from Gujarat to Coromandel.

But these conquests were like a ship which cleaves the bosom of the ocean and leaves the gathering waters in its wake so placid that there seems to be no trace of the ship having ploughed them. This was nothing more than a military tour of the Khilji commander. In 709 A.H. (1309 A.D.) one of his officers named Malik Kafur subjugated the Karnatik.

Later on in 727 A.H. (1232 A.D.) rose the Vijayyanagar kingdom which served as a barrier to protect southern India from the onrush of the Muslims of northern India. The small Islamic principality established in Ma'bar (Coromandel) in connection with Malik Kafur's conquests, merged into the Vijayyanagar kingdom after a life of forty years.

But further away from this dreadful carnage and terrible holocaust, there were colonies of Muslim Arabs and 'Iraqis who did not come to the South by the land route from the North but travelled on the sea-coast until they settled down in those parts.

It is an open fact that long before the Muslims settled down in northern India there were Muslim colonies in southern Inida; and the history of these colonies really goes back to the era of commercial relations. Not only did Muslims from outside settle down in these areas but even the native inhabitants began to embrace Islam.

There are various traditions regarding this impact of Islam and they are recorded in history-books and travel - diaries. What is common to these traditions is that this impact was due to two forces - one, the coming and going of Arab merchants; the other, the spiritual influence of the Sufis and Dervishes who came to see the footprint (Adam's footprint) in Sarandip (Ceylon).

Ceylon, the First Muslim Centre

Firishta has written that since the Arabs came to these islands as merchants and the inhabitants of these islands went to Arabia even at a time when Islam had not yet dawned upon the world, the Raja of Sarandip first became familiar with Islam. In 40 A.H. (the beginning of the seventh century A.D.) during the time of the revered Sahabis (those who had seen the Prophet) he embraced Islam.[1]

Firishta does not mention the source of this quotation but this fact is fully corroborated by an old book written in 300 A.H. and known as 'Aja'ibu'l-Hind (Wonders of India). Buzurg bin Shabryar Nakhoda (sailor) who used to sail round about these islands, writes in his description of Sind:

> "There are many kinds of yogis and ascetics in India. One kind of yogis is known as Bikur."[2]

They originally belonged to Sarandip and they entertain kindly feelings towards the Muslims. They remain practically stark naked during summer and wrap round the waist a loin-cloth only four fingers long; they cover their bodies with mats in winter; they sew for themselves a motley coloured cloth and wear it; they besmear their bodies with the ashes of burnt corpses. They shave the head and beard and grow hairs on other parts of the body; they hang a human skull round their necks and eat their food in that skull for the sake of humility and edification.

Other statements of Arab travellers leave no manner of doubt that they were Buddhists. Arabian traveller goes on to tell this story:

> "When the people of Sarandip and places round about learnt about the Prophet of Islam they sent an intelligent person from among themselves to Arabia for inquiry. When at last, he reached Madína the Prophet was already dead."

The period of Abu Bakr's Caliphate was also over and Hazrat Umar was the Caliph at that time. The messenger from Sarandip met him and inquired about the Prophet's life. Hazrat Umar gave him the details. While the messenger was on his way back, he died at Makran (near Baluchistan). He had with him a Hindu servant who came back to Sarandip safe and sound.

He described everything about the Prophet, Hazrat Abu Bakr, and Hazrat Umar and also how they lived like dervishes. He said that humility marked their character; they wore patched clothes and slept in the mosque. The reason why the people of Sarandip have kindly feelings towards the Muslims is, thus, explained.[3]

There is a third corroboration of this tradition that when at the end of the first century A.H., Hajjaj was the Governor of 'Iraq and ships hovering round the south of India came from the harbour of 'Iraq, the Raja of Sarandip (also called by the Arabs 'the island of rubies') sent in a ship to 'Iraq, as a token of goodwill and friendship towards the Muslims, among other presents, those Muslim women and girls whose fathers had come as traders and died, leaving them guardianless in a strange land.[4]

This proves that, as early as the first century A.H., there were Muslim colonies in Sarandip. Abu Zeyd Seyrafi (300 A.H.) has mentioned the sojourn of Arab travellers in this island and their coming and going towards the end of the third century A.H.[5] From a study of these various traditions one conclusion emerges: that on this side of the globe the first colony of Islam and the Arabs was established in Sarandip. Its history covered the period from the first century A.D. to the seventh century A.D.

Maldive: the Second Centre

The second centre of Muslim and Arab colonization on this side of the globe was Maldive, sometimes called 'jaziratu'l-Mehl' by the Arabs. The Arabs called the collection of these small islands by the name of Deybat.[3] Ibn Batutah has given the fullest account of these islands. During the time of Ibn Batutah, that is, during Muhammad Tughlak's reign (700 A.H.), all the inhabitants were Muslims; there were settlements of the Arabs and native Muslims; and the island was ruled by a Bengali woman named Khadijah. At that time there were in that island many scholars and navigators from Yaman and other places.

Ibn Batutah has recorded, as he heard it from them, the story of how the idolatrous island embraced Islam. Every month a terrible spectre used to emerge out of the sea. When the people of this place saw the spectre they left a virgin, adorned and decorated, in the idol-house situated on the sea-shore. But this dreadful calamity was averted by the blessings of an Arab of Morocco named Shaikh Abu'l-Barakat Barhari Maghribi who arrived here by accident.

Thereupon Raja Shanuraza and his subjects became Muslims and the Shaikh initiated them into the faith. Ibn Batutah says that he found the following inscription upon the archway of the mosque built by this newly-converted Raja.

> "Sultan Ahmad Shanwara became a Muslim, Abu'l-Barakat Maghribi having initiated him into the faith."

In short, from that day to this all these islands are inhabited by Muslims and the majority of them are Arabs of mixed blood.

Malabar: the Third Centre

It is proved by different traditions that the third centre of Arab colonization is the extreme fringe of India known in Ancient India as Kerala and later on as Malibar (Mali - mountain; bar - country). As described by Arab geographers, it extends from the end of Gujarat to Kolam in Travancore.

The following is the version of Tuhfatu'l Mujahidin recorded by Farishta. Before and after the advent of Islam, Jewish and Christian merchants used to come here and settle down. When two hundred years had passed after the advent of Islam, a band of Arab and Persian dervishes (all Muslims) was going to Ceylon to see Adam's footprint. As chance would have it, their ship, tossed by the winds, reached the town of Kadanklur (Kadanganur). The Raja of the place (Zeymur) treated them very courteously.

In the course of conversation there was mention of Islam. The Raja said:

> "I have heard from the Jews and the Christians an account of your Prophet and religion."

Now I want you to describe all these things:

> "The way the dervishes explained their religion was so impressive that it touched the deepest chords of the Raja's heart. The Raja took an assurance from them that they would halt at his town on their way back. They fulfilled their promise by halting at that town. The Raja assembled his nobles and chiefs and declared that he wanted to consecrate the rest of his life to the worship of God. He distributed his lands equally to all officers, went away secretly to Arabia with the dervishes, and became a Muslim. He told the dervishes that, in order to propagate Islam in Malabar, it was necessary to establish commercial relations with Malabar, and gave a letter of recommendation addressed to his nobles."

Later on, the treat these foreign merchants courteously and provide every means of convenience. Help them in every piece of pious work. Permit them to build their houses of worship and treat them in such a way that they may be inclined to reside there.' From that time onwards Arab merchants came and settled down in Malabar.

There is another version (which is believed by *Firishta* to be more reliable than this, but which I personally do not think to be so reliable) to the effect that this event took place during the Prophet's life-time. However, the dervishes again came to Malabar and built a mosque in Kandankar. Some settled down in that town; some migrated to Kolam and built a mosque there too. They built mosques and established their colonies in Hili Marawi, Jarpatan, Darpatan, Findarniya (Pindarani) Faknur and Mangalore.

This is the summary of Firishta's statements. A few extracts from Tuhfatu'l-Mujahidin throw light on the conditions as they prevailed in later times: Plenty of merchants have come from different countries to parts of the western coast of India. New towns sprang up; the trade of the Muslims has increased the population; plenty of houses have been built.

The Raja and his chiefs abstain from adopting an unkind attitude towards the Muslims. Though the chiefs and their soldiers are idol-worshippers, still they revere the Muslims and their faith. This friendly feeling amazes us all the more when we think that the Muslims number only a tenth of the whole population. Generally speaking, the Hindu Rajahs of Malabar adopt an attitude of respect and kindness towards the Muslims, as the establishment of many towns is due to the Muslim traders having settled down in those parts.[6]

These are the Muslim Arab traders and merchants who left their homes and became known in India as moplahs and Naits. They held in their hands the reins of naval supremacy before the Portuguese became masters of the sea. The native inhabitants who became Muslims or intermarried with the Moplahs entered their fraternity.

It lies in modern Travancore. Arab navigators have been mentioning it from very early times. They said

> "this is the last town of the land of spices."

Ships used to go from this place to Aden. There was a locality in which the Muslims resided. The Muslims had their mosque here.[7]

Ma'bar Coromandel: the Fourth Centre

In Madras, the coast on the opposite side to Malabar is called Ma'bar by the Arabs. Its famous modern name is Coromandel. Ma'bar was notably known to Arab sailors and merchants. Ibn Sa'id Maghribi has mentioned it as a place which lies at a distance of three or four days' journey east of Kolam and leans towards the south.[8]

Zakarya Qizwini (686 A.H.) has mentioned it in the seventh century as 'Mandal' and has praised the ambergris of this place.[9] He mentions Ras Kamran (Cape Comorin) as situated near Ma'bar or Coromandel and hence ambergris was known as 'Kamrui 'ud' or Comorin ambergris.[10]

Abu'l-Fida (732 A.H. or 1313 A.D.) has mentioned 'Ras Kumari' as 'Ras Kumahri [11] and has thus defined the boundaries of Kolam:

> "It lies east of Malabar at a distance of three or four day's journey and its boundary begins from Kolam.[12] The name of its capital is 'Birdai' (Birdhol). Horses are brought here

from outside.''[13]

It seems that this part of the coast came into Arab use after a few centuries. We find its name mentioned from the end of the sixth century onward.

In the seventh century the Arabs seem to have given an appreciable amount of power and influence in that place. Wasaf (d.728 A.H.) and Rashidu'd-din, the author of jami'-ut-tawarikh (d.718 A.H.) both wrote their books at the end of the 8th century. Both write almost unanimously upon this subject. M'abar (Coromandel) extends for 3 farsangs on the sea-coast from Kolam to Silwar (Nellore). It contains many towns and hamlets. The Raja is called by his subjects 'Diwar'which means 'a wealthy person.' Large Chinese ships called 'Janah' bring here valuable goods and cloth from China, Sind and Hind (India) and carry silk and odoriferous wood from Malabar. Large pearls are taken out of the rivers. The products go to 'Iraq, Khurasan, Syria, Rum, Byzantium and Europe. It produces red and odoriferous grass. There are plenty of pearls in its temples. Ma'bar is the key of India. A few years ago Sunder Pandey was the Diwan of the place.

He, together with his three brothers captured power and influence in various directions. Malik Taqiu'd-din bin Abdu'r-Rahman bin Muhammad-at-Tayyabi, the brother of Skeykh Jamalu'ddin, was the minister and adviser of this Raja who entrusted the kingdom of Patan, Mali Patan (Patam and Mali Patam) and Badal to the care of his minister. Since good horses were not found in Ma'bar, the Raja caused a contract to be made that Jamalu'd-din Ibrahim should fetch him fourteen hundred Arab horses of fine mettle from the port of Kaish (Qais[14]).

Every year ten thousand horses, each costing 220 gold mohurs (dinars) came from other parts of the Persian Gulf - Qatif Al-Hisa, Bahreyn and Hurmuz. In 292 A.H. (1293 A.D.) the 'Diwar' (Raja) died and his wealth was distributed among his ministers and advisers. It is said that Skeykh Jamalu'd-din, who succeeded him, got seven thousand bullock-loads of gold and jewels and Taqiu'd-din, according to the contract, became his representative.[15]

At about the same time, when Marco Polo came here the kingdom was ruled over by five Hindu Rajas but he found that the

Muslims commanded a powerful commercial influence. Regarding the import of horses from Arabia he says :

> "Horses are not found in this land. Merchants bring horses every year from the parts of Aden and Hurmuz. Every year two thousand - horses are imported by the five Rajahs and each horse costs five hundred dinars."

Soon after, Sultan 'Alau'd-din Khilji's army devastated the whole country between Gujarat and Coromandel. Then for the first time in Indian history, the 'Iraqis and Arabs who were in the service of the Raja of Coromandel, who had his capital at Birdhul, fought against the invaders who were Muslim turks. Amir Khusru of Delhi has recorded this event with much detail in Khaza'-inu'l-Futuh[16] in the course of a colourful but meaningless history of these conquests of 'Alau'd-din Khilji.

The Muslims who had pledged themselves to the service of the Raja fought desperately against the Muslim Turks, but the latter proved more than a match for the former. The Raja was defeated and Malik Kafur, 'Alu'd-din's general, annexed the country. Malik Kafur wanted to chastise the Muslims who had fought against him, but they declared their faith by shouting the Kalimah and reciting extracts from the Qur'an. [17]

In the second volume of his book Elliot has given a summary of Khaza'inu'l-Futuh under the title of Tarikh-i-Alai. In connection with this incident he has translated a sentence of Khusru thus:

> "These Muslims were half-Hindus and quite ignorant of the principles of their religion."[18]

But this interpretation is entirely erroneous. They real fact is that with poetical fancies and rhetorical flourishes Amir Khusru has reprehended the Muslims for siding with the Hindu Raja. In no way does this condemnation mean that they were half-Hindus.[19]

Gujarat : the Fifth Centre

The fifth theatre of the Arabs commercial activities was the territory covered by Gujarat, Kathiawar, Cutch and the Konkan. It was ruled over by Wallabh Ra'i or Raja Bilhara, beloved of the Arabs, who had his first capital at Wallabhipur, which was a large town near modern Bhaunagar and is always called by the Arabs Mangar or Mahanagar.

Modern archaeological researches prove that the circuit of this town covered an area of five miles. Some Rajas were Buddhists and some Jains and it was religious animosities and jealousies which paved the way for the downfall of this kingdom. Under the sheltering care of this kingdom the region of Cheymur, called Seymur by the Arabs, was in a highly flourishing condition. Khambayat and other regions came next in importance.

The first Arab traveller and merchant, who completed his travel-diary in 235 A.H., i.e., Suleyman, has showered praises upon Wallabh Rai. He writes:

> ''He and his subjects entertained very good feelings towards the Arabs and the Muslims and they believed that the longevity of their Rajas is due to the love and affection they show to the Arabs.''[20]

This shows that very friendly relations existed between the Arab merchants and settlers on the one hand and the children of the soil on the other. This explains why there were plenty of Arab settlements in various towns of this kingdom and also why they existed right up to the end. Of the Rajah of Taqan or Dakhan or Dakhan he states:

> ''Like Bilahar he too treats the Arabs lovingly.''[21]

Of the Rajahs of Gujarat proper he says:

> ''They are the enemies of the Arabs.''[22]

At the end of the third century A.H. and the beginning of the fourth, the ships of Buzurg bin Shahryar Nakhoda sailed on this side and he found here a large population of Arabs and Muslims. He also met a newly converted Muslim navigator whose ships had earned a large fortune and who had gone on pilgrimage too.[23] He also met one Muhammad bin Muslim, a merchant of Seyraf, who had lived in Thana (near Bombay) for more than twenty years, had visited many towns of India, and was familiar with them.[24]

In Cheymur (Seymur in Gujarat) he met one Abu Bakr, a Muslim of Fasa (in Persia).[25] The courtier of the Rajah of Goal (called Chandanpur by the ancient Arabs) was a Muslim named Musa.[26] This is a Persian word which denotes 'a man of skill' but the Arabs used it in a particular sense. Dropping the final dal they called it Hunarman and formed the verb 'Hunarmana' (which meant 'to be skilled'). Technically it meant a Muslim qadi or consul appointed in non-Muslim lands by their governments to decide cases concerning Muslims. When the Arab and Muslim governments attained their meridian of grandeur, they enjoyed in non-Muslim lands special privileges and prerogatives similar to those enjoyed in Asia and Africa to-day by Europeans, whose cases are not decided in the courts of non-Europeans. There are signs of such distinctive privileges in Turkistan, Rum (Byzantium) China and India.[27]

However, this qadi or consul, or the Muslim officer appointed by a non-Muslim government, was called 'Hunarmand'. At the end of the third century A.H. and the beginning of the fourth, the Arab population had grown so large in Cheymur that the Raja had to appoint for them a 'Hunarmand' whose name was 'Abbas bin Mahan.[28]

The Kingdom of Vallabh Rai

Mas'udi came to India at the beginning of the fourth century A.H. he came to Khambayat in 303 A.H. He visited many other towns of Gujarat. His evidence about the Vallabh Rai kings is the same as recorded sixty or seventy years before by Suleyman the Merchant. He says, ''In no other kingdom in Sind or in India are the Arabs and Muslims treated with so much respect as in the kingdom of the Bilahara Rajas.

Islam is safe, immune and secure in this kingdom. There are mosques and Jami'mosques in which the faithful congregate in large numbers to offer prayers. The Rajahs rule for forty or fifty long years and the people believe that this longevity is due to the justice and respect with which they treat Muslims. The Rajah of Gujarat is a blatant enemy of Islam, while in the kingdom of Taqan or Dakhan the Muslims are treated with the same respect.[29] In Seymur (a town in Vallabh Rai's kingdom) the population of Arabs, and Muslims of mixed blood, was increasing day by day. When Mas'udi came here (in 304 A.H.) the Muslim population numbered ten thousand in this town alone.

Beysar

This is a puzzling word but Mas'udi defines it as the Muslims born in India. Its plural is Beyasarah. The following is an important extract from Mas'udi: ''In 304 A.H. I went from Lar in the kingdom of Bilahara to Cheymur (Seymur). The name of the ruler of this town at that time was 'Janch."

At that time, there was a population of ten thousand Muslims which was composed of those who were born in India (called Beyasarah), in Seyraf, Oman, Basrah, Baghdad and other places, and who had settled down here. Among them there are respectable merchants like Musa bin Ishaq of Sandalun (Sandapur?). Abu Sa'id Ma'ruf bin Zakarya filled the post of 'Hunarmand.' Hunarmand means the Sirdar (chief) of Muslims and the Rajah selects one of the Muslim nobles to whom are entrusted all matters concerning the Muslims. Beyasarah means the Muslims born in India." [30]

Thana

Ibn Sa'id Maghribi, a contemporary of Sultan Shihabu'd-din, was writing in 585 A.H. in Morocco and Egypt a book on the geography of the heavens (astronomy) like Beruni's Laws of Mas'udi. He has mentioned in it the names of some towns of Southern India. He says in the description of Thana, "this is the last town of Gujarat (Lar). Its name is on the tip of merchants' tongues. The inhabitants on this Indian coast are idolworshipping Hindus but they also let Muslims settle down there."[31]

Khambayat

He describes Khambayat, thus, this is among the coastal towns of India. Traders use to come here; there are Muslim inhabitants too.[32] Soon after, during the time of Sultan Shamsu'd-din Iltamash (625 A.H.) Awfi, the author of Jami-ul-Hikayat, perhaps, went from Sind to Khambayat. He says:

"There is a population (in Khambayat) of pious and conscientious Muslims and they have a Jami 'mosque too and an Imam. The Rajah of Gujarat who lived in Nahrwalah treated them with commendable justice."[33]

Khambayat to Cheymur in the Fourth Century

Ibn Hauqal of Baghdad, who travelled from Gujarat to Sind, says:

> "The rule of Raja Bilahra extends from Khambayat to Seymur...The Hindus form the majority of the population, which includes Muslims too, who are ruled over by a

> Muslim gentleman appointed by the Rajah to look after them ..There are mosques in the kingdom of Vallabha Rai in which Juma` (Friday) prayers and other prayers are offered and the call to prayer is openly shouted.''[34]

Khambayat to Coromandel in the eighth century

The conquest by Malik Kafur of the territories from Gujarat to Coromandel was a whirlwind which swept the land and passed away. But the flag of Alau'd-din's conquests, once planted, could not be rooted out. But they both became independent. The hundreds of miles between Gujarat and Coromandel were usually under Hindu Rais and Rajahs.

Gujarat was added for ever to Islamic possessions but Hasan Keythli and his successors ruled over Coromandel (Ma'bar) for forty years right up to the middle of the eighth century. Coromandel was finally conquered by Vijayyanagar.

Ibn Batutah, the famous traveller of Morocco, who came to India at that time and was going to China with a reply embassy from Muhammad Tughlaq, went from Delhi to Khambayat, and from Khambayat to Coromandel whence ships sailed to China. He has mentioned the Islamic settlements on his route and their rulers. His account shows the places where Muslims lived under Hindu governments and also describes their condition.

Khambayat

Passing through Daulatabad and Sagar Ibn-Batutah reached Khambayat, which was a large port of Gujarat. Though this port was nominally bound up with the Delhi empire, yet all commerce, business, and influence was commanded by the merchants and sailors of Arabia and Iraq who had been long settled here.

There were plenty of the Muslims of Arabia, Iraq and Persia in every direction and there were mosques and monasteries built by them. Ibn Batutah says:

> ''This is the finest town in respect of its mosques and other buildings. The reason is that the majority of the inhabitants have trade relations with foreign countries. They always build fine buildings and handsome mosques and try to vie with one another.''

Among stately buildings is the palace of Samari Nestling to it is a mighty mosque. The house of Gazaroni, the prince of merchants, is also very large and there is a mosque attached to it. The house of the merchant Shamsu'd-din Kulah-doz (cap-sewer) is very large. In the town is the monastery of Haji Nasir who was an inhabitant of the town of Diyar-Bakr in 'Iraq. Another monastery is that of Khwaja Ishaq where provisions are distributed to beggars.[35]

Gawi and Gandhar

Gawi and Gandhar were both ports attached to Bharuch ('Ain-i-Akbari). Ibn Batutah left Khambayat and first reached Gawi and then Gandhar. He says that both these coastal towns are under the possession of Raja Jalini who is under the supremacy of Islam. He finds Muslims here, most of whom were the courtiers and officers of the Raja. One of them was Khwaja Bahrah, another was Nakhoda Ibrahim, who owned six ships. Ibn Batutah boarded one of the ships of Nakhoda Ibrahim and his brothers. The names of the ships were Jagir and Manurat. There were fifty thousand archers and sixty Negro soldiers in the ships.

Beyram

This is a small island four miles off the Indian coast (this is not the Beyram situated near Aden). It was formerly in Hindu hands; later, it came under Muslim possession. At the time of Ibn Batutah Gazruni, the prince of merchants, built it and populated it with Muslims.

Gogah

Gogah or Ghogah (near modern Bhaunagar) was governed by Raja Dankil. There were large markets in this large town. He saw here a mosque ascribed to Hazrat Khizr (believed by the multitude to be the saver of the drowning). There was a band of Haidari faqirs.

Chandapur

Our traveller leaves Gogah for Chandapur, called Sandapur by the Arabs and which I took to be Singapur on the ground of verbal resemblance; but really it lay near Goa. He finds here a State ruled over by a Muslim, Sultan Jamalu'd-din Hanuri whose father Hasan was a navigator. Sultan Jamalu'd-din owed allegiance to Raja Harib (the correct name is Harir and he was the ruler of Vijayyanagar).

Here there was a separate locality for the Hindus and a separate locality for the Muslims. Here there was a stately mosque which, in the eyes of Ibn Batutah. equalled the mosques of Baghdad. Near Chandapur was a small population on the coast which had a church too. He saw in an idol house there a Muslim sufi in the guise of a yogi who talked only with signs and gestures.

Hanur

Hanur called Haunur and still existing in the district of northern Kanra within the boundaries of Bombay, was the real centre of Sultan Jamalu'd-din's power. Ibn Batutah met here Shaikh Muhammad Naguri, a pious founder of a monastery, and the theologian Isma'il, who was a teacher of the Qur'an, Nuru'd-din 'Ali Qadi and an Imam. He found one strange thing here, that men and women alike were educated. He saw in the town 13 girls' schools and 23 schools for boys.

The Muslim women of Hanur, like the Hindu women, wore 'saris.' Trade was the means of livelihood. Here Ibn Batutah got a message and a present for the Muslim yogi, The inhabitants were followers of Imam Shafi'i, which means that they were Arabs or their descendants.

Malabar

Ibn Batutah's ship starting from Hanur touched the coast of Malabar. He says that there is a distance of two months' journey between Chandapur and Kolam, which is the extent of these lands. This is the land of pepper.

There are twelve Hindu Rajas, great and small, in this land. The powerful Rajas have an army fifty thousand strong, while the small ones have a force three or four thousand strong. A wooden gate with the Raja's name upon it marks the frontier between two States.

In spite of Hindu government in these places, the Muslims are held in high respect. Between Chandapur and Kolam at every half mile there is a wooden house with shops and mounds where every traveller, Hindu or Muslim, takes rest Near every house is a well where a Hindu gives water to all people. The Hindus get water in pots, the Muslims in 'uk' (a wooden contrivance through which water flows).

The Hindus do not allow Muslims to be shown into their homes, nor do they allow them to eat in their pots. if they let any Muslim eat in their pot, they break it or gave it away to him. But in places where there are no Muslims they cook food for Muslims, and serve it on plantain leaves. They give away what remains of the food to kites, crows, and dogs. At every manzil (halting-place) there are Muslim inhabitants with whom travellers stay. They buy everything for them and cook food for them .

If the Muslim population did not exist at different places, it would have been difficult for Muslims to travel. Even if a Hindu sees a Muslim wayfarer on the road, he takes to flight.

Abi Sarur

He mentions the town of Malabar which he first enters as Abi Sarur. Abu'l-Fida has written it as 'Yasrur Ibn Batutah, says : "It is a small port. There is a population of Muslims here, too. The greatest among them is Shaikh Juma'ah widely known as Abi Sittah. He is a very generous man and he has distributed his wealth among beggars and poor people.

Paknur

From Abi Sarur he comes to Paknur (This is a place in Madras in the South, famous as Barkur. At the time of Ibn Batutah it was under the rule of the Vijayyanagar kingdom). He says that the name of the Raja of this place is Basdeo. He had thirty warships, but the admiral, who was a Muslim, was not good-natured and used to rob merchants. When a ship comes here the Raja exacts something as port duty. The Raja treated Ibn Batutah very courteously. Huseyn Salat is an eminent man in this town. There are qadis and khatibs and there is a mosque, too, built by Huseyn Salat.

Mangalore

He leaves Paknur and casts anchor at Mangalore. He says, this is the largest port of Malabar and many merchants of Persia and Yaman land here. The Raja of this place is Ramdeo. There are four thousand Muslims here, and they live in a separate quarter of their own. Sometimes they fight with the native inhabitants, but the Raja intervenes and a compromise is reached. There is a qadi here of fine parts. He is very generous; his name is Badru'd-din; he is a native of Ma`bar (Coromandal) and belongs to the Shafi`i faith. When the Raja sent his son as a hostage in the ship, I landed at the Qadi's request and I was entertained for three days.

Hili

Though no port of the name of Hili exists today, yet sixteen miles away from Cannanore a fringe of mountain juts out towards the North into the sea and is known as 'Koh-i-Hili' or the mountain of Hili. Ibn Batutah says:

> "It is a large and handsome city. Giant ships come here and ships from China halt here."

It is sacred both to the Hindus and the Muslims, and all the shipmen make offerings in the mosque. There is a treasure of offerings which is under the care and supervision of one Huseyn, the Imam of the mosque. Huseyn Wazzan is the Sirdar (leader) of the Muslims. A number of students get their stipends from the treasury of offerings in the mosque. There is a house of provisions connected with the mosques and food is distributed to poor Muslims." Ibn Batutah met here a dervish from Africa who had travelled in India, China and Arabia.

Jarpatan

This was a place within the area of Malabar and perhaps now known as Kandapuram. Among the mosques built in Malabar on the conversion of the Raja of Malabar to Islam one was built here also. Ibn Batutah says:

> "The name of the Raja of this place is Koel. He is a powerful Raja in Malabar and his ships go to Persia, Yaman, and Oman."

He saw here a scholar of Baghdad, whose brother was a rich merchant and who left a large fortune behind him.

The Hindu Rajas do not levy any death-tax upon Muslim inheritance which is entrusted to the Sirdar of Muslims on the death of a person. Ibn Batutah says that when he left the place the scholar was leaving for Baghdad with all the goods and riches of his dead brother.

Dah Patan

This too is under the supremacy of Raja Koel and is a large town on the sea-coast. There are plenty of gardens; cocoanuts, pepper, betel, and 'arwi' (a kind of vegetable) are found in abundance. There is a very handsome tank excavated by one of the ancestors of Raja Koel, in which red chiselled stones are set. There are four domes on all the four corners of the tank and near it is a mosque built by one of the forebears of Raja Koel. The Muslims bathe and perform ablutions in the tank and offer prayers in the mosque.

It is said that the Raja was a Muslim. Ibn Batutah heard from the inhabitants the story of the Raja's conversion to Islam. At the place where the mosque stood there was a tree which shed every autumn leaves bearing the Kalimah ("There is no God but God and Muhammad is the Messenger of God"). The Hindus and the Muslims divided among themselves these leaves which were efficacious in curing the sick. Impressed by this miracle, the Raja embraced Islam. He could read the Arabic script. His son, who did not take to Islam, had the roots of the tree cut down. But the tree again shot up. At the time of Ibn Batutah, the tree was standing near the mosque. There was an archway in front of it.

Budh Patan

The ship, starting from Dah patan, reached Budh patan where there was a mosque built by the converted Muslim Raja of the first century A.H. Ibn Batutah says that this, too, is a large town on the sea-coast (perhaps this is the town of Chalyam situated near modern Beypur). Ibn Batutah says that the Brahmans, who form the majority of the population, are open enemies of the Muslims. There are no Muslims.

Outside the town there is a mosque on the sea-coast. Muslim travellers stay here. The reason why this mosque, too, is spared is this. Once a certain Brahman demolished its roof and set the beams to his own house. His house caught fire and he was burnt to ashes together with his house, family and effects. Since then no Brahman wishes ill to this mosque; rather they guard it. There is an arrangement of drinking-water for travellers. There is a network on the door to ward off birds.

Pindarni

Starting from Budh Patan our traveller reaches Pindarni which he calls Findarinah and which lies sixteen miles north of Calicut. He says, it is a very large town. There are three localities inhabited by Muslims and in each locality there is a mosque. On the sea-coast there is a spacious Jami`mosque facing the sea. The Qadi and Imam is a native of Oman. Ships from China halt here in summer.

Calicut

Now our traveller arrives at Calicut, the famous port of Malabar. He says:

> "This is the largest port in Malabar. Merchants of China, Java, Ceylon, Maldive, Yaman, Persia, nay, of the whole world, come here. The port is among the largest ports in the world. The Raja is a Hindu and his title is Zeymur (Samri). He shaves his beard as do the Europeans whom I have seen."

But the chief of traders and merchants is a Muslim whose name is Ibrahim Shah-Bandar. He is a native of Bahreyn, of scholarly tastes, and of a generous disposition. Merchants from all sides have their meals at his board. The Qadi of the town is Fakhru'd-din `Uthmani and the head of the monastery is Shihabu'd-din Gazruni.

The people in India and China who vow to make offerings to the memory of Abu Ishaq Gazruni come to this monastery to make offerings. Nakhoda Mithqal who lives here is a very famous and wealthy marine merchant and he has his own ships which fetch commercial commodities from India, Yaman, China, and Persia."

The Raja's representatives Shaikh Shihabu'd-din and Ibrahim Shah-Bandar welcomed him as the ambassador of Muhammad Tughlak with drums and trumpets and banners. Ibn Batutah says that the Raja of Calicut is very just and impartial.

Once the nephew of the Raja's vicegerent snatched away the sword of a Muslim merchant. The merchant complained to his uncle who, after making inquiries, ordered his nephew to be sliced in two pieces with the same sword.

Ships of China start from this place. Ibn Batutah had to wait for months for fine weather. The owner of the ship was Suleyman Safdi. By his mistake Ibn Batutah's goods and luggage were loaded in the ship while he was left on the coast. He started by land for Kolam where he boarded the ship.

Kolam

Kolam is included in modern Travancore. Ibn Batutah says:

> "that this is the handsomest town in the whole of Malabar. The markets, too, are fine. The merchants are so rich and influential that they buy whole shiploads at a time and keep the wares in their godowns to sell them."

There are plenty of Muslim merchants here, the most influential of whom is Alau'd-din, a native of Ava. There is a considerable number of Iraqis here. The Qadi of the town is a learned scholar from Qazwin.

The wealthiest Muslim in the town is Muhammad Shah Bandar whose brother (Taqiu'd-din) is a very learned scholar. The Jami`mosque here is good and handsome. The name of the Raja is Taruri. Banate deyri' means Raja in this language. He respects the Muslims very highly and is very just-minded. here there is a monastery of Shaikh Fakhru'd-din, son of Shaikh Fakhru'd-din.

Chalyat

On account of the destruction of ships Ibn Batutah had to come to Calicut by the same route. He halted at Chalyat, called Shalyat by the Arabs and now known as Shalyah. It was situated near Calicut. Ibn Batutah praises the fine quality and design of cloths woven here.

Leaving this place he reached Hanur, from Hanur to Chandapur (Goa). He learns that the Raja (perhaps the Raja of Vijayyanagar) has fought against Sultan Jamalu'd-din Hanuri and annexed that State. Boarding the ship here, Ibn Batutah left for Maldive.

Maldive

There was a large population of Arab Muslims and they were ruled over by Sultan Khadijah. It has been already described.

Ceylon

From Maldive he went to Ceylon. The Raja at that time was Arya Chakravarti. He had many ships which sailed up to Yaman. He understood the Persian tongue. On account of the footprint (of Adam) there was a constant incoming and outgoing of Arab and Persian dervishes.

Gali

After a lot of wandering he reached Gali (Qali), the harbour of Ceylon. Even today ships start from this place to Europe and Australia. This owner of the ships of this port was Nakhoda Ibrahim. Boarding the ship at Colombo and Batala he came again to Ma'bar, (Coromandel) on the Indian coast in the ship of Nakhoda Ibrahim.

Ma'bar (Coromandel)

When Ibn Batutah reached Coromandel its ruler was Ghiyasu'ddin Wamoghani. It is the same government that was established here after the conquests of Malik Kafur, 'Alau'dd-din Khilji's officer. It was probably 741 A.H. (1341 A.D.). At the end of this century the Raja of Vijayyanagar exterminated this Islamic government. Madura was its capital.

Dwar Samandar

The Hosyala dynasty ruled over the country covered by the modern Mysore State. They had their capital at Dwar Samandar. The reigning Raja at that time was Balaldeo. Ibn Batutah relates that his army was one lac strong. The army included twenty thousand Muslims, all of whom were, says Ibn Batutah, fugitive criminals, thieves and robbers. But it is not known whence they came.

Perhaps Ibn Batutah has written all this in the fury of rage since they were fighting at that time against Ghiyasu'd-din who was the ruler of Coromandel and the husband of the sister of Ibn Batutah's wife.

Vijayyanagar

The mighty Hindu kingdom of Vijayyanagar extended from the river Kistna to the sea-coast. It is an amazing fact that while, on the one hand, it was perpetually at war on land with the Islamic kingdom of the Bahmanis, on the other hand, by sea it had relations with the Muslim kings of Arabia and Persia Mirza Shahrukh, son of Timur, had sent an embassy here. Maulana Kamalu'd-din 'Abdu'r-Razzaq was the leader of the deputation.

On coming back, he wrote an account of the glory and grandeur of Vijayyanagar which has been quoted by Khavind Shah in the last portion of Raudat-us-Safa and in the geographical portion of Habibu's-Seyyar under the names of Mangalore, Calicut, and Vijayyanagar army and the Raja respected them on account of their military sense. The Rajas had a mosque built and the Qur'an was held in reverence.[36]

Sind: the Sixth Centre

As has been already mentioned the Arabs conquered the territory stretching from Deybal (Thath) onwards at the end of the first century A.H., but the fact is that, even before this conquest, nay, before the invasion, there were Muslim inhabitants in Sind. Five hundred Arab Muslims under the leadership of an Arab Sirdar fled away from Makran to Raja Dahir of Sind. Muhammad bin Qasim conquered Sind and Multan at the end of the first Muslim century.

After that, for a century and a quarter, this country became a province, first of the Damascus Government and then of the Baghdad Government. Towards the middle of the third century A.H., after Mu'ta-sam bil'llah, the weakness of the centre gave rise to fissiparous tendencies and Arab governors become independent in a way.

After this the Hindus annexed some parts and the Muslims founded little States at various places. Some Muslim States existed in Sind right up to the days of the conquest of Sultan Mahmud of Ghazni and two of them were, comparatively speaking, large ones. One was situated in Mansurah on the border of Sind and the other in Multan on the extreme boundary of Sind.

The Arab travellers, who came here till the end of the 4th century A.H., describe both these Islamic States. Before Mahmud, there were scores of Muslim scholars and traditionists in Multan, Mansurah, Deybal and other towns. One of them was Abu Ma'ther Najhih of Sind, who flourished in the second century and who was a student of the prophet's biography. He was so much respected that, when he died the Khalifah Al-Mahdi led the funeral prayers.

A famous Arabic poet (of Sind) of the same age was Abu 'Ata Sindhi whose pronunciation was not admirable but the merit of whose Arabic verses was admitted even by the Arabs. If the name of other celebrities be recounted, a volume would be made. Hence I leave out other names.

After the conquest of Sind the Arabs established their settlements. The tribes of Qureysh, Kalb Tamim, Asad and various bribes of the Hijaz and Yaman settled down in sundry towns and their government existed, in some form or other, from Multan to the sea right up to the middle of the third century A.H. The jealousies and rivalries and civil wars between the Arabs of Yaman and those of the Hijaz annihilated them and many lands slipped out of their hands. But the States of Multan and Mansurah (Sind) existed till Mahmud's invasion I want to describe these with some details.

Multan

It has been mentioned above that this town was annexed by the Arabs in the first century A.H. (7th century A.D.) and remained from that time to Mahmud's time under Arab rule. Every Arab traveller of the third and fourth centuries has mentioned it. Even at the time of Mahmud's invasion and afterwards there were Muslim settlements here. In the beginning, this town, like other towns of Sind, was within the ambit of the Omayyad dominions.

After thirty or forty years the wheels of fortune took a new turn. In 132 A.H. the 'Abbasids replaced the Omayyads and held in their hands the reins of the Islamic empire. The centre of government shifted from Damascus to Baghdad. Multan remained bound up with the Abbasid Government till Mu'tasam's time. Then it happened that whenever a king was powerful he kept intact his possession over distant towns. If the king was weak, the governors of the towns became independent. Multan remained under the governors of Sind and Mansurah for some time; but later threw off the yoke of Sind and became a self-governing State. The date of this independence is probably the middle of the third century A.H.

Multan denotes not a single town but a whole province which was sometimes a State, nay, a kingdom. Mahalabi, Minister of Egypt, wrote in the fourth century A.H.: Its boundaries are wide. It extends up to Makran on the west and up to Mansurah (Sind) in the south.[37] The Kannauj, which lay near the river Sind, was included in Multan in 300 A.H.[38] According to census reports there were one lac and twenty villages within the orbit of the Islamic State of Multan.[39] It has been a rule more often than not in old kingdoms that the non-official sects of a religion flee for refuge to the borderland.

The fire-worshipping Iranians and Christians of Byzantium did so. Such was the case with Muslim Arabs.

In Qazdar, there was a population of Khariji Muslims and they had their own government. So Multan, too, became the refuge of a sect of Shi'as known as Isma'ilis who, later on, established their government there. They were pure Arabs and called themselves the descendants of Samah bin Lu'i.

Banu Samah

Among the early ancestors of Qureysh there was one Lu'i bin Ghalib. One of his descendants was Samah. This family was known as Banu Samah.[40] In the history of Islam this family attained to grandeur during Mu'tadad's time.

In the province of Oman in Arabia there were plenty of Kharijis (Schismatics). Muhammad bin Qasim, who was sent to chastise them, defeated them and established his government in Oman where the Sunnah became the ruling force. He is the first Amir of his dynasty and after him his descendants ruled over that State.

In 305 A.H. their natural jealousies led to internecine strife. The Qaramitah who were gaining strength in Bahreyn made capital out of the situation so much so that in 317 A.H. Abu Tahir Qaramati annexed Oman to the Qarmatian possessions.[41] The sea-trade between Oman and Sind had existed for a very long time and the relation of the Samanid with Sind was of long standing. A slave of the Samanid, Ghulam Fazl bin Mahan and some members of his dynasty ruled over Sandan in Sind from Ma'mun's time to the time of Al-Mu'tasam billah, but fratricidal warfare put an end to this rule.[42]

It would be no wonder if, after the extinction of their kingdom in Oman, the Samanids, fleeing from the Qarmatians, had migrated to Sind and from Sind to Multan where God blessed them with a new kingdom. However that may be the Samanids were the nobles of Multan. We first find mention of their independent State at the end of the third century A.H.

Banu Manbah

First of all, Ibn Rastah, whose date is 290 A.H., says in the geographical portion of his book Kitabu'l-a'laq-un-Nafsiyah:

> "There is a people in Multan who claim descent from Samah bin Lu'i.[43] They are called Banu Manbah. They are the rulers there and in the Khutbah they mention the Amir-ul-Mu'minin. When Indian Rajas attack them they, too, move forward with their large army from Multan, fight with them and, by virtue of their strength and wealth, overpower them."[44]

Ten years later Mas'udi arrives at Multan in 300 A.H. The Amir of Multan (I have mentioned that the government is in the hands of Samah bin Lu'i bin Ghalib) has an army, and he is powerful. Multan is among the great frontier provinces of the Islamic Empire. Under the control of Multan there are a hundred thousand and twenty villages which have been reckoned. Here there is the famous idol-house..... The income of the Amir of Multan mostly depends upon the sweet-smelling wood which is sent to this idol-house from distant places.

Whenever Hindus attack Multan and the Muslims are not prepared to face the attack they give out the threat of demolition of the idol-house, whereupon the Hindu armies go back. I went to Multan after 300 A.H. and the ruler at that time was Abdulah Manbah bin Asad Qarshi Sami.[45] Forty years after Mas'udi, Istakhri came to India in 340 A.H. He says:

> "The town of Multan is half of Mansurah. There is an idol-house here; pilgrims come from distant places and they spend large sums upon it and its guardian priests. The idol-house is situated in the most flourishing part of the bazaar - (Then there is a description of the idol). Whatever comes here is taken by the Amir. He spends some money upon the priests and saves some for himself."

Whenever any Hindu Raja intends to attack him, he holds out the threat of demolishing the idol-house. The Raja retraces his steps. Were it not for this fact, the Hindu Rajas would have harried Multan? There is a strong rampart-wall on all sides of Multan. Outside the town, at a distance of half a farsang there are many buildings named Jandrawan. It is a military camp. The king lives here. He goes to Multan only on Fridays. He goes to the town on an elephant to offer Friday prayers. He is by birth a Qureysh and is descended from Saman bin Lu'i. Multan is in his possession and he does not owe allegiance to the Amir of Mansurah or to anybody else. He mentions in the Khutbah the name of the Caliph.''[46]

Twenty-seven years after Istakhri, Ibn Hauqal, arrived at Multan in 367 A.H. He has recorded a good many things about Multan, but he gives no account of the Batinis and Isma'ills though this new feature deserved mention.

Eight years after Ibn Hauqal, Bashari Al-Muqaddasi set foot on the soil of Multan. He says, "The people of Multan are Shi'as. They shout hayya 'ala kheyri'l-'amal in the call to prayer and call 'takbir' (Allahu Akbar-God is greater) twice when standing up to pray.[47] In Multan the people mention in the Khutbah the Fatimid Caliph of Egypt and everything is managed according to his orders. Presents are always sent from this place to Egypt.[48]

These statements, besides other events, go to prove that during Ibn Rastah's time (290 A.H.), again during Mas'udi's time (as he is silent) and during Istakhri's time the government was in the hands of Sunnis and the Khutbah used to mention the Caliph of Baghdad.

Till 367, nothing had happened. But in 375 the government appears to be in the hands of the Isma'illis and under the influence of the Fatimid Caliph of Egypt who was an Isma'ill. It is obvious that this religious revolution of the ruling dynasty of Multan took place in 340 A.H. or between 367 and 375 A.H. This hypothetical history is corroborated by the fact that the kingdom of the Fatimids was established in Egypt at the same time, i.e.,in 258 A.H. and that their capital shifted from Tripoli to Egypt in 361 A.H.

At that time, the Islamic world was divided into two camps. The Sunnis owed allegiance to the 'Abbasid Caliph of Baghdad while the Shi'as recognized the Fatimid Caliph of Egypt. These two Caliphates vied with one another to extend their influence in the various Islamic countries. This rivalry existed even in Mecca and Madinah.

Whenever an Islamic kingdom was established the advocates and propagandists of both Caliphates started their propaganda. It was the period of the decay of the Banghdad Caliphate and of the fame and grandeur of the Caliphate in Egypt.

The 'Abbasid kingdom had grown old and effete, while the 'Fatimid kingdom was in the heyday of glory. But the 'Abbasids had their compensation. The new Turkish kingdoms founded in the East recognised the suzerainty of the 'Abbasids. The Samanids of Bukhara were under their influence.

In the middle of the fourth century A.H. the Ghaznawids appeared on the scene; and, forty or fifty years later, the banner of the Seljuqs was unfurled; and they all, in spite of their great military strength, bowed before the 'Abbasid Caliph. With the rise of Sultan Mahmud's fame the Caliph of Baghdad sent him, first in 387, and then in 390, rich robes, and gave him the titles of Aminu'sl-Millah, Yaminu'd-daulah.

In 396 A.H., the Sultan arrayed his forces against the Isma'illis and arrested the Qarmatian Amir. Probably it was this which led the Egyptian Fatimids to send their ambassador to Mahmud. Mahmud had him arrested on the way and placed him in charge of the famous Sayyid Huseyn bin Tahir bin Muslim'Ulwi who had him put to death.[49]

The Qarmatians of Multan

Now the question arises, was the Isma'ili dynasty which came upon the scene after the Arab Sunni dynasty of the Banu Manbah, which Arab geographers describe as the ruling dynasty of Multan, the line of the Arab Banu Manbah converted from Sunnism to Shiaism? or was it some other dynasty?

The heaps of books before it do not give any clue, but Abu Reyhan al-Biruni writes, while describing the idol-house of Multan, in Kitabu'l-Hind, which he wrote in 424 A.H.:

> "When the Qarmatians (Isma'ilis) became rulers of Multan, Jalam bin Sheyban, who had gained the upper hand, took the Jami' mosque of Muhammad bin Qasim to be an Omayyad relic. He demolished the shrine and built a mosque on its site."[50]

It transpires that this Qarmatian dynasty which gained supremacy at the end of the fourth century was new one. The founder was Jalam bin Sheyban and, as the name indicates, he was an Arab, Al-Biruni says:

> "The period of these Qarmatians is nearly a hundred years behind us."[51]

Kitabu'l-Hind was written in 424, A.H. and a hundred years behind this date would be 324, A.H., and a hundred years behind this date would be 324 A.H. Hence 324 A.H. marks, not the date of the possession of Multan by the Qarmatians, but of their appearance on the coasts of the Persian Gulf.

The fact is that the names of three Islamic sects have become mixed up - the Qaramitah, the Isma'iliyah and the Malahidah. Though all three sects are branches of the Shi'a faith, there are slight distinctions which separate them one from the other. The dates of their births, too, are different.

First of all, at the end of the third century, the Qarmatians made their appearance in Bahreyn, the Persian Gulf and 'Iraq; the Isma'ilis appeared in Africa in 296 A.H., but came to Egypt in 356 A.H.; the Malahidah, also known as Batiniyah who were followers of Hasan bin Sabbah appeared in Khurasan after 483 A.H.

The Fatimid Isma'ili Caliph, Al-Hakim bin Amri'llah founded a new sect in Syria, known as the Duruz (Druses). The question arises: while it is certain that the sect which held the reins of Multan Government was of the Isma'ili Shi'a persuasion, to what subsect did it belong? The historians who have called them Qaramitah and Malahidah did so on the strength of certain resemblances. The period when the ruling sect became powerful in Multan (after 340 A.H.) was everywhere a period of decay and downfall for the Qarmatians.

Secondly, the Qarmatians only nominally recognised the leadership of the Fatimid Caliphs of Egypt, while the people of Multan fully recognised it. Thirdly, Bashari Muqaddasi, a religious scholar, mentions them, not as Qarmatians, but as Shi'as and under the influence of the Fatimids.

Then again, *Hayya'ala kheyri'l-'amal* in the call to prayer and the particular characteristies regarding Friday prayers and the Khutbah were not found among the articles of the Qarmatian faith, but all these things, according to Muqaddasi, were included in the practice of the Isma'ilites of Multan. The Druses are a product of the years between 376 and 411 A.H. - a much later development. The sect of Malahidah or Batiniyah founded by Hasan bin Sabbah was born a hundred years later. So it is entirely erroneous on the part of some historians to describe them as Malahidah.[52]

The name of the ancestor of the Isma'ili dynasty which ruled over Multan at that time was, according to Persian histories, Shaikh Hamid. It is not known from what source *Firishta* has written that the early Muslims who came here at the time of the invasion of Afghanistan could not go back and began to intermarry with the Pathans of the Khyber mountains. Two tribes, the Lodis and the Surs, sprang from this Arab-Afghan progeny. Shaikh Hamid belonged to this very Lodi tribe.

The whole story, like other baseless things relating to the origin of tribes, is pure invention. The Lodis never appended 'Shaikh' to their names. Nor were their names anything of this sort. That they embraced Islam can be hardly recognised. The truth is that Persian historians were entirely unfamiliar with Arabic histories.

So they could not help taking the Muslim nobles to be Afghans. Shaikh Hamid and others had no connection at all with the Afghans and were probably descended from Jalam bin Sheyban as has been just mentioned with reference to Al-Biruni. Further detail follows.

It is written in Firishta that when Alaptagin and his successor Sabuktagin started invading the country of the Afghans the latter sought help from Raja Jaipal of Lahore. Raja Jaipal consulted the Raja of Bhatiya and decided that since the Indian army could not endure the biting cold of Frontier winter, the Pathans should be brought here and made to settle down.

Shaikh Hamid Lodi was awarded the Jagir of Lamghan and Multan. Shaikh Hamid appointed his officers and, in consideration of his Jagir, performed the service of defending India against the invasions of Alaptagin in 351 and 365 respectively.[53] In this incident the story of bringing Pathans to settle and of mentioning Shaikh Hamid as a Lodi, is pure fiction.

When Sabuktagin became king after Alaptagin in 365, Shaikh Hamid, seeing the growing power of Ghazni, made peace with Sabuktagin and became a tributary of that Amir. When Sultan

Mahmud sat on the throne of Ghazni in 390 A.H. and when he was attacking Bajrao, Raja of Bhatiya, the kingdom of Multan was in the hands of Shaikh.

Hamid's grandson, Abu'l-Fath Da'ud bin Nasir bin Shaikh Hamid who is mentioned as a heretic and a Qarmatian. Perhaps, seeing the growing ambition of Sultan Mahmud, Abu'l-Fath Da'ud wanted to defend himself by alliance with Hindu Rajas. On the occasion of the invasion of the territory of Bhatiya, Abu'l-Fath helped Bajrao.

This year the Sultan watched all this silently, but, next year in 396, he resolved to punish Abuj'l-Fath. He wanted that, instead of going direct to Multan, (i.e., through Dera Ghazi Khan), he should go from Peshawar to Punjab, and from the Punjab to Multan and take Abu'l-Fath by surprise. This led the Sultan to ask Anandpal to permit this army to pass through his country to Multan.

Other historians relate that Abu'l-Fath, having learnt the Sultan's intentions, sought Anandpal's aid. The Raja went from Lahore to Peshawar to persuade the Sultan not to carry out his intentions. But the Sultan's army defeated Anandpal, passed through his country to Multan. Abu'l-Fath shut himself in the palace; and, at last, the people of the town intervened and made a compromise on condition that a fixed tribute should be sent from Multan to Ghazni.

Abu'l-Fath recanted his faith and promised that the principles of Sunni faith, and not of Isma'ili, should be current in the land. A few years after (before 402 A.H.) the Sultan again attacked Multan and annihilated the Isma'ili faith. He seized Da'ud bin Nasir, took him to Ghazni, and imprisoned him in the fort of Ghor where he died.[54]

This is the summary of Firishta's statement. But Gardizi whose history. Zeynu'l-akhbar was written about 441 A.H. in the time of the Ghaznavids and at the capital, says:

> "The Sultan intended to start from Ghazni for Multan and thought that, if he should go direct to Multan, Da'ud bin Nasar (not Nasir), the Amir of Multan, might perchance get the news and make arrangements for his safety. So he took

> another route. Anandpal's dominion lay on the way and Mahmud sought that road. Anandpal refused. A fight ensued. Anandpal fled to Kashmir. The Sultan reached Multan and besieged it for seven days.

At last the inhabitants made peace on condition that they would hence forward pay a tribute of twenty thousand dirhams. The Sultan went back. All this happened in 396 A.H.-Then, again in 401 A.H., he went from Ghazni to Multan and conquered the remaining unconquered portion of Multan. He arrested the majority of the Qaramitah (Isma`ilis) who lived there, killed some, chopped off the hands of some, and punished them very severely. And that very year he arrested Da'ud bin Nasar and incarcerated him in the fort of Ghor.[52]

In trustworthy Arabic histories there is a very brief account of this affair and there is divergence of opinion on some points. But there is unanimity so far as the important points are concerned. Ibn'Athir (555 A.H.-630 A.H.) says:

> ''This year (396 A.H.) Sultan Mahmud invaded Multan. The motive behind this invasion was the fact that the Sultan had come to know of the heresies and unorthodox opinions of Abu'l-Futuh the ruler of Multan. He also learnt that he had given his subjects an invitation to believe in his heresies and that his subjects had responded to his call.

This led the king to wage a holy war against him and to bring him down. He started from Ghazna and found in the way many rivers and brooks which were overflowing with water.

It was difficult to cross Seyhun especially. Hence he sent word to Anandpal asking him to let him pass through his country to Multan. When he refused, the Sultan attacked him first. Anandpal fled away to Kashmir. When Abu'l-Futuh heard of the Sultan's march, finding himself not equal to the task of facing him, he sent all his fortune to Ceylon and left Multan. When the Sultan arrived here, he found the people enveloped in the Cimmerion darkness of heresy. He besieged them conquered them, and fined them twenty thousand dirhams.[56] Ibn Khaldun, too, has repeated these events in his history.[57]

This extract gives us the correct name Abu'l-Futuh instead of Abu'l-Fath. Secondly, we get to know the reason why, instead of going direct from Ghazni to Multan the Sultan took the route through the Punjab. But the incident of Abu'l-Futuh having sent his treasures to Ceylon is baseless.

Perhaps the historians of those days did not know the distance between Multan and Ceylon. Possibly it is that in the original MS. there was the name of some town which was wrongly transcribed as Sarandip (Ceylon). After this, in 403 A.H., the Fatimid Caliph of Egypt wanted to establish relations with Sultan Mahmud, but the latter declined and the ambassador was killed, as has been described above.

In this connection, a very important thing is a passage from the holy book of the Druses. In a writing of the year 423 A.H. we find:[58]

> "Addressed to the Indian believers in the unity of God generally, and to Skeykh ibn Saumar Rajah Pal in particular."

423 A.H. is the period of Mas'ud, the son and successor of Sultan mahmud (d.421 A.H.).

This shows that even after the Ghaznavid conquest of Multan, Multan was a centre for Schismatics. Even it appears as if, after the weakening of the Ghaznavids, Multan again was possessed by the Isma'ilis since, in the time of Shihabu'd-din Ghori, we again find the Isma'ilis ruling over Multan. In 572 A.H. the Sultan had to snatch away Multan from the Qaramitah (isma'ilis).[59] At last Multan became incorporated with the Delhi Government.

References

1. *Firishta*, Vol, 2, Discourse No. 8 p. 311. (Nawal Kishore Press).
2. Probably this very word is described in one place as Beykarjin and some where else as Beykarnatin in *Kitbu'i Badau't-Tarikh* and the travel-diary of Suley man the Merchant.
3. *Aja'ibul-Hind*, pp. 155-157.
4. *Futuhu'l-baldan* by Balazri, dated 279 A.H., p. 435 (Leiden).
5. Abu Zeyed Seyraff, p. 121 (Paris).
6. *Tuhfatu'l-Mujahidin* (quoted from Dr. Arnold's *Preaching of Islam)*, pp.882, 883.
7. *Taqwimu'l-buldan*, p. 361.

8. *Ibid*, p. 361.
9. *Atharu'l-bilad* by Qizwini, p. 82.
10. *Taqwimu'l-buldan,* p. 355.
11. *I bid*, p. 354.
12. *Ibid*, p. 355.
13. The date of the authorship of *Tarikh-i-Wasaf* is 707 A.H. 1307 A.D.), Elliot, Vol. 3, p. 44.
14. A full description of this island has been given in my article on Commercial relations.
15. Elliot's translation of *`Jami-ut-Tawarikh,* pp. 69,70.; Vide Wasaf's book,Vol. II, pp. 32-53.
16. *Khaza'inul-Futuh* by Amir Khusru, edited by the Jamiah Milliah Islamiah (Aligarh), dated 1927 A.D., pp. 157, 1962.
17. *Ibid.*,Vol, 3, p. 90.
18. *Khazainu'l-Futuh*, pp. 161,162.
19. *Ibid.*
20. *Ibid.*, pp. 26,27.
21. *Ibid.*, p. 29.
22. *Ibid.*, p. 28.
23 .*Aja`ibu'l-Hind*, p. 16.
24. *Ibid.*, p. 152.
25. *Ibid.*, p. 157.
26. *Ibid.*, p. 157.
27. Ibn Hauqal, p. 233.
28. *`Aja'ibu'l-Hind*, p. 144.
29. *Muruju'dh-dhahab* by Mas`udi, Vol, 1, pp. 382, 184.
30. Muruju'dh-dhahab by Mas'udi, Vol, 2, pp. 85, 86.
31. With reference to Taqwimu'l-buldan by Abul's Fida, p. 359.
32. *Ibid.*, p. 257.
33. The manuscript copy of `Sufi's *Jamiu'l-Hikayat* existing in Daru'l-Musan-nifin, (Azamgadh).
34. Ibn Hauqal, p. 233 (Leiden).
35. *Safarnamah-i-Ibn-i Bhatutah `Arabi*, published by the Kheyriah Press in Egypt, Vol. 2, pp, 128,129.
36. *Firishta*, vol. I. p. 333.
37. *Taqwimu'l-buldan* by Abul'l-Fida, p 350, (Paris).
38. Mas1udi, vol. I, p 372, (Paris).
39. *Ibid.*, P. 375.
40. Ibn Khaldun has often made it clear that many etymologists do not recognize the descent of Banu Samah from this Samah bin Lu'f Ibn Khaldun, Vol. I, p. 325 and Vol. I, p. 93.
41. Ibn Khaldun, Vol, I, p. 93.
42. Baladhari, p. 446 (Leiden).
43. Some historians and travellers have written, instead of Samah,

Asamah which is incorrect.

44. *Al A'laqu'n-Nafiyah* by Ibn Rastah.
45. *Muruju'dh-dhahab* by mas'udi, Vol. I, pp, 375, 376, (Paris).
46. Istakhri-quotation from *Mu'jamu'l-buldan* by Yaquit,
47. *Ahsanu'l-taqasim* by Muqaddasi, p. 481.
48. *Ibid.*, p. 485.
49. There is an account of this Fatimid embassy given in *Zaynu'l-akhbar*, p.71(Berlin).
50. *Kitabu'l-Hind*, p. 501 (London).
51. *Ibid.*, p. 56 (London).
52. The word is often used as a general term for any hereties "LC" Edition.
53. The whole story is given in Firishta, vol. I, pp. 17,18 (Nawal kishore Press).
54. *Tarikh-i-Firishta* Pp. 25, 27 (Nawal kishore Press)
55. *Zeunu'l-Akbar* by Gardizi, pp. 67. 68 (Berlin).
56. Ibn Athir, *Kamil*, Vol. 9, p. 132, (Leiden).
57. Ibn Khaldun, Vol 4, p, 366, (Egypt).
58. Supplement to Elliot's *History*, Vol. I p. 491.
59. *Firishta*, Vol., I, p. 56 and Vol, 2, p, 324, (Nawal kishore Press).

Part - II

Muslim Kingship after the Muslim Conquest

Chapter - 7

Muslim Conquest of Delhi

Nako, a land of beasts, birds, fish, men and serpents, was ruled by a *Badshah* named Muhammad Shah of Alamanja.[1] He had no son. Once he feasted some *faqirs* and *Pirs* with great cordiality and earnestness, and prayed to them as follows:

> "I have three hundred wives, but still I have not been blessed with a son. Please consult the scriptures and tell me what I am to do."

The *Badshahs* rest under the shade offered by the wings of the bird Hurma which lives on rhinoceros and elephants. The bird has a horn on its back. Sometimes before its death the bird goes about with an elephant pierced through the horn. The elephant dies afterwards, and maggots breed on its carase which enter the entrails of the bird and eat them up. The bird dies in consequence. Sarol is another bird of that place. The grandees make hubble-bubbles of the eggs of these birds. The price of each egg comes up to rupees one hundred or two hundred. Shah-Morog is another species of bird found in that country.

Before its death it flaps its wings on the ground in quick succession; the friction produces fire in which the bird is consumed to death. There is another bird named Sereng which assumes a white colour in the morning, crimson in the afternoon and black at night; and they are kept by the grandees for their amusement. There is another bird named Murtaskhor. It swallows live charcoal of burnt fuel, wood and bamboos, without scalding its mouth. The rats and mice of that place are very sweet-scented. The nobles of the land use coats and garments made of their skins which they sew and convert into dresses. Their pillows are also made of the same stuff, and they become cool in summer and warm in winter. Their price ranges from one hundred to two hundred rupees. Diamonds are also found in that country. The faqirs and pirs replied:

> "What means shall we suggest? There is one *Pir* named Marda Sher Khan Ali[2] who wanders about in disguise from city to city on an Iraqi horse. If you can recognise him when he comes to your city, you should pray to him for a son, and he will fulfil your wish."

As luck would have it Sher Khan Ali halted at the city and the Badshah honoured him and offered the saint large quantities of food articles.

> The pir asked the Badshah, " I hope you are perfectly happy"
>
> Badshah: "I have everything complete, but I am unhappy having no son. I have three hundred wives, but still no son has been born to me."
>
> Pir: "In your previous life you had stolen the son of another man, and sold him to a degenerate infidel who must have killed and devoured the child. For this sin you have not been blessed with a son. Now, if you, desirous of a son, offer one lakh of golden pieces to mecca you will surely have one."

The *Badshah* did accordingly and got a son, who was named Rangaddin.[3]

The Munificence of Rungaddin Badshah

After some time, Alamanji Muhammad Shah died, and he was succeeded by his son Rungaddin. With regard to his own kingdom he enquired:

> "How long have we been Badshahs of Nako?"

He could trace the date of origin to the wars between the Kauravas and the Pandavas and not further than that. Nobody could say how long they were wielding the sovereign power. The Badshah ordered the articles in the royal store to be counted, but the counting could not be finished.

Rungaddin Badshah said to his *Wazir*, Farteijang Khan, and his *Karzi*, Sul Marda-dadulla:

> "I investigated into the antiquity of our dynasty of Badshahs. The records testify to its existence at the time of the war between the Kurus and the Pandavas. No date could be

> traced earlier than that Armageddon. The articles of the royal treasury were also computed, but the counting could not be finished. So I ask you both to give me such advice as will conduce to my well-being in the life to come as well as in the present life, so that my soul may be blessed."

The two ministers said to the Badshah:

> "Make more liberal presents to Mecca and to other holy places with due discrimination. Bestow gold, silver and clothes on faqirs, pirs, beggars and the poor. If this is accomplished you will earn blessings in the after-life. Arrange and reconstruct the city in the proper order. Keep more soldiers, so that you may subjugate the frontier Rajas and Badshahs and exact tribute from them. Find out a kingdom greater that Nako: invade and occupy it, and become its Badshah. If this can be done, you will earn fame and glory in this world."

Accordingly, the Badshah made more liberal presents to religious places, exercising proper judgment and discretion; gifts of gold and silver and apparel were made on a more extensive scale to faqirs, beggars and the indigent. The wives of mendicants wore bracelets and anklets of gold and silver. The city walls, the fort and the forum were constructed with marble stones.

Rungaddin's War Equipments

The Badshah then commanded Farteijang Khan to recruit and maintain officers and servants, which was done accordingly. There were 30,500 officers consisting of *Wazirs, Dewans, Nawabs, Bukshis* and *Mansabdars*; a cavalry of 700,000 soldiers using Iraki, Arbi, Sujarnis[4] and Turki ponies, 3,500 elephants; 42,000 canons; 84,000 muskets; 28,000 chandravans; 100,500 beldars, and innumerable merchants, shopkeepers as well as camels, bullocks and asses.

Rungaddin's Expedition of Conquest

After subduing all the Badshahs and Rajas on the frontiers of his kingdom, Rungaddin marched against Sher Pingal, King of Rum. Before storming the entrenchments and garrisons of Sher Pingal Badshah, Rungaddin halted at a distance of three days journey and despatched messengers to the King of Rum with a letter to the following effect, I am the Badshah of Nako, and my name is

Rungaddin. How dare you rest in peace after having heard my name? Have you not received reports of the invincibility and splendour of my soldiers and my arms and weapons?

Even now there is time for you to come and make friends with me by offering due submission otherwise he prepared for war. If your back in war materials, just ash of me and I will send them to you. Anyhow I demand war. The above message formed the subject-matter of the letter which was delivered to the Badshah by a courier.

Sher Pingal's Reply

Sher Pingal became furious on the receipt of the letter and said:

> "My name is Sher Pingal, which denotes a tiger. Why should an ordinary human being brag before a tiger? Why should I supplicate you for war-equipments? The splendour of your army has led you to utter these words of pride and disdain, which will be humbled at the sight of the magnificence of the forts of my kingdom. I have three fortresses, one of copper, another of iron and the third of stones; if you can come after passing these three citadels I will then ask you for supplies of war."

To this the Ukil made the reply:

> "Have you not heard the name of Rungaddin Badshah? He has humbled numerous Badshahs and Rajas. The three forts of which you have just spoken will not stand you in good stead. Man has constructed them, and man will demolish them."

So, do not remain in peace by counting upon their impregnability. Go and offer your homage to him everything will go well. If you oppose nothing will be saved. Your assertion that Sher Pingal means a tiger is inauspicious, as elephants, rhinoceros and tigers are all killed by men."

After having said so the Ukil was turned out of the Badshah's presence, and he reported the whole matter to Rungaddin Badshah, who presented the Ukil with a pony and ten thousand rupees, saying:

"Well done, Ukil."

Crossing of the invincible forts

After this, the *Badshah* despatched Farteijang Khan, a senior Nawab and a commander of twelve thousand, at the head of twelve Nawabs and a large army. At the sight of the copper fort, the general placed in the van large sheets of iron to serve as walls for the soldiers who marched under the shelter thus afforded, unhurt by the showers of arrows and bullets. The cavalry riding on Iraki and Sujarnis ponies then reached the foot of the copper fort, when they crossed the fort and went over to the other side. The inmates of the fort perished or took to their heels. The copper fort was destroyed by Farteijang Khan. The invaders then attacked the fort of iron. Here also they posted the iron screens in front. The *poladars* served as screens for which they could not assail the fort The *beldars* or sappers cut open a path with thin steel hoes through which the sepoys, the elephants and other men passed, and occupied the fort.

After this the invaders stormed the stone fort. There was a Nawab who had once been wronged by Sher Pingal; he now came and made friends with Farteijang Khan. The general gave him large presents and asked the methods of successfully attacking the iron fort. The Nawab replied:

> "There is a secret passage; and horses and elephants cannot pass through it as it is very narrow. A hundred or two men only can pass through the passage."

Some two hundred soldiers versed in magic were then requisitioned for service. They entered the royal apartments by a stratagem, and transported Sher Pingal Badshah bodily with his bedstead, and handed him over to Farteijang Khan, who in turn despatched the captive monarch to the presence of Rungaddin Badshah.

Sher Pingal Offers Submission

Rungaddin Badshah brought Sher Pingal to the *Darbar* and said:

> "Well, Sher Pingal, you did not consult men proficient in the ways of the world, nor did you act as one should do when he is in danger and misfortune. Hence you are now facing all this misery."

Sher Pingal replied:

"O Badshah, I bow to thee, What you have said is proper and reasonable. You have heard what sort of a man I, Sher Pingal, am. Even Jungam-Shahan Badshah could not stem the tide of misfortunes;[5] what am I to say now? Do as you think proper."

Rungaddin then said:

"Well, Sher Pingal, do not be afraid in the least. I shall leave this place after seeing that you are properly established."

Having said so, Sher Pingal was allowed to dine at the royal banquet, and to attend the assembly of the Wazir and the Dewan. The elephants, horses and other spoils seized by Farteijang Khan after destroying the three forts were taken with him. He left two Nawabs in charge of the place and proceeded to the presence of the *Badshah.* Sher Pingal took his oath in accordance with the injunction of the Musalmans, and Rum became bound to pay an annual tribute of five corers of rupees. Sher Pingal was presented with a sirpao or robe of honour, after which he was allowed leave to go. The son of Farteijang Khan was appointed Subedar or governor of the place. Rungaddin Badshah said to Sher Pingal:

"I assure you there is no cause for alarm. Pay the stipulated sum of money annually to the Subha."

To this Sher Pingal replied,

"*Badshah salamat*, you have bestowed a second life upon a dead person. I will act as you have commanded me."

Farteijang Khan was rewarded with presents of elephants and horses, and a purse of one lakh of rupees; the twelve other Nawabs were also rewarded according to their desert. After the subjugation of Rum, Rungaddin Badshah encamped on the bank of the river Narmada, where Nasir Beg blew the naubat.

Pithor Raja of Delhi

Rungaddin's spies then went far and wide to survey the countries. A messenger returned from Delhi and reported to Rungaddin Badshah:

"Pithor Raja rules at Delhi. He is a powerful chief, and his kingdom is a prosperous one. All the commodities wanted by the Badshah are available in his territories. In ancient times it was the kingdom of the Kurus and the Pandavas. It is inhabited by men of all castes, Brahmans, Kshattris,

Vaishyas and Sudras, and other Hindusthanis. That place is fit for the establishment of your throne."

Rungaddin Marches against Delhi

Having heard this the Badshah asked the Wazir for his opinion. The Wazir replied, I hear Delhi has insurmountable fortresses, great warriors and diplomats. Still, if you resolve, you can occupy the throne of Delhi.

The Badshah then despatched Jambur Khan by the route through the Maru river at the head of one lakh of sepoys, while Harjubar Khan proceeded by the way through Rachanpur in command of an army of one hundred thousand soldiers consisting of Rohella-pathans and others. The Badshah went in the middle. Bahlol Khan Nawab marched at the head of a large force of thirty thousand sepoys a journey of six dandas in advance, Rungaddin Badshah marching in the rear.

The Rajputs Prefer War to Submission

The general of Rungaddin Badshah captured some forts within the jurisdiction of Pithor Raja's territories. The soldiers stationed at those forts reported to Pithor Raja, king of Delhi :

> "The powerful sovereign Rungaddin Badshah, son of Muhammad Shah of Alamanja, King of Nako, whose capital is Mazitpur, has come with a large army, and is marching towards this direction after capturing our garrisons."

Then Pithor Raja conferred with the Rajas of Amber, Bandhab, Haro, Rana Raja, Gar-Chitor, Jharkhand and other powerful chieftains, when he said:

> "Rungaddin Badshah is a very mighty prince. After subduing numerous potentates he is now coming to invade our kingdom. Please advise whether we should offer our homage to him."

The Rajas assembled replied in one voice:

> "We are *Kshattriyas* and Rajputs. We are not prepared to derogate our name for fear of our lives. Besides, the Raja of Delhi has never submitted nor paid his homage to any other prince. Death in battle is preferable to submission. So make preparations for war, and we shall fight."

Exchange of Embassies between Rungaddin and Pithor Raja

In the meantime Rungaddin Badshah's Ukil arrived at the court of Pithor Raja with a letter containing the following message:

> "I am the son of Muhammad Shah Badshah of Alamanja, and my name is Rungaddin Badshah. Have you heard or not of the magnificence of my army and of my subjugation of the Rajas and the Badshahs of the territories through which I have passed ? You should now come and establish friendly terms with me, and I will go back after having settled you in your territories, and you will live in peace by paying me presents and tribute. If you do not submit I will invade Delhi and take possession of the same, and you will be deprived of great opportunity."

Pithor Raja, King of Delhi, sent the following report :

> "The Badshah is a great man to himself, what is that to me? He is the Badshah of a kingdom and I am also the Raja of mine own. He should not have written like this." The Ukil then said: "What you have said and written betrays indiscretion. Everyone has heard of the prowess and strength of Rungaddin Badshah. Now that you have spoken so, you will have no loophole to escape."

Clash between the Muhammadans and Rajputs

The Ukil reported the whole matter to Rungaddin *Badshah*. The *Badshah* marched to the battle, and so did Pithor Raja. The Raja despatched the Rana-raja with a numerous army to meet the forces of Jambur Khan, while the Raja of Gar-chitor marched at the head of a large contingent of soldiers and chieftains against Harjubar Khan, Raja Pitholdas was sent with another detachment, six dandas in advance.

Pithor Raja himself marched to the eastern front personally to conduct the battle against Rungaddin Badshah. Then the advance guards of the Raja and of the Badshah caught sight of each other. The emissaries of the two sovereigns sent report to their respective lords.

The battle commenced at a distance of seven days' journey from Delhi. There ensued a terrible encounter between Jambur Khan and the Rana Raja with heavy casualties on both sides. Jambur Khan and the Rana-raja were engaged in a duel on horseback, and they both perished by their swords. This was followed by a furious contest between the Raja of Gar-Chitor and Harjubar Khan.

On one side were ranged Rajput sepoys who were of very hard metal they would never retreat even at the cost of their lives; on the other side were the Rohilla-Pathans, riders of sujarnis horses; they would perish by the sword, but would never yield. There was terrible slaughter on both sides.

The Raja had a brother named Surat Sangha. A Nawab was fighting from the back of an elephant. Surat Sangha crept under the elephant and speared the Nawab to death. The remnant of the Nawab's army fled and joined the forces of Rungaddin. After slaying Hurjabar Khan, Unmatta Sangha joined the ranks of Pithor Raja.

The Death of Pithor Raja

Then ensued a terrific contest between Maharaja Pithor and Rungaddin Badshah. It commenced with the firing of muskets from both the hostile camps, which was followed by a battle with bows and arrows. Then came the battle of the elephants, and horses, which was followed by those of spears, swords, daggers and targets. The struggle continued for one full year in which varieties of weapons were used. Then the Rohella and Pathan cavalry of Rungaddin Badshah, riding upon Arabian and Sujarnis horses, destroyed the elephants and horses of the Hindu Raja, whose men were also killed by thousands. The Raja from an elephant's back hurled his own chandravan (discus?) which fell back on himself and killed him.

After his death, the cries of his subjects crossed the barriers of heaven. The Raja's brother Rana Sangha and his son Kumud Sangha burnt the dead body of the Raja on a pyre made of aloe-wood. The queens of the Raja who numbered 120 accompanied their lord. Several hundred pitchers of ghee were poured upon their bodies, and the fire reached the summit of the sky. Ten crores of rupees in gold and silver and ten thousand cows, as well as clothes, were presented to Brahmans and Vaishnavas for the spiritual well being of the deceased sovereign.

Rungaddin's Victorious Entry in Delhi

Adam Fartu Khan, brother of Rungaddin Badshah, and Shah Adil Khan, his son, met the Raja's brother Rana Sangha and his son Kumud Sangha in a serious combat. All the four perished by their swords. Thus ended the war between the two armies. Rungaddin won the day, while Pithor Raja encountered a defeat. The remnant of the army of Pithor Raja surrendered to Rungaddin Badshah who inspired them with confidence and goodwill.

The victorious Badshah then proceeded towards Delhi. On an auspicious day and moment he made his entry into the walls of Delhi. All the gold and silver and other articles that belonged to Pithor Raja were plundered and seized.

The prince who was left behind by Rungaddin Badshah in his native land was known as Sultan Muhammad Mazum. The Badshah now sent to him presents of precious articles of Hindustan, as well as a sceptre and umbrella with the command appointing him Badshah of Nako.

Rungaddin retained two lakhs of sepoys with him, and sent back the rest to his own kingdom of Nako, after having presented them with gold, silver and clothes. With regard to the two lakhs of sepoys kept by him, he doubled the number of mansabs. Pithor Raja's crown, worth three lakhs of rupees was presented to Farteijang Khan. Others were amply rewarded.

The Rajas and chieftains of various ranks who fought on the side of Pithor Raja either perished in battle or survived. The brothers and sons of those who were killed were appointed Rajas. They were all given presents. Further they were assured his support, and allowed to live in their old dignity and rank. He enquired into the respective status of his subjects, and allowed them to retain the same.

Rungaddin's Respect for Hindu Traditions

Rungaddin Badshah invited Sarbabhaum-Chandra, the family priest of the late King Pithor Raja, and said:

> "This Delhi was ruled by Hindu sovereigns for a very long time. I was the Badshah of Nako at a distance of six months journey from Delhi."

The Almighty God has now placed a Musalman Badshah to rule here in place of the Hindu Rajas. You should advise me in a manner which will lead to the continuity of our rule here.?

Then said Sarbabhum-Chandra : " O Badshah, what shall I say? You are yourself acquainted with all laws and traditions. God has created the nations of the earth in separate groups, each different from the other; and he has not provided uniform customs and religions for all. If the different castes and creeds are protected, God will protect you also, and you will be able to remain at Delhi without any trouble or fear."

Rungaddin Badshah then said: "Thanks very much, Pandit. You have given me wholesome and salutary counsel." The Badshah presented to the priest rewards and four thousand rupees, and made the following declaration: "The laws and traditions which existed before will remain unaltered."

The Organisation of Mansabs

After this, Rungaddin Badshah ordered Farteijang Khan:

"We have two lakhs of horse of our native kingdom, and four lakhs more recruited in this country, coming up to a cavalry of six lakhs strong. Now you should proceed to group them under Nawabs, Mansabdars and Fauzdars."

Farteijang Khan accordingly created Nawabs with various grades of Mansabs, such as hafthazari, Chai-hazari, *Panch*-hazari, Chari-hazari, tin-hazari, dui-hazari and ek-hazari. Mansabs were also created with eight hundred soldiers and five hundred guns, and fauzdars with three hundred, and one hundred and fifty respectively.

The new system was recorded on paper and communicated to the Badshah. Farteijang Khan was further commanded to despatch soldiers to different localities, the number being proportionate to the exigency of the place, and to make gifts to all the people. Then all the inhabitants of this country were given a sufficient quantity of gold, silver and clothes irrespective of their castes and classes.

Divisions of the Palace

The Badshah then enclosed his compound with ramparts built of stone, and commenced the construction of his quarters. First came the Mardana-mahal where the Badshah sits and reclines or confers with the males, so it is called *Mardana-mahal*. Then came the *Zanana-mahal*, where the Badshah sleeps and amuses himself with the *begums*, where males have no access. Then came the *Dewankhana* where the Dewan holds his court, superintends his affairs and communicates to the *Badshah* when necessary.

So it is called *Dewankhana*; then came the hall of the *Khan-saman* on the north, where is situated the store for the articles of the Badshah, hence it is called *Khan-sama*. On the west is the *Roz-dewan* where the Badshah receives reports of affairs of countries far and near, and issues his ordersand decisions with regard to places as occasion demands.

In front of the hall, there is a place enclosed by gold railings, with two pillars of gold, near which the two Wazirs take their seat; the Dewan sits within the enclosure.

After this we have the silver enclosure with twelve pillars of silver against which lean the commanders of seven thousand and six thousand. Then comes the copper enclosure meant for the panch-hazaris and chari-hazaris; then the brass enclosure intended for the tin-hazaris and dui-hazaris; and last the iron enclosure for the *ek-hazari* Nawabs. On the south is situated the *Roz-adawlat* where the *Badshah* enquires into the petitions of complaints.

The Badshah's Weekly Routine

The Badshah proceeds to the *durbar* when ten dandas have elapsed, and rises when there are two dandas for the commencement of the second prahar. On Mondays and Saturdays he conducts affairs of the State sitting at the Roz-dewan. On Sundays and Wednesdays he decides the applications of complainants. On Tuesday he enquires into the income and expenditure of the royal treasury. On Thursday he holds his court at the Hall of State called Khirnawat where he investigates matters relating to the sacred shrines of Musalmans and Hindus. On Fridays he visits the hall of Prayer to take the name of God.

Hindu sovereignty ended at Delhi with Pithor, and Musalman usages commenced from the time of Rungaddin, who became Badshah in the era of Sakaditya 843. Here ends the narrative of the country of Nako.

References

1. *Thana Panjar* in another text.
2. *Muhammad Ali* in another text.
3. *Rukundin* in another text.
4. *Sujarnis* is obviously a misnomer for *Sumarnis*, the name given to poniesimported from Sumyran; Mujanas occurs in *Ain-i-Akbari*; see Hobson Jobson, under *Turkey*.
5. In another text, "During the conflict I could not recuperate myself, being avictim of drive misfortune."

Chapter - 8

The Kingship of Timurlang

After the death of the Daigati Nawab, his grandson Timurlang became afflicted with extreme poverty. His mother earned her bread by spinning cotton yarn for others, and Timur tended the goats of a local blacksmith; thus did the mother and her son live somehow on what they earned by their own labour. Timur took the goats to the field every day; at noon his mother gave him in the field his breakfast consisting of one-quarter seer of bread the same amount of bhang[2] and the same amount of water.

Blessed by a Prophetic Faqir

One day a faqir of the Lohalangar (iron-chained ?) order went on shouting at the place where Timur's goats were grazing to the following effect:

> "The person who will give me bread, bhang and water, each measuring one quarter of a seer, will be appointed by me Badshah of Delhi."

Timur's mother was then proceeding to give her son his noontide repast.

Timur, on hearing the cries of the faqir, went to give him the bread, bhang and water. The mother dissuaded her son from doing so, saying:

> "You will suffer from hunger. Do not part with your bread to the faqir."

Timur disobeyed his mother's bidding and gave his breakfast to the faqir, who ate it and became extremely pleased. The faqir then said to Timur:

> "Lie flat on the ground with your face downward."

Timur obeyed, and the faqir inflicted seven strokes on Timur's body with the iron chain that girdled his person, saying:

> "I confer on you the kingship of Delhi for seven generations."

Saying this, the faqir vanished. Timur became afflicted with pain from the strokes of the iron chain that he received from the faqir, and his mother said:

> "I forbade you, and you disobeyed my words. Now, you are throbbing with pain from the blows of the mad faqir."

Then the mother and son went home.

Timur's Master Dreams the Site of Hidden Treasures

Some time after, Timur's master the blacksmith said one day to Timur:

> "I have no man to-day to heat the furnace. So you should work with me in the forge to-day."

The furnace was heated and the smith, after hammering iron for some hours, became exhausted with fatigue and fell asleep peacefully with his mouth wide open. Then an insect as big as a black bee with the colours of gold, silver and diamond, issued out of the smith's mouth and flew into the house.

Timur saw the insect and chased it. The insect, after flying over to the ruins of the fort of Khattam Shah Badshah, entered again into the mouth of the smith. Timur returned to the smithy and began to blow the bellows. The smith awoke from his sleep and said:

> "I have dreamt a dream. I wandered over the rampart of Khattam Shah Badshah and saw gold coins strewn all over the fort."

Timur then said:

> "You have seen something in your extreme fatigue. Besides, a day-dream is always false, and never true."

A Miracle at Timurabad

At night Timur with his mother excavated a part of the old fort and came upon piles of gold mohurs strewn all over the place. The mother and son extracted a basket of coins and deposited them in their house. Timur saw a dream that very night in which a faqir said to him:

> "Exhibit the gold mohurs to the people and you will be Emperor of Delhi."

Then Timur during the self-same night took with him baskets of mohurs and scattered them in the thoroughfares of the town. The next morning the people became astonished at the sight of the gold mohurs strewn all over the *bazars*. A *waqayanavis* in the service of the Badshah of Delhi lived at Timurabad, and he reported the matter to Jalal Hussain, Emperor of Delhi, in the following words:

> "There have been elephant like piles of gold mohurs at Timurabad last night."

On receiving this news the Badshah became astonished.

Occupation of the Throne of Delhi

Timur then maintained a large number of elephants, horses, cannon and sepoys and became the proprietor of the fort of Khattam Shah Badshah. The Badshah of Delhi heard this news and despatched a Nawab to capture Timur and take him to Delhi. The Nawab proceeded to Timurabad, fought with Timur, but being repulsed he returned to Delhi. Timur pursued him as far as Delhi with 80,000 soldiers and camp-followers.

Then the Lohalangar faqir, who had partaken of the bread, bhang and water from the hands of Timur went to Delhi. There was a man named Sharif Muhammad, and he was the preceptor of the Delhi Badshah. The Lohalangar faqir said to him:

> "You say you are the preceptor of the Badshah. I will play a practical joke upon the Badshah, save him if you can."

The preceptor of the Badshah said:

> "Wherein lies your power ? Better save your own life and remain silent."

Then, the Lohalangar faqir struck three blows on the earth with his iron chain, and instantaneously the Badshah with the Raja of Peshowa flew up into the air, and dropped down again on the earth. Then the imperial preceptor paid his homage and reverence to the Lohalangar faqir and departed from the place. The Lohalangar faqir went to unknown quarters after placing Timur on the throne of Delhi.

Timur thus became the Emperor of Delhi. After his death, he was succeeded by his son (descendant) Shah Babar who was succeeded by his son Shah Humayun who was succeeded by his son Shah Akbar, who was succeeded by his son Shah Jahangir.

References

1. The name Rungaddin or Rukundin is found in the list of the rulers of Delhi from Judhisthir to Aurangzeb inserted in many Assamese chronicles. According to one list Rungaddin vanquished the Rajput Raja Udayamaila; according to another he defeated Pithor Raja. The period of his reign, viz. 23 years, 9 months and 8 days, is uniform in all Burannjis; though the starting date varies, 1st Ashar, 787 *Saka*, in one; and 11th Ashar, 764, *saka*, in another. This, I believe, is a serial mistake as 764 *plus* 23 makes 787. The Kali era when he commenced his rule at Delhi is given as 3944. Rukundin's successors in Delhi according to these lists are Bahuddin, 25 years; Samruddin, 29 years; Kutubuddin, 27 years, Shahabuddin, 21 years; Samruddin, 29 years; Kutubuddin, 27 years, Shahabuddin, 21 years; Bibi Rabiya, 7 years 3 months, 10 days from 891 Saka. The list will be published later on. The text of Chapter I, has been collected carefully from three manuscripts.
2. *Bhang* has been described by Manuceei, Irvine Vol. II page 7, as a :"Beverage made of the leaves of dried hemp ground down, which intoxicates as soon as taken. Aurangzeb wanted to suppress this disorder."

Chapter - 9

Humayun's Flight and Restoration

Humayun King of Delhi used to say frequently while sitting at the *Durbar*, I do not know of any man likely to thwart my sword. Daria Dadulla Kazi could not stand this repeated bragging of the Emperor, and he said:

> "Why do you vaunt in a manner irritating to the Almighty Allah?

Now you say there is no man to thwart your sword; such a man will come out whose strength you will not be able to oppose, and for whom you will have to flee leaving the throne of Delhi. He will become the Badshah of Delhi. Thus it has been enscrolled in the scriptures.

The Future Rival of the Emperor

The King was seized with apprehension and he said to the Kazi:

> "Would you be able to show me the Nawab's slave who, you say, will measure my strength in future?"

The Kazi replied:

> "I cannot undertake to show him in the ordinary fashion, saying, Here is the man."

I shall be able to show him after having identified him with the marks specified in the scriptures. The King said:

> "I am prepared to act as you recommend, please state your suggestions."

The Kazi replied:"

> Please arrange the necessary provisions for holding a banquet and I will show you the man there."

At the instance of the Kazi the King collected food provisions and invited his nobles. He made the Kazi sit near him, and ordered the guests to partake of the cheer which consisted of bread and vegetables.

One Sher Khan, a trustworthy sepoy serving under a *panch-hazari* Nawab, brought out a knife with which he cut his bread and ate. The Kazi pointed him out, saying:

> ''O King-Hazarat, this is the man who will baffle the prowess of your sword.''

The Badshah beckoned his confidants near him and said:

> ''Now, mark this attendant of the Nawab, you shall have to recognise him hereafter.''

Attempts to Capture Sher Khan

Four days after this feast the Badshah despatched a messenger to the Nawab asking the latter to see His Majesty the following morning, in the company of his sepoy Sher Khan. Having received this command of the Badshah the Nawab summoned the sepoy to his presence and said:

> ''The other day you cut and ate your bread before the Badshah; for this I have been commanded to take you with me.''

You are a servant in our family for the last three generation; how can I inflict upon me the sin of causing your death by making you over to the Emperor? Do as you think proper. For your sake, I am prepared to face whatever the Badshah may be inclined to do. Having said so he caused the flight of the sepoy.

The Nawab proceeded to the presence of the Badshah on the next day. The Badshah asked the Nawab whether he had brought with him the sepoy, Sher Khan, to which the Nawab replied:

> ''O! Badshah - Hazarat, I have despatched him to the interior and I have sent for him yesterday on the receipt of the Badshah's command. I will present him before His Majesty when he comes back.''

The Badshah then said:

> ''I have not summoned him with any evil intention. It is for his good that I want him in my presence. So please bring him quickly.''

The Nawab acceded to the request, saying that in obedience to the command of the Badshah he would deliver his servant within eight or ten days. The Nawab has himself imparted secret counsel to the slave and caused his flight; will he now capture and deliver him to the Badshah The Nawab simply made a false statement before the Emperor, and tried to gain time so that the slave might flee further still. On the expiry of ten or twelve days, the Badshah asked the Nawab:

> "How is this that you have not yet brought Sher Khan sepoy to me?"

To this the Nawab replied:

> "I sent messengers to the *perganah* to which he had gone. He could not be found there, and I searched for him in other places too. There is none who can give any clue regarding his whereabouts. He might have heard of the Badshah's summons, and have consequently fled to some unknown place."

The Badshah then said to the Nawab :

> "If Sher Khan cannot be procured, you will be looked upon as Sher Khan, and you will not be spared. Despatch a larger force to the place whither he has gone, and find him out. Get accurate information about his movements and report the same to me. In case Sher Khan is not found, remember that your days are numbered."

The Nawab deputed men to search for Sher Khan at the instance of the Badshah.

Sher Khan, a Fugitive in Sewa

After some time, the messengers sent in quest of Sher Khan came back and reported to the Nawab that the sepoy had taken shelter in Sewa[1] and avowed that the information was correct. The Nawab reported to the Badshah:

> "The men who went to search for Sher Khan sepoy have returned, and they have informed me that they have positively known that he has sought refuge in Sewa."

The Badshah said to the Nawab:

> "All this is your trickery."

The Nawab was dismissed and imprisoned. The Badshah summoned to his presence his Kazi, Daria Dadulla and said. Sher Khan sepoy, of whom you once said that he would oppose me in strength, has now been living in Sewa; I have received authentic report of this fact. The Kazi replied:

> "I have said: I found in the Scriptures. That is all I have to say. What shall I say more ?"

Sher Khan Defeated by the Badshah.

The Badshah despatched a panch-hazari Nawab with forces to seize the person of Sher Khan and bring him to the Emperor's presence. On the arrival of the Nawab, Sher Khan, with the help of an army, encountered the imperial troops. A terrible battle ensued between the two armies. Sher Khan won, and the imperial commander of five thousand perished in the battle. Half the soldiers were also killed, and the other half somehow preserved their lives. Sher Khan marshalled his forces and marched against Delhi with the object of invading it.

On receiving the intelligence, the Badshah came forward to oppose the invaders. The advance troops of the Emperor fought with the troops of Sher Khan, who, being unable to hold his stand, returned once more to his place of refuge. He again collected his forces and marched against Delhi where he encountered the imperial army in a deadly battle. A large number of men were killed on both sides. Sher Khan, being unable to resist, retreated from the battlefield.

Correct Methods of Warfare.

Sher Khan deserted his comrades and fled alone. Losing all hope of victory, he took shelter in the house of an old woman of the city. Sher Khan said to the old woman:

> "Here is the money, go to the bazaar and buy for me a dish of rice of a quality which is generally taken by well-to-do people."

The old woman did not know that her guest was no other than Sher Khan. She went to the *bazar* with the money and purchased a platter of rice which was placed before Sher Khan.

Sher Khan was extremely hungry and why should we blame him if he lifted the morsel from the middle of the pile of rice ? The old woman said, Sher Khan falls upon the centre of the troops of the Delhi Emperor; and being unable to stand, he finally retreats from the field. If he rounds up his enemies commencing from one side only, the Badshah of Delhi will be surely defeated. If rice is eaten from one side, the quantity gradually diminishes and one's hunger is also appeased. Sher Khan remembered this timely hint of his hostess, and commenced his operations by rounding up the enemy from the confines, and halted at his camp facing the Narmada.[2]

Sher Khan's Victory over the Imperial Troops

The Badshah marched with an army against the rebel, and there were numerous engagements between the two forces. For full one year there was no decisive victory or defeat on either side. A band of jugglers used to display their feats in the camp of Humayun Badshah as well as in that of Sher Khan. Sher Khan said to the jugglers:

> "I will reward you a huge sum of money if you can find out and inform me at what particular moment, out of the eight divisions or *prahars* of day and night, the army of Humayun Badshah remains in an unguarded condition."

At the instance of Sher Khan, the jugglers went to the camp of Humayun Badshah and inquired into the camp-life of the soldiers and came to know that they remain watchful throughout the eight *prahars* and that at the fourth *danda* of the early morning, nearly ten-sixteenth of the men remain unguarded; only one-sixteenth remain vigilant. This fact was communicated to Sher Khan by the jugglers. Sher Khan took with him a hundred and forty soldiers selected from the pick of his army; and having crossed the Narmada at night fell upon the Emperor's troops in the early part of the morning. The soldiers of the Badshah, being unguarded at the moment, dispersed in what ever direction they could. The fugitives were killed wherever they could be met.

Humayun took refuge with the Badshah of Rum, and Sher Khan sat on the throne of Delhi with the name Sher Shah. The Nawabs and Omraos of the older regime were neither dismissed nor killed, but they were retained in their former offices. Humayun Badshah fled alone, leaving his wife, son and dependents at Delhi.

Sher Shah Retains the Rank of Humayun's Consort

Sher Shah once said to the Begum and Prince Akbar:

> "You should consider Humayun to be the real ruler of Delhi, Humayun is my father and you are my mother, and Akbar is my brother. You should eat and dress as you used to do before, and I shall not reduce your supplies."

A water-jug was lying somewhere there, and Sher Shah said to Humayun's consort:

> "Please pass on the jug this side, as I want to drink water."

The Begum handed over the pot and Sher Shah drank water therefrom.

Sher Shah's Magnanimity

While sitting at court Sher Shah said to his *Wazir* and his Dewan, "By the grace of God I have become the Badshah of Delhi: nothing can be higher in the destiny of a mortal, and for me there is nothing else to be achieved. I drank water from the pot given to me by the Begum of Humayun Badshah I have made the exalted consort of the Emperor of Delhi do service to me, and that I regard as the meridian of my good fortune." The Wazir, the Dewan and the assemblage at the durbar praised Sher Shah, saying: God has blessed you with good fortune on account of this noble intelligence of yours. Your preservation of the family of Humayun in their former dignity and style will perpetuate your fame as long as Delhi exists."

Humayun's Indignities at the Persian Court

> Humayun Badshah stood at the gate of the Sultan of Rum and sent the following message: "Humayun, the Badshah of Delhi, is waiting at your door."
>
> The Badshah of Rum said: "Why should the Badshah of Delhi come to me? It must be false. Let him say positively who he is?"
>
> Humayun replied: "I am really the Humayun of Delhi. The reason for which I have deserted my country and taken shelter here will be communicated to you in detail."

The King of Rum did not first admit Humayun to his Durbar, but allowed him separate quarters and supplied provisions for food with the remark:

> "Let him stay there for this day. He will be given audience at the court some time after."

Humayun refused to take the food supplied to him by the Rum Badshah as it was unworthy of the ex-emperor: "this was partaken of by his retainers." Humayun said to the noble deputed by the Sultan to attend on him: "Bring me the food taken by the Badshah, and I will pay what it may cost," and handed over a gold mohur to the latter. The food was brought accordingly.

The courtyard facing the audience-hall of the Badshah of Rum was covered with mud, and Humayun saw the mud when he was conducted to the court through that way. A servant ran up and rubbed Humayun's feet with oil. The Badshah of Rum observed that after Humayun had crossed the courtyard the servant wiped off the mud from the Emperor's feet.

Humayun stood in front of the Badshah of Rum and seeing that no seat was offered to his lord, a servant laid a shield on the floor and covered it with a cloth and Humayun Badshah took the seat thus prepared for him.[3]

The Sultan of Persia Denounces Humayun

After some time the Badshah of Rum addressed Humayun, O Humayun, Badshah of Delhi, how many attendants like this had you at Delhi. Humayun said : "By your blessings, I had a large number of followers like this."

The Badshah of Rum then said : "Why did you flee from Delhi, fortunate as you were in the enjoyment of the services of faithful servants like this one ?[4]" You have been the rulers of Delhi for three generations, you had such blessings and opportunities, still you would not hold your stand, and had to flee for life. At least a hundred thousand men would be found who would have willingly sacrificed their lives for you if you had only asked them to do so. During your Kingship you must have regarded the gratification of your desires and pleasures as of supreme importance, without investigating into the weal and woe of your subjects.

The minds of the people therefore became disaffected towards you on the slightest provocation. This disgrace of yours will last as long as Delhi exists, and your name will be an object of ridicule among the Musalmans. You are a man to be severely condemned. You are lifeless, what is the harm if severe strictures are passed upon you?" Humayun Badshah made the following reply :

> "Of all the hated persons in the world, I am the one who merits the severest reprobation. My disgrace has spread over the whole earth. By coming to the deliverance of this reprehensible one you will earn eternal fame to last as long as Delhi exists. With what words shall I contrive to please you ? Whatever you say of yourself fully maintaining your

prestige and fame will be effected.''

Humayun Invades Delhi with Persian Troops

The Badshah of Rum offered Humayun a seat worth one lakh of rupees. The Badshah handed over from his throne a martial robe, and all the necessary articles of food, as well as a good place for residence, with the following words, that you have taken refuge with me in solicitation of my help, you have nothing to say, everything rests with me now. He gave to Humayun Sawars and Nawabs to the extent of three lakhs, making up a total of seven lakhs of soldiers with musketeers, shields men and others, saying : "Go now and occupy Delhi.'' Humayun returned with this army and attacked Delhi.

Humayun again Defeated by Sher Shah

Being unable to oppose Sher Shah in strength, Humayun fled a second time to Rum. The Badshah of Rum said to Humayun : "Formerly you said that you would be able to reoccupy Delhi with an army of three lakhs of soldiers only, now, you have not been able to retake it even with seven lakhs of soldiers.'' Having said so to Humayun, the Badshah inflicted appropriate punishments upon his Mansabdars, Nawabs and soldiers who were found delinquent.

The Badshah supplied to Humayun a fresh army of twelve lakhs strong, including six lakhs of horses, manned this time by veteran Nawabs. With this vast army Humayun was sent back to Delhi. The Badshah addressed his men as follows:

> ''If that ordinary individual, a fit object of our compassion and favour, wins victory over two *Badshahs* the discredit will ring through ages. Knowing this, act in a manner which will enable you to occupy Delhi.''

With these words he granted leave to all with appropriate presents and gifts.

This army in full force attacked Delhi. A series of battles were waged with Sher Shah. First came the battle with big guns, then the battle with ponies and riders and then of the shieldsmen; but Sher Shah could not be vanquished in any way. Sher Shah conferred with his men and said:

> ''All right, I will deal in a manner which will prevent the soldiers of the Rum Badshah from coming here again.''

Saying so, he selected seven hundred horsemen with him, and with swords in both hands he made a sudden attack upon the enemy in the early part of the morning, and massacred a large number of horses and men. The rest of the imperial army took to their heels and fled to Rum. Instead of going to Rum, Humayun Badshah retired to the interior on this occasion.

Humayun's Restoration to the Throne

Sher Shah sent a man with a letter containing the following message to Humayun:

> "You need not wander about from place to place, leaving your wife and son, and afflicting your body with pain. You are my father, and I am your son. I would invite you to come back to Delhi, and I will retire to Agra. The empire will be divided into two parts, one of which will go to you and the other to me I will make a solemn vow in accordance with the injunctions laid down in the scriptures. If you agree to this proposal, you should come immediately to Delhi.''

On receiving this invitation Humayun came to Delhi. Sher Shah entered into a sacred covenant by which he divided the empire into two parts, and Humayun ruled at Delhi and Sher Shah at Agra. This is how the Kinghsip of Delhi was partitioned into two portions. Sher Shah and his descendants ruled at Delhi for three generations, covering a period of 20 years, 6 months and 10 days.

References

1. Sewa was most likely Bijapur, *Sabai* or *Savai* being the surname of the first Adil Shahi Sultan, Abdul Muzaffar Yusuf. See *Hobson Jobson under Sabaio*, and also *Ain-i-Akbari*, Vol. I., pp. 586, 600.
2. The story of acquiring the correct method of military operations from the analogy of dishful of rice is attributed to Timurlang, with precisely the same details, in *Manucci*, Irvine, Vol. I., PP. 99 110.
3. This story is repeated in Manucci, I, page 114, though the provison seat was made "by cutting open the covering of his quiver and spreading it in front of the royal seat. On this cloth Humayun at once sat down.
4. It is curious and surprising that this statement of the chronicler writing in an obscure corner in Eastern India, is an exact repetition of what we find in Manucci, I, pp 114-5, "The Persian King asked King Humayun how he could lose his kingdom when he had such attentive and well-affected servants."

Chapter - 10

The Accession of Jahangir

On the death of Humayun his son Shah Akbar became the Badshah. On Akbar's demise his son Jahangir became the Badshah. Akbar had two Wazirs, Nazahat Khan and Matamad Khan. On the accession of Jahangir to the Badshahate, Nazahat Khan Wazir was removed from office, and Sayid Khan appointed in his place. The Badshah conducted the affairs of the State with Matamad Khan and the newly appointed Wazir. Jahangir Badshah one day asked his two Wazirs:

> ''Let me know the names of the countries with their Rajas and Badshahs who paid homage to Emperor Akbar but have refrained from doing so during my reign.''

The two wazirs consulted the records and said:

> ''You have lost sovereignty over the following chiefs and territories, - Muhammad Murad Khan Badshah of Hussain-abdal, Shahdul Badshah of Piran, Raja Bitholdas of Bund, Mohan-Madhur Singha of Rameswar-Bandar; Achinta Zemindar of Jaleswar Bandar; Kiledar Khan,-Nawab of Benares Sarkari; Hussain Khan Badshah of Gaur in Bengal, and the kingdom of Bengal with their Rajas and Zemindars.''

The Emperor commanded that Subhas with forces be despatched against the refractory rulers with the object of subjugating them. The Wazir said:

> ''We have only two tanks of coins, one of gold mohurs and the other of silver, accumulated during the period from the reign of Timurlanga to Akbar Badshah. The gold and silver mohurs of the two tanks should now be extracted, with which alone you will be able to conduct the wars in all quarters simultaneously by maintaining a large army of sepoys and officers.''

Akbar Badshah was very prodigal in expenses. We have searched in the treasury and have found there only seven crores of rupees, besides one more crore representing your own earning. With these eight crores of rupees it will be difficult to carry on the campaign in all the theatres of war at the same time. Jahangir Badshah then replied:

> "It will bring disgrace to my father if the money from the tanks be raised and spent. People will say Akbar Badshah was bankrupt as his son had to carry on his Badshahship with the help of ancestral wealth. This report will gladden the hearts of our enemies."

Proposal for the Invasion of Gaur

The Wazir then said, "Let the campaign against foreign enemies be postponed for the present; specially because the Rajas and Badshahs of those territories live at a considerable distance from us. At present there is Hussain Shah Badshah of Gaur, a highly refractory chief. Kiledar Khan Nawab of Baranasi and the Zemindars and Rajas are also of a hostile disposition. They are not very far from Delhi. After their subjugation you should take up the subjugation of Hussain-abdal, Piran-Maluk and others. Bengal is an extensive territory where you will acquire a vast amount of wealth and property, with which you will be able to subdue other countries.

Besides, in a dish of rice, one can eat up the whole pile without burning his fingers if he commences from the four corners. If, in a hurry he thrusts his hand right into the very middle of the platter, he will only scald his fingers and his tongue. There is Mandhata, Raja of Amber, a commander of 8,000, whom you have deputed against the countries of the Sultans, which he has accordingly invaded and subdued by this time. Summon him back, and despatch him to the war against Hussain Shah, who has impregnable forts and garrisons. None but Mandhata will be able to subjugate him.

Man Singha Starts on his Expedition

The Emperor agreed to the proposal of the two Wazirs, summoned Mandhata from his campaign, honoured and rewarded him with rich presents, and despatched him to the Gaur war. Mandhata first visited his own principality of Amber where he collected the Rajputs to whom he said:

> "My kinsmen who are deputed to the wars under the orders of the Badshah do not get any time to build up their

strongholds; and it transpires, that for doing so, they will have to wait for a period of time intervening the planting of a mango sapling and the enjoyment of its fruits. He is afraid lest, in a period of recess, I construct my forts and assume independence. I am despatched to all the wars, and I do not get any time to rest; my soldiers are harassed and they curse me.''

Then Raja Mandhata, marched to Bengal, at the head of an army consisting of 70,000 imperial soldiers, 22 Omraos of senior and junior ranks, his own contingency of 20,000 Rajput warriors, as well as his brothers and nephews. He paid his respects to the image of Kesavrai Gosain at Mathura where he arranged for the construction of a temple; he also ordered the erection of a brick house at Brindaban for the shelter of the monkeys. He performed Sraddha at Gaya, after which he reached Benares.

Subjugation of Benares.

Mandhata despatched two Rajput envoys to Kiledar Khan of Benares with the following message. You have eaten the salt of Emperor Akbar, but you have turned your face against his son Jahangir Badshah, a monarch of great prowess and valour. You will not know any peace in your life here and hereafter. If you desire your welfare, come and offer your submission to me, and I will protect you in the hands of the Badshah. If not, remember you are but the husk of corn before my army.

On the receipt of this letter Kiledar Khan thought within himself, it will be disastrous if I court the friendship of Mandhata, the Badshah will surely kill me. And if I flee I will not be able to escape. Mandhata has come with an army befitting a Badshah. Under these circumstances, death in fighting is preferable.'' He did not send any reply.

On the other hand the two messengers were turned out with blows and the letter torn to pieces. The two messengers cried out, '' The Musalmans dare to turn us out with blows! We shall prove the mettle of Rajputs.'' During the scuffle the Ukils killed a number of nobles and also rushed at the Nawab with a view to kill him; but they were inflicted with spear wounds of which they died. On receiving report of this tragedy, Mandhata became furiously incensed, and despatched Thakur Amar Singha, Thakur Kesor Singh,

Thakur Rahiraman and five Nawabs. They marched towards the fort, and their troops surrounded it on all sides.

Kiledar Khan then collected seven thousand sepoys with whom he waged a furious battle with the invaders. The Nawabs said to the three Thakurs; Ask Mandhata to send us some muskets like those of Kiledar Khan, we have too many big guns. We shall gain victory if we fight with small guns. The three Thakurs replied:

> "We have a numerous army, and it may be possible to achieve victory with the help of muskets. But such a fighting will be uncustomary and unjust. Fighting with elephants and horses will be advisable."

A battle then ensued between the two forces. The Nawab lost a large number of his soldiers. Thakur Kesor Singh fought with Nawab Kiledar Khan on horseback for a considerable time. Kesor Singh killed the Nawab by piercing him with a spear. His two sons were killed by gun-shots. The children and dependants as well as the belongings of the Nawab were despatched to Delhi. The remnant of his forces surrendered to Mandhata who enlisted them in his army. The general after creating confidence in the hearts of the place, after which he marched against Hussain Khan.

The Fortifications of Gaur

Mandhata then reached the territory of Sobhachand Thakur, situated on the east of Muger. Mandhata had married the daughter of the Raja of Jaintapur which had been renamed by the Bengals[1] as Adamabad. As a mark of this relationship Raja Barish-sal came with precious presents and submitted to Mandhata. Mandhata honoured the Raja with presents and said: "As commanded by the Emperor, I have come to subjugate Gaur. How can I successfully attack its forts ? What is the number of strongholds in Gaur? How impregnable are the forts? What is the strength of the army?" Raja Barish-sal replied."

One will be amazed at the splendour of the soldiers and the arms and weapons. The forts are made of stone and brick and are extremely insurmountable. There are three passages leading to the fortifications; one runs along the entrance of the fort, this is one path leading to the first fort; there is another on the left by the route through Sikarpur; there is a third way on the right through Pura-Perganah which will lead you to another fort.

The stronghold of Hussain Shah can be reached after crossing these three fortification. There is a zemindar at Dacca named Ise-Khan-Masandali. He is a very influential potentate and poses as the Badshah of Bengal. I can also arrange his submission to you.'' Raja Mandhata then despatched Nawab Pardal Khan with eight thousand sepoys and camp-followers by the Sikarpur route. Nawab Ayaz Beg and Uzbeg proceeded by the route through Pura-Perganah, in the company of twelve thousand sepoys, and Thakur Bitholdas and the son of Raja Barish-sal. The general Raja Mandhata with Raja Barish-sal marched by the middle route with all his army.

Message to Ise-Khan-Masandali

Then letters were despatched to the zemindar Ise-Khan Masandali by the followers of Raja Barish-sal's son, one from Raja Mandhata through the retainers of Ayaz Beg, another from Raja Barish-sal himself through Thakur Bitholdas. The message ran as follows:

> ''We have come to fight against Hussain Shah Badshah, and you should come and join us.''

Raja Barish-sal wrote:

> '' As there has been long friendship between yourself and me, I have spoken well of you to Raja Mandhata. The Raja is a great warrior, and has subdued many countries. You should come and be friends with us, otherwise you will be subjected to misery in future.''

Ise-Khan's Reply

Ise-Khan then sent a wakil with a reply, as well as precious gifts, ''I am a zemindar, and hence unconcerned with wars. For the present please accept my friendship conveyed through this note. On Raja Mandhata's arrival at Dacca, I will offer my submission in person.'' He wrote to Barishtha-sal, '' If I meet the Raja personally now, I shall also be commanded to take up arms, which is a bad thing for the future. We are zemindars, and war complications are not safe for us.

Mandhata permitted the messengers of Ise-Khan Masandali to depart after having bestowed on them rich presents, and asked them to send with Ayaz Beg and Bitholdas men who were acquainted with the routes and interiors. The request was accordingly communicated to Ise-Khan Masandali by his messengers. He despatched large quantities of rice, pulse, mug for Ayaz Beg and Bitholdas, as well as a man who was versed in the knowledge of the routes and defiles.

Man Singha's Ultimatum to Hussain Shah

Proceeding by the central route Raja Mandhata sent a Wakil to Hussain Shah of Gaur with the following message:

> "Your forefathers were on friendly terms with the Emperors of Delhi. Now, what pride has prompted you to turn your back against the Emperor Jahangir? Specially I am Mandhata, Raja of Amber. I have borne in my armpit dozens of Badshahs like yourself; I have caused the death of many, while others have been released through me. So you should come and offer your submission to me. Our family has never been known to have harmed any body: still if any one persists in being unfriendly I shall certainly destroy and exterminate him."

Hussain Shah despatched the following reply:

> "Jahangir is the Badshah of Delhi, and so am I of Gaur. There was friendly interchange of embassies before. He had discontinued sending men, and so have I. Mandhata is only an Omrao; why should I, a Badshah, pay my homage to him? What touch of genius has led him to pen such a letter ? If he has come for war, let him come."

The letter of Mandhata was torn to pieces and his envoy expelled. On this Raja Mandhata rushed to the attack of the advance fortifications; by mere display of valour he caused the soldiers of the garrison to flee back to Hussain Shah.

First Encounters

There were battles at the forts situated on the way through Pura-Perganah by which Ayaz Beg and Bitholdas had marched. There were severe massacres at these encounters, when many soldiers of the garrison of Gaur were killed. Then the soldiers of Ayaz Beg and Bitholdas riding on Tazi and Sujarnis ponies scaled the forts and took possession of them. The remnant of the garrisons made good their escape and joined Hussain Shah Badshah.

The soldiers at the forts situated on the Sikarpur route, through which Nawab Pardal Khan had marched, strenuously opposed the attack of the imperialists for three days, after which they also took to their heels. Pardal Khan encamped on the northern side, well prepared to face the attack of the enemy; Ayaz Beg and Bitholdas halted on the east, while Raja Mandhata stood in readiness on the western side.

The artillery were posted as follows: rows of cannon on the front, then of muskets, and *chandravans* and rai-bahs, then the sepoys and spearmen, by which they encompassed the enemy on all sides. Hussain Shah in person stood in front of the forces of Raja Mandhata: while his son Jalal Hussain was posted in front of the army of Pardal Khan; and his nephew Paris Muhammad against Ayaz Beg and Bitholdas. Sporadie encounters, lasting for two or four days continued for six months.

The Support of Rajas and Zemindars

Hussain Shah Badshah sent the following message to Ise-Khan Masandali, to the Zemindar of Sala, to the Raja of Jharkhanda, to the Raja of Morung of the north to the Raja of Cooch-Behar and Raja Raghunath. From ancient times Gaur and Delhi have been ruled by separate Badshahs. It is unjust on the part of Jahangir Badshah to despatch Mandhata.

The imperialists have besieged Gaur for six months in order to occupy it, blocking the passage of our traders and retainers, for which my subjects are in great distress for food. So I want to attack the intruders by issuing out of our garrisons. You should all support me in the project. We shall fight from the front, and you should march by the three routes and kill the imperialists, with the object of repulsing and driving away Mandhata. Otherwise, having attacked me today he will proceed to attack you the next day. To this Ise-Khan Masandali replied:

> "I am a zemindar to whom wars are not proper. Whoever may wield the sovereign power I am his subject. It is befitting for you Badshahs to engage in mutual conflicts."

The Raja of Jharkhanda and other Rajas deputed messengers to say:

> "All right, we shall fight from the rear."

Victory of Raja Man Singha

On the receipt of these assurances, the forces of Hussain Shah came out of the fortifications on the three sides and fell upon the imperialist. A furious contest ensued. Hussain Shah lost a large number of his soldiers who were killed by the canon-shots of

Mandhata. War-elephants armed with huge iron clubs rushed at the soldiers and destroyed many of them. Soldiers were also killed with *Chandravans* and *dabas*.

Then ensued a terrible fight on horseback attended by heavy massacres and losses on both sides. Neither did the imperialists nor did the troops of Hussain Shah prefer to retreat from the fight. Raghunath Raja, the Cooch-Behar Raja and others who promised to fight from behind did not turn up, saying:

> ''Mandhata is a great Raja. It will be disastrous to us if we fight with him and thereby assume the designation of rebels.''

In the evening engagement Hussain Shah fought mounting on an elephant. Thakur Chandraval, uncle of Mandhata, who was riding on a Sujarnis pony, whipped his steed and spurred him on. The horse following the hint lifted its two legs and placed them on the forehead of the elephant. Thakur Chandraval then struck Hussain Shah with his spear, and threw him down, and thus perished the Badshah of Gaur. Thakur Dipsing riding on horseback severed the head of the elephant, which died. The garrisons on the north were also defeated. His son perished in the battle, the army on the eastern route was vanquished. The nephew of Hussain Shah fled. Raja Mandhata won victory in the battle

Hussain Shah's wives and children fled. After collecting the belongings of Hussain Shah, Mandhata made an inventory of the articles seized, and after sealing them properly, he submitted his waqaya to Delhi. He then retired to Dacca. Ise-Khan Masandali came and submitted his homage to Mandhata. Raja Raghunath, and the Raja of Cooch-Behar as well as other chiefs paid tributes to the Badshah and established friendly terms with Mandhata, who renamed Dacca as jahangir nagar, and appointed Ise-Khan Masandali as zemindar, to whom he made suitable presents. Mandhata then returned to Delhi.

The Recital of Markendya-Chandi

On his way Mandhata saw Brahmans reading the Chandi on the bank of the Ganges.

> The Raja enquired: "What is this book that you are reading?''
> Brahmans: "It is Chandi, a portion of the Markhandeya Purana.''

Mandhata: "What is the result of the recital of this book?''
Brahmans: ''The man who hears the recital of three rounds of Chandi goes to Kailasa or heaven. If it is recited more, the result is unmentionable.''
Mandhata: "Then please, recite three rounds of the book in my name.''

Saying thus, the Raja offered to the priests a reward of one thousand rupees. During his march, the Rajas who resided near about interviewed Mandhata with presents for himself and the Badshah. Mandhata also offered presents to them, and assured them of his protection and aid.

Man Singha's Eulogy of Hussain Shah

After subduing Bengal and the territories around it, Raja Mandhata proceeded to Delhi and paid his respects to Emperor Jahangir who bestowed on him high honours and costly presents. He was retained in his former mansab of the rank of a commander of eight thousand, and was given a cash reward of three lakhs of rupees for eating *pan* and *tambul*. The Badshah then said to Mandhata:

> ''From your experiences of military operations in diverse localities, tell me of the magnitude of Hussain Shah's heroism as a warrior.''

To this Mandhata replied:

> ''Hussain Shah is the greatest of all the soldiers I have encountered in my military engagements in different places. His courage is indomitable, and he fights without caring for his life. He has been killed only through the prowess of the Emperor. He is peerless in heroism.''

Jahangir's Conquest of Secunderabad

Salutation to Sree Krishna. On the death of Humayun Shah Akbar became the Badshah. On the death of Akbar his son Jahangir assumed the title of Badshah. The Emperor Jahangir after ascending the throne went out on tour to visit places being accompanied by 500,000 soldiers. After some time he marched towards the Deccan.

Some *bairagis* or itinerant mendicants who had travelled in various places said to the Emperor:

> ''There was a king named Sekendar Badshah. He constructed a city and a bazaar named Secunderabad with beautiful

> stones of diverse colours by engaging lapidarists. That place is fit for the Emperor. The kingdom is now ruled by a monarch named Nasir Muhammad Badshah. He does not pay tribute to anybody, and with regard to the peace and prosperity of his kingdom he is unrivalled.''

On hearing this from the bairagis the Emperor Jahangir marched towards Secunderabad, and from a distance of three days' journey he despatched a courier to Nasir Muhammad with a letter to the following effect:

> ''The city of Secunderabad which has been built by Sekendar Badshah is fit for us, and not for you. So please move to some other quarter. I will establish a camp at Secunderabad. If soft words cannot move you will be afflicted with distress when I invade and occupy your territory.''

On receiving this letter Nasir Muhammad Badshah sent the following reply:

> ''Jahangir Badshah has become mad. Such a letter should be addressed to bondsmen and slaves. He is a sovereign, and I am also a sovereign. He thinks that I will desert this place out of fear; such an idea should never find quarter in his heart.''

The Imperialists Cross Impassable Dikes

The reply seriously infuriated the Emperor and he proceeded towards the capital of Nasir Muhammad, and came upon a huge ditch which was as broad as a river. It was impossible to cross the ditch there being no place to moor the boats. Being amazed at the sight of the ditch, the Emperor said to some of his swift horsemen, let the horses first attempt to cross the ditch being fitted with howdah-like seats, and they will be followed by Potla, Suluf, and Batel boats carrying soldiers who will attack the hostile fort.

In obedience to the command of the Emperor, horses harnessed with seats were made to swim over the ditch. Crocodiles and sea-horses had been let loose in the ditch, and they seized and devoured many of the horses and soldiers of the Emperor, and dragged down others beneath the waters. The Badshah seeing their sad plight asked the wazir of the reason of the disappearance of the soldiers under water, to which the minister replied that they were eaten up by the sea-monsters roaming about in the ditch.

The Badshah enquired of the means by which the dike could be crossed, and Sabre Khan Uzir replied:

> "There are two huge cannon at Delhi, named *Killa-shikist* and *Koh-shekan*. Let us fetch them from Delhi, and place the guns on the sides of the ditch on a mound constructed at a higher level than the hostile fort. If we fire the two guns towards the rampart of Nasir Muhammad by loading them with stone-balls, his fort will be destroyed, his soldiers killed, and on hearing the roar of the guns the crocodiles and sea-monsters will disperse; then our men will be able to cross the ditch safely."

In accordance with the suggestion of the wazir, the two big guns were brought from Delhi and mounted on a mound higher than the elevation of the hostile fort. They were loaded with stone-balls and splinters of bricks and potteries, and then fired. The men and soldiers of the enemy's camp were blown off. The guns roared with a terrific blast which rent the earth into chasms, broke down the trees and produced waves on the waters. Many of the alligators and sea-horses perished, while the rest dipped below the waters. The soldiers of Jahangir Badshah now crossed the ditch without any difficulty, and attacked and occupied the fort.

Establishment of Court at Secunderabad

Then the King Nasir Muhammad retreated with the remnant of his army to another fort, and remained in preparedness for a contest. Jahangir after occupying the first fort marched against the next, in the precincts of which he secretly laid powder mines and covered them with grass.

During the darkness of night Nasir Muhammad issued out of his fort with an army intending to inflict a surprise attack on the Emperor's camp. Jahangir also came out and set fire to the mines. The soldiers of Nasir Muhammad were burnt to death. Being victorious in war the Emperor captured the fort of Nasir Muhammad and occupied the throne of Secunderabad. He then gave suitable presents to all the nobles there, including the revenue officials, such as Chaudhauris and Patwaris, and firmly established his suzerainty at Secunderabad.

The Emperor appointed a Court there with Sher Khan Bahadar, Amir-ul-Omrao, a Commander of seven thousand, at the head of the following Nawabs: Hasan Khan, Dasil Khan, Sarif Khan, Latif Khan, Yusuf Khan Siparsalah. He also established a garrison there with eight thousand soldiers, having the usual quota of Ek-hazaris, Do-hazaris and Tin-hazaris. The total strength of the imperial detachment left at Secunderabad, including the seven thousand soldiers of Amir-ul-Omrao Sher Khan Bahadur came up to 15,000. The emperor then returned to his capital Delhi.

Conquest of Secunderabad by Siliman Badshah

There was a vast wilderness in the midst of the sea covered with dense forests. Sekendar Badshah who was formerly in the country of Iran, went and settled there, from which he earned an income of rupees forty lakhs and fifty-thousand. He named that country Secunderabad.

After living in that place for some time Sekendar Badshah came back to his throne at Iran, leaving Muhammad Galib Khan Nawab, a commander of 9,000 in charge of Secunderabad. Secunderabad measured 220 kos in length, and 103 in breadth. The town was built with stone and brick and renamed Hiranagar or the city of Diamonds. It was situated at a distance of three months' journey from Delhi. In the shops were sold pearls, coral, rubies, emeralds and other precious articles. Aquatic horses came out of the sea in winter to bask on the sands. Men used to capture and tame them. They used to be called Dariaighoras or sea-horses, and their price ranged from rupees 1,000 to rupees 1,500 each. The pigs of that country were of the size of horses, their hoofs and feet being like those of horses.

All the inhabitants, there are Musalmans, there being no Hindusthani person there. People lived on maize and eggs of china ducks. There was no paddy or rice. It could be had only when some merchants from this part placed it on the market ; its price used to be rupees three or four per seer.

Siliman Badshah Intends to Conquer Secunderabad

There was a port named Faranga, where lived Siliman Badshah. One day the Badshah said to his wazir:

> "Secunderabd is a beautiful place, fit for the residence of a Badshah. There is a Nawab there named Muhammad Galib. It is reported that Sakendar Badshah is now dead. So

> I intend to attack and occupy Secunderabad. What means do you suggest ?''

The wazir replied:

> ''That country can be conquered only by the most dexterous expedients. It was formerly a forest in the midst of the sea, full 220 kos in length and 103 kos in breadth. Sekendar Badshah had brought men from all quarters and settled them there. It has an army of 60,000 soldiers, who use Turki, Tazi, Sujarnis, Arbi and Dariai ponies.''

The kingdom is surrounded on all sides by sea water. Its three sides can be traversed by boat in one-and-a-half *prahar* and ten *dandas*. We have the sea on one side, where we have expert soldiers trained in the art of fighting by boats, such as Batel (Patil), Suluf (Salb) and other kinds of war-boats. The country has four forts on the east, west, north and south, all made of bricks and stones. It has, besides, a rampart of trees, which have been planted close to each other, so that they have now assumed the shape of a compact wall the trunks touching one another.

There is another rampart of thorny bamboos whose trunks have also become compact. There is an encompassing ditch in the shape of a circle studded with floating batteries. There is also the wall of the sea. In the heart of the kingdom is situated the capital of the Padsha, which has walls and forts made of stone and brick. Big cannon resembling the trunks of plantain trees have been mounted all round the wall at intervals of twenty-five cubits. Hence the place is very impregnable and dangerous.

It can be conquered only by the employment of diplomacy and tact. The kingdom is so invincible that no one has been able to conquer it. You will not also succeed in occupying it unless you take recourse to diplomatic stratagems.

Siliman Badshah's Plan to Conquer Secunderabad

Siliman Badshah convened a meeting of his counsellors and said, I want to invade and conquer Secunderabad. Do confer, and let me know the means by which we shall be able to achieve success.

The ministers assembled came to the following conclusion after a prolonged deliberation, ''Secunderabad can never be conquered by open warfare. Let five hundred of our most clever and trustworthy soldiers proceed to Secunderabad and live there in the service of the Nawab. They should study the strength and position of the soldiers, and forts and other military resources of the place. Let some of our merchants proceed there with ships loaded with merchandise, and let them live there, being engaged in peaceful commercial pursuits. Let a damsel in disguise be palmed off on the Nawab as the grand-daughter of the Badshah, with instructions to kill the Nawab somehow or other. Then fight, and occupy his territory.

Siliman Badshah's Diplomatic Proposal

After hearing this device suggested by the wazir and other ministers, Siliman Badshah despatched the following message to Muhammad Galib Khan, Nawab of Secunderabad, We live in the country known as Farang, and Muhammad Galib Khan lives at Secunderabad, almost in our neighbourhood. We are designated as Badshahs and he as Nawab, this is the only difference between us. On the other hand he has a larger assortment of war-materials and weapons. I have no influential friend and ally. If the Nawab has no objection I wish to establish friendly relations with him.

This has been necessitated by the report that the Pathans are contemplating to invade his territories as well as mine. I will stand by him when his kingdom is overrun by the enemy, and he will do so when my kingdom confronts such an unfortunate plight.

The messengers of Siliman Badshah proceeded to Secunderabad and handed over the letter to the Nawab who became highly delighted, and honoured the ambassadors with rich presents. The Nawab presented his daughter named Gul-Makhmal to the son of Siliman Badshah with a dowry of precious robes and articles.

Nawab Galib Khan's Reply

He sent her with his envoys who also carried the following message to Siliman Badshah:

> "I am extremely delighted to receive your message. You have written about the establishment of cordial relations between the two States. This desire has been cherished by me for a long time. I wish the friendship which existed before between Saiyid Badshah and Arbal Khan Badshah should now be re-established between you and me."

You are far from the truth when you assert that there is no difference between a Nawab and a Badshah. A horse is thin and slender in body, yet it flits in war with the speed of hurricanes; the Telengi bullock is of enormous bulk and handsome features, but can it stand comparison to a horse. The horse is a horse and the ox is an ox. How do you expect that you and I will be each other's peers?.

Siliman Badshah became extremely delighted on the receipt of this reply accompanied by the gift of the Nawab's daughter. She was admitted and kept with due honour and dignity. The Badshah in his turn sent with his messengers one Lolin, very handsome and ingenious in all things, who was palmed off as the Badshah's niece intended for the Nawab, who believed her to be really a beautiful a clever scholar and married her.

Farangi Spies at Secunderabad

The Badshah then deputed five hundred soldiers to live in disguise. They went to the advance fort of Secunderabad, and informed the inmates that they had come to see the Nawab with the intention of employment in his territory as underlings. The soldiers living at the forts informed the Nawab accordingly who invited the supplicants to his presence. The soldiers were all young men, and properly trained in the wielding of arms and weapons. As they looked smart and handsome, the Nawab employed them as servants on good pay. They soon won the confidence of their master.

After this the Badshah sent five ships loaded with valuable merchandise for carrying on trade. The captain of the boats presented precious articles to the Nawab and earned his estimation, who then permitted the merchants to trade in his dominions.

The Badshah also prepared a fleet of Jalia, Batel and Suluf boats and equipped them with arms of war. The Jalia boats were harnessed with quilts of straw looking like deer-skins; they were then stuffed with fish-scales and attached to the sides of the boats, leaving sufficient space for the oarsmen to ply the vessels. The Batel boats were constructed to accommodate elephants and horses.

Murder of Nawab Galib Khan

Then Lolin, who was presented to the Nawab, spread a sheet of poison-cloth on the body of the Nawab at the time of sleep. The Nawab died. The miscreant then escaped early next morning and took shelter in the ships of the merchants. The news was communicated to Siliman Badshah, who came post-haste in boats attended by soldiers. The soldiers of the advance fort came to inform the Nawab, but they found that the Nawab had already breathed his last. The brothers and sons of the Nawab, hearing the report, asked the informants not to allow the invaders to proceed.

Siliman Badshah Occupies Secunderabad

There was hard fighting between the forces of the Nawab and of the Badshah. First, there was an engagement on boats. The soldiers of the Nawab hurled arrows and gun-shots, but they produced no effect as they were small and struck only the quilts stuffed with the scales of fish. The oarsmen pursued the Nawab's boats and came near them. Many soldiers of the Nawab perished by the arrows and bullets of the Badshah.

The Nawab's army saw that arrows and bullets could not retard the advance of the enemy; and this time they met the latter with long spears as the enemy approached the precincts of the fort. There was severe fighting attended by heavy casualties on both sides, but neither of the belligerent forces turned their face.

When Siliman Badshah discovered that the fort could not be captured though he had fought in so many ways, he deputed some reliable emissaries to instruct his own soldiers and the merchants of the ships and boats as follows. This is the opportune moment, and they should act in Whatever way they think proper.

On this, the five hundred Farangi sepoys who had accepted service under the Nawab, acting in concert with the men of the boats, set fire to all the places, including the bazaar and the fort and cut down the enemy on horseback. They created a confusion inside the fort; where also they massacred a large number of the Nawab's men. The soldiers posted at the fort fled of their own accord.

Then the Badshah, winning a victory in the naval fight, got on land and conquered all the forts. The kinsmen of the Nawab all perished in the battle. Siliman established his court at Secunderabad and lived there, protecting the subjects. From that time till now (say 1682 A.D.) Secunderabad has continued to be the territory of Siliman Badshah. Some time afterwards his son was placed in charge of the Faranga country.

From this territory of Siliman Badshah, Delhi is situated at a distance of three months journey. Muhammad Ali is a Mogul of that place. He is a very great scholar, and knows all the *loghats* or languages, Arabic and Persian. He taught the sons of Mansur Khan, and for this he received an honorarium of full rupees one hundred per month. The above incidents have been taken from his mouth.

References

1. The ward *Bangal* is applied by the Assamese to all people outside Assam proper. Even a Duropean is ealled a Baga Bangal, or a white Bangal.

Chapter - 11

Aurangzeb's Accession to the Throne of Delhi

Emperor Shah Jahan had four sons: the eldest was Dara Shah with mansab 20,000. Sawar 20,000; Shah Shuja with mansab 15,000, Sawar 15,000. Aurangzeb with mansab 12,000, Sawar 9,000 and Murad Buksh. Shah Jahan had his future calculated by astrologers to whom he said, "How many years shall I live more?" The pandits consulted their books and reported that he would live for ten years more. Dara Shah said:

> "O father, I have heard the astrologers saying that you will live for ten years more. I am now fifty years old. O father, if you live for another ten years I shall be sixty years old. Of what use is the Badshahship of Delhi to a sexagenarian? If my father has compassion upon me he should abdicate the throne for ten years and made me Badshah."

Shah Jahan Divides his Empire

Emperor Shah Jahan then placed Shah Shuja at Rajmahal in charge of the twelve divisions of Bengal; Aurangzeb at Aurangabad; Murad Buksh at Kabul. He further instructed his three sons as follows:

> "I have conferred the emperorship on Dara now when I am in good condition. Nobody should object to this arrangement as long as I live. You should act as you like under my orders."

He said to Dara:

> "You should not accept the imperial revenues due from the three places."

With these instructions he despatched his three sons to their respective charges. He placed Dara on the throne and himself saluted his emperor-son. Shah Jahan lived inside the fort of Delhi having constructed his quarters properly. He said to to Dara:

> "Pay me every month the sum of rupees one lakh and twenty thousand. The amount should be paid to me on the appearance of the new moon."

The principal Begum of Shah Jahan, the mother of the four *Badshahzadas* said one day to her husband:

> "I am not accompanying you to your new quarters. I have now come to considerable age. Through your favour I have enjoyed all the pleasures which can fall to the lot of a mortal. Four tiger cubs have been born of me. They will not abide by the arrangement you have made, and they will die by the hands of each other. What is the good of my being burnt in the fire of affliction and sorrow? I will die with the name of God on my lips."

Saying thus the Begum prepared herself for death; and uttering the name of Khoda she put an end to her life by swallowing poison.

Sultan Dara Sukah Imprisoned

Six months after this Shah Shuja attacked Delhi with an army of 1,00,000 sawars, but his forces were defeated, and he fled back to Rajmahal being unable to take his stand. Aurangzeb said to Murad Buksh:

> "I have already made up my mind to become a faqir, and I will not bid for the Badshahship now. If the Almighty God allows I will make you Badshah instead. I have been a faqir before and I will remain as a faqir. Put me in some corner, and I shall live in the religion of a faqir."

To this Murad Buksh said:

> "You are my elder brother. Keep me in any fashion you like, and I will abide by your counsel."

Having said so Murad Buksh marched to Delhi by the western road. Dara came out of Delhi and encountered the forces of his brothers at a distance of two days' journey from the capital, and waged a severe fight with the army of Aurangzeb. There were heavy losses on both sides. Murad Buksh reached Delhi by the southern gates. Being attacked on both sides Dara could not resist the combined forces of his brothers and fled. He was captured and enchained in golden fetters. Murad Buksh was placed on the throne and made Badshah. Aurangzeb in concert with Murad Buksh informed Shah Jahan:

> "We two desire to pay our respects to our father."

Shah Jahan replied:

> "My words have not at all been honoured; so you need not salute me now. You may salute me afterwards if you preserve the life of Dara."

Aurangzeb and Murad Buksh used to take their dinners together. Aurangzeb dined occasionally at the residence of Murad Buksh; so did Murad Buksh at Aurangzeb's. Noticing the undivided friendship of the two brothers the people also ceased to look upon them as two brothers the people also ceased to look upon them as two different individuals.

On one occasion Aurangzeb invited Murad Buksh to dine with him. Cakes of numerous varieties were prepared, as well as delicious jellies. On the arrival of Murad Buksh, Aurangzeb said:

> "O Badshah, take some cakes, and rest here for a while, we shall have our dinner when it is ready."

Murad Buksh said:

> "All right, I shall rest after partaking of the cakes."

When he slept, he was seized with intoxication, and could not regain his senses by any means.

Aurangzeb then posted his men in order, and said:

> "The Badshah is sleeping, you should not make any noise at all."

Having cast his glance he saw that the new Badshah had lost his consciousness, due to severe intoxication. He was then chained with golden fetters.

Sultans Dara and Murad Murdered

Aurangzeb then placed Dara and Murad Buksh on the back of an elephant and displayed them to the people by beating drums. As the people might be provoked to sympathetic action after they had known that the two brothers were living, Aurangzeb decided to put an end to their lives.

Aurangzeb brought a dish of gold and with a knife beheaded his two brothers, Dara and Murad. With their blood imprinted on his forehead, Aurangzeb sat on the throne and became the Badshah.

Mir Jumla's Expedition against Sultan Shuja

Then the emperor despatched Mir Jumla to Bengal with his son Sultan Muazzam, 1,00,000 horse, elephants, cannon and all necessary war materials. The general was presented with a sirpao and received the following mandate of the Badshah, "Direct your efforts to the extermination of Shuja. I also appoint you subha at Dacca. Shaista Khan Uzir is my maternal uncle whom you should see on your way." Mir Jumla agreed to pay a visit to Shaista Khan at the instance of the emperor, whom he requested to issue orders to Shaista Khan to grant an interview to the general at any time and dismiss him very quickly. The emperor agreed to ask his uncle not to detain Mir Jumla very long in the interview.

Mir Jumla Insulted by Shaista Khan

Mir Jumla then retired to his own residence and conferred with his confidants saying:

> "I have no mind to go to Shaista Khan. At the same time I cannot but go, as the emperor has commanded me to see his uncle. How can I see Shaista Khan?"

Mir Jumla's friends gave the following advice:

> "We have heard that Shaista Khan remains engaged in cleansing his teeth up to the fourth danda of the day. If you go to him at that time he will certainly bid you farewell from the door."

In obedience to the command of the emperor, Mir Jumla stood one morning at the door of Shaista Khan and said to the janitor at the door:

> "Please ask a servant to tell Shaista Khan that Mir Jumla is at the door, and wants leave at once."

The door-keeper asked a servant to tell the nawab that Mir Jumla was waiting at the door and that he wanted leave at once. The servant did not communicate the message to the nawab, but reported falsely that Mir Jumla was asked by Shaista Khan to wait for some time at the door as he was then engaged in brushing his teeth. Mir Jumla said:

> "It is surprising that such a shirker is attached to a durbar like this. Well, door-keeper, please send for another servant to carry the message."

The door-keepre asked another servant, who told the Nawab that

Mir Jumla was at the door and that he wanted leave at once, and Shaista Khan said:

> ''Mir Jumla knows all these things. How is this that he has come to see me at this ungodly hour? However, call him in.''

Mir Jumla paid his greetings to Shaista Khan, but the latter did not give up rubbing his teeth, nor did he leave his seat, and neither did he place his hand on the breast. Shaista Khan said to Mir Jumla:

> ''I repeat what the Badshah has taught you. You may think that you have been deputed to subdue Shuja because there is no other nawab at Delhi. You have no bread in this land: the Badshah, out of compassion, is providing your descendants with bread. Try to to perpetuate this bread.

If the mission with have been denuted be crowned with success then only people will know that you are a trusted man. People do not know you now, whether you are honest or wicked.'' Saying so, Shaista Khan bade farewell to Mir Jumla, and despatched to Mir Jumla's quarters horses, swords and robes as presents to the general; but they were worthy of a commander of 5,000. Mir Jumla went home and said, "The prestige which I managed to acquire during these seventy years of my life has all been burnt to ashes in the hands of Shaista Khan.''

Sultan Muazzam's Marriage to Fatima

Mir Jumla and Prince Muazzam then attacked Shah Shuja, and had a series of daily engagements with the latter. Shuja seizing an opportunity sent a messenger to Sultan Muazzam with the following proposal:

> "My daughter Fatima is a captivating maiden, and Muazzam should come and marry her.''

That was a fraternal war, and Prince Muazzam hearing of a beautiful maiden and himself being of an amorous disposition could not resist the temptation. He visited Shuja in the company of 10,000 horses. On the arrival of Sultan Muzzam, Shuja thought he had practically won a victory. Shuja married his daughter to his nephew Muazzam and kept him there.

Mir Jumla's Warning to Prince Muazzam

Aurangzeb received the intelligence of Sultan Muazzam's marriage to Fatima and the Prince's stay in Shuja's residence. The emperor wrote a letter to Mir Jumla:

> "Alas! The war against Shuja has been well completed. Indeed, Mir Jumla has not even been able to keep my son. If he thinks he is unable to do anything, let him say so, and I will despatch another nawab with forces."

To this Mir Jumla sent the following reply:

> "I will bring the war against Shuja to a victorious termination, and I would ask the Badshah not to entertain any doubt or apprehension. As regards the blame he has pinned on me for the desertion of Sultan Muazzam, I would like to inform the emperor that if I, Mir Jumla, only shake the sleeves of my cloak dozens of such Badshahzadas will come out."

Mir Jumla despatched a man to Prince Muazzam with the following message:

> "Do you think that Shuja will ever occupy the throne by ousting the Emperor Aurangzeb? If not, act in a manner that will ensure your safety and well being in future. You said you would join me in the war from the south. The words of a great man are never violated. Act properly; then only you will remain in peace and happiness."

Flight of Prince Shuja

On the following day, while proceeding to war, Shuja speared Rashid Khan the senior from behind. Rashid Khan turned back and said:

> "At whose instance have you done this, O Shuja? Now I realise that you have been bereft of all hopes, and Aurangzeb has become Badshah without any obstruction."

Having said so Rashid Khan breathed his last. On another occasion, Shuja proceeded to the battle-field riding on an elephant. There ensued a terrible contest with heavy bloodshed. Rashid Khan's son who was holding the marchula, or fly-whisk made of peacock's tail, said:

> "O Badshah, everything will be thrown to the winds if you are fired at from a distance. So you should dismount from the elephant and ride on a horse."

There was severe fighting as soon as Shuja became a sawar after alighting from his elephant. Shuja was defeated. Having heard of the prince's defeat his soldiers deserted their ranks and joined the forces of Mir Jumla. Shuja boarded a boat and escaped to the country of the Mags.

Having received this intelligence Aurangshah presented a sirpao to Mir Jumla and conferred on him the title of Majum Khan. The Emperor commanded the general to remain as Subha of Dacca with an army of 40,000 horse and to despatch Sultan Muazzam with the rest of the troops to Delhi.

Mir Jumla's Invasion of Assam

Majum Khan wrote to the Badshah, as to my appointment as Subha of Dacca, I will remain at that place only after I have subjugated Cooch Behar which has become disloyal as well as Assam which has wrested back Kamrup. I solicit the orders of the Badshah. Sultan Muazzam having reached Delhi was despatched to remain in charge of Gwalior.

The Badshah commanded Majum Khan to leave his son Muhsud-ami Khan (Muhammad Amir Khan) at Dacca and subjugate the two provinces by conducting the expedition in person. The Badshah on receiving the intelligence of Majum Khan's entrance into the country of Gauhati after the subjugation of Cooch Behar conferred on him the title of Khan-Khana. Having heard of Mir Jumla's march through Assam, Aurangzeb said to Shaista Khan:

"The Khan-Khana has marched to Assam without my orders." Shaista Khan replied:

> " He has no bread in this land. He has thus acted to provide for his children and descendants."

Death of Mir Jumla

Having reached Pandu on his way back from Assam, the general was honoured with the title of Khan-Khana Siphar-Salah Siramauli. When he reached Bouroitola he died. Dilal Khan with the remnant of the army proceeded to the presence of the Badshah, having taken Muhsud Ami from Dacca. They took with them the elephants and princess which were brought from Assam, and paid their respects to the emperor. The Badshah said to Dilal Khan:

> "Well Dilal, you have come, but where did you leave the Khan-Khana ?"

The Badshah put this question twice; he wiped away the tears from his eyes and said to Muhsud Ami:

> "I bestow on you all the property which belonged to your father as well as the rank of a panch-hazari. You should remain with me. I appoint Shaista Khan Subha of Dacca."

Then turning to Dilal Khan the emperor said:

> "Well, Dilal Khan, you have come back after under going severe hardships. Go and remain as Subha at Aurangabad."

He was also honoured with the present of a sirpao. Here is finished this episode.

Mir Jumla's Career from Golconda to Garhgaon

Salutation to Sree Krishna. Hasan Muhammad Khan, the Badshah of Golconda, had no son though he was far advanced in years. He adopted the son of a nawab who was his wife's elder brother. The old Badshah said:

> "People would have obeyed you if you had been my son, but they will hesitate to do so as you are the son of a nawab. So you should bring the people under your obedience during my life-time."

All the nawabs and officers accepted the adopted son as their future king. Mir Jumla dewan, the son of Mirza Hazru, happened to be the only dessentient. So attempts were made to seize the person of Mir Jumla.

Mir Jumla Aids Aurangzeb

Having heard this, Mir Jumla, accompanied by 400 elephants, horses and troops fled with the object of going to Delhi. Aurangzeb was then living at Aurangabad; he detained Mir Jumla at his court. In the meantime Shah Jahan had abdicated the Badshahship and conferred it on his eldest son Dara, which gave rise to enmity among the four brothers. Shah Shuja was at Dacca and Murad Buksh at Kabul. Aurangzeb said to Mir Jumla:

> "Let us proceed to attack Dara at Delhi."

To this Mir Jumla replied:

> "I have come from Golconda with my allegiance mentally offered to the emperor of Delhi, and I will not lift my sword against His Majesty. I will proceed to any other quarter you order me to go."

With these words Mir Jumla gave to Aurangzeb 100,000 gold coins, saying, "You may spend this amount and attack Dara." Besides, Mir Jumla bore all the expenses of Aurangzeb's campaigns which amounted to eighteen crores of rupees.

Aurangzeb vanquished Dara and Murad Buksh, and staying at Delhi he summoned Mir Jumla to his presence. On his arrival the emperor said:

> "You should proceed to attack Shah Shuja who is at Dacca. I send my eldest son Sultan Muazzam to accompany you, besides 100,000 cavalry. You should also take with you elephants and cannon, and all necessary materials for war."

Mir Jumla's Humiliation at the Hands of Shaista Khan

The Badshah honoured Mir Jumla with numerous presents and gave him leave to depart, saying:

> "The general should on his way see Shaista Khan Wazir who is my maternal uncle." To this Mir Jumla replied, "Yes, I will see him, as commanded by the emperor. But he should ask Shaista Khan to grant me an interview at any time I choose to go, and give me leave quickly."

The emperor promised to ask his maternal uncle to dismiss Mir Jumla after a short interview. Mir Jumla retired to his residence and conferred with his trusted friends, saying:

> "I have no mind to go to Shaista Khan. At the same time I cannot but go, as I have received commands from the emperor. But I have also procured the Badshah's orders that Shaista Khan should grant me an interview at any time I go, and dismiss me quickly from his presence. I solicit your counsel on this subject."

His friends discussed the matter jointly and said:

> "Shaista Khan remains engaged in cleansing his teeth up to the fourth danda of the day. If you go to see him at this time he may give you leave to go by simply admitting you to his presence."

Accordingly Mir Jumla waited at the door of Shaista Khan early in the morning. He beckoned the duwar-dar or door-keeper and asked him to summon an attendant and send the information to Shaista Khan. The servant did not inform the nawab, but he said, as coming from the nawab:

> "Mir Jumla should wait for a while at the door. I am engaged in datwan or brushing of my teeth."

Mir. Jumla said,

> "It is curious that such a servant is permitted to reside in

> such a durbar; well, duwardar, you should beckon another personal attendant of the nawab to give him the information.''

The janitor called an attendant and sent information a second time. The servant informed Shaista Khan accordingly, who said:

> ''Mir Jumla knows all these things. But how is this, that he has come at this unseasonable hour? How-ever, call him in.''

Mir Jumla offered his muzura or greetings to the nawab, but the latter did not give up rubbing his teeth, nor did he leave his seat, and neither did he place his hand on his breast. Shaista Khan said to Mir Jumla:

> ''I repeat the instructions delivered to you by the emperor at the time of despatching you to fight with Shah Shuja. Do not think that you have been deputed by the Badshah of Delhi to subdue Shuja because there is no other nawab in this country. You have no ruti or bread in this land; the Badshah, out of compassion, is providing your descendants with bread. Act in a manner by which you may perpetuate your bread or position. If you can accomplish the mission with which you have been deputed by the Badshah, then only people will know your merits. They do not know you now as either honest or wicked.''

Who were Ram Singha's brothers and nephews. He also took with him 80,000 Rajput sepoys as well as numerous gunners, beldars, dafadars, labourers and shieldsmen. The total strength of his army was 300,000 and with them he proceeded to the Sewa campaign. On reaching the jurisdiction of Sewa, Ram Singha despatched messengers to the Sewa Raja with a letter to the following effect:

> '' I am the grandson of Maharaja Mandhata, and the son of Mirza Raja Jai Singha, and my name is Ram Singha. You must have heard the sound of our family's swords. There exists also a long-standing friendship between your family and mine. Our family has never shown its back in any war. You are also familiar with the prowess of the Emperor Aurangzeb. The nawabs who were sent before against you failed in their mission; so some of them have been executed and others expelled. The emperor wanted to send his son Sultan Muhammad, but I dissuaded him from coming, and

> I have come myself on account of the long friendship subsisting between us. So come, and let us meet at a convenient place: if on the other hand you want war, be prepared for the same, and do not delay.''

Ram Singha's Victory over Sewa

Kandarpa Singha, the Raja of Sewa, received the imperial ambassadors, and sent the following reply to Ram Singha's message:

> ''The arguments which you have set forth in your letter are true and wholesome. But if I enter into any friendly terms with you, people will laugh at and upbraid us both saying that we have become friends being unable to oppose each other in strength. So war seems to me the better course.''

Then there ensued a terrible contest between the two parties. The soldiers of Ram Singha were great experts in spear-fighting. They were insensible to pain even when they received wounds from weapons on account of their bodies being saturated with opium of which they were habitual consumers. They preferred death to retreat from battle.

On the other hand, the soldiers of Sewa took to their heels when they had to face a very hard contest. So in the war a large number of the soldiers of Sewa fled from the battle-field or were killed. Seizing an opportunity during the thick of the fight, the bheel soldiers of Ram Singha surrounded the Raja of Sewa. Ram Singha defeated Sewa Raja in the war.

The Sewa Raja then enquired what Ram Singha was going to do with him, whether he would be taken to the presence of the Badshah or be let off. Ram Singha said:

> ''This is out of the question now, as you did not act before according to our advice. You will be taken to the presence of the emperor. But I will intercede on your behalf with the Badshah so that no harm may be done to you. You shall place your head below and I will place mine on top of yours.''

Ram Singha wrote a detailed despatch on the war and sent it to the emperor, who asked Ram Singha to escort the Sewa Raja to the court after having left Jumsher Khan in charge of the army. Ram Singha accordingly appeared before the Badshah with the Sewa Raja. Ram

Singha was honoured with rich presents. The emperor asked the Sewa Raja:

> "You are the great chief of Sewa, and of a very long standing too. Your ancestors had served mine. You have now become unfaithful to us. May I know the reason ? Are you defying me on the strength of any secret alliance you have formed with any other power? Or do you think I am impotent in my authority ?"

Thus replied Kandarpa Singha, the Raja of Sewa :

> "My forefathers never served your forefathers in person. They only sent articles and supplies through their envoys according to time-honoured customs."

On ascending the throne you have insisted on the payment of tribute, and you have introduced the system of obligatory personal service. This is why we have ceased to be under your vassalage."[1]
The emperor said:

> "You did not serve before, nor did you pay any tribute. We have now seized your person. Wherein now is your honour gone? I can now kill you, or do whatever I like with you. So consent to accept our allegiance, and live in peace and plenty by paying us tribute. Otherwise you will be killed, being trodden on by elephants."

Sewa Raja hurled the following retort:

> "I cannot do what we never did before nor can I accept your suggestion even on pain of death."

The emperor, being indignant, ordered the raja to be put under the feet of elephants. But Raja Ram Singha implored the emperor on behalf of the Raja of Sewa, and asked the Badshah not to kill the raja, who was accordingly imprisoned, being chained with shackles of gold.

Kandarpa Singha's Escape from Prison

After staying in prison for some time, Kandarpa Singha said to Ram Singha:

> "You brought me here with assurance of safety. I cannot understand why I am now detained in prison, and I do not know what else is in store for me. All this is due to you. I have in my life subdued many people."

Ram Singha earnestly entreated the emperor to release the raja but in vain, and Ram Singha became sorely grieved at heart.

A son was then born to Ram Singha, who was named Keshore Das. On that occasion Ram Singha used to send out articles of food and ornaments, loaded in huge boxes of copper, brass and silver, to the rajas and nawabs. He cut asunder the chains of the Sewa Raja, put him in a box and sent him back to his kingdom and it was not detected at any of the imperial gates and outposts.

Ram Singha's First Offence

The emperor ascribed the escape of the raja to Ram Singha and accused the latter, saying: "What have you done with the Raja of Sewa? To this Ram Singha replied:

> "I implored you so earnestly on his behalf and, as you were not willing to let him off, he has made his escape."

The Badshah replied: It is you who allowed him to escape to which Ram Singha said:

> "If you think I have been instrumental in the escape of the Sewa Raja, he is under my thumb, and there should be no fear on that score."

The Badshah did not say anything, but remained silent, cogitating within himself.

The Sikh Guru Teg Bahadur Escapes from Captivity

Then there was a saint of the faith of Guru Nanak, and he became the guru of a large number of brahmans and kshattriyas. He would not take the name of Ram or Krishna, nor of any god or goddess. On meeting a disciple of his own faith he would simply say: "Om, ai, Guru; Om, ai, Guru," and nothing else. The brahman Bhattacharyas or priests and the Kazis of the Musalmans reported to the Badshah:

> "This man does not belong to any particular school or faith; he goes about ravaging the country."

The emperor asked the guru to appear before him, but he did not come.

On the other hand, he defied the authority of the Badshah, and roamed about plundering and destroying the country, attended by thirty thousand Nanak-panthi sepoys. The Badshah became indignant, and he deputed Alo Khan Pathan who captured the guru. The Badshah ordered the guru to be executed, who for fear of his life sought the protection of Ram Singha, who became a surety for the Sikh leader. But the aforesaid Nanak-panthi guru also made his escape.

Ram Singha's Second Offence

The Badshah accused Ram Singha, saying:

> "How is this that you have allowed the guru to flee, though you yourself stood a surety for him?"

To this Ram Singha replied, "

> What is he ? Only a raja or a nawab is worthy of your vengeance. He is only a mendicant faqir. To accuse me for his escape will cause people to laugh when they hear of it."

Hearing the explanation offered by Ram Singha with regard to the escape of the Sikh guru, the Badshah said to himself:

> "This Ram Singha has begun to commit one misdeed after another. Remembering the services rendered to the State by his father and grandfather, I cannot say anything to him. Besides, any punishment inflicted on Ram Singha may lead to a concerted action on the part of the rajas against me, and I shall be alienated from them all."

Thus thinking, the Badshah did not propose to do anything to Ram Singha.

Dangers of Assam Wars

And it came to pass that the Swarga Maharaja of Assam attacked the fort of Gauhati and captured the nawab Sayid Piroz Khan. On receiving this intelligence the Badshah said to Ram Singha:

> "Raja Jai Singha, son of Raja Mandhata, fought in the Bengal war and subdued that province. Now, you proceed to the war with Assam."

The reason for which, the Badshah said thus to Ram Singha was this not a single nawab who had been deputed to the Assam war could ever come back safely; some died of themselves, while others were killed in the battle; the waters of Assam are poisonous, its air unhealthy and its hills are covered with dense forests; and the emperor wanted that Ram Singha should die in Assam. Devising this plan the Badshah deputed Ram Singha to Assam.

Ram Singha Deputed to the War against Assam

The Raja took with him the Rajput bheels of his owe State; Rashid Khan Nawab and others, and took leave of the emperor. The Badshah appointed two of his own men as dewans to accompany

Ram Singha in his expedition, Mirza Saiyid Saf, the dewan of the Perganas, and Mir Raji, the dewan of the laskars and sepoys.

The emperor also deputed Bahlol Khan, the Daroga of seven hundred Iasols, and Sultan Ali the Daroga of three hundred Ahudis. Mir Gazar Beg Hazi was appointed waqaya-navis of the expedition and the emperor said to him:

> "Ram Singha is an untrustworthy man. He may enter into a collusion with the Swarga Maharaja. You should send regular reports to me regarding his movements, and the success or ill-fate of the expedition."

The raja halted on the way with his detachment. The nawabs who were commissioned to accompany the raja joined him subsequently with their quota of suppplies. There was a garden at Patna founded by Ram Singha's father Jai Singha. The Raja stopped there for a week awaiting the arrival of the remaining portion of his army.

Ram Singha Warmly Received by Shaista Khan

From Patna, Ram Singha proceeded towards Jahangirnagar in order to have an interview with Amir-ul-Omrao Shaista Khan who was the sworn friend of the raja's father Jai Singha. On account of this old friendship Ram Singha came to Dhaka. On hearing of the approach of the raja, Shaista Khan welcomed him with great cordiality and splendour.

The son of Aburnamir Khan and the two dewans, Raja Nandalal and Rai Muraridhar, escorted the raja with elephants and horses, marching to the notes of the five musical instruments. The path lying on the march was splashed with water by a host of chikabardars and the roofs of the houses in the bazaars through which the raja passed were covered with golden and silvery cloths.

The court chamber of Shaista Khan was also draped with costly carpets up to the ceiling. There were placed six hundred incense pots fuming with the vapour of burnt aloe. In every room tassels of pearls and corals were placed six hundred incense pots fuming with the vapour of burnt aloe. In every room tassels of pearls and corals were suspended from the overhanging canopies.

The raja approached the nawab and, addressing him as uncle or chacha, saluted the latter by touching his feet. Shaista Khan clasped Ram Singha to his bosom by twining him by the neck, and kissed the raja's head. The nawab presented to Ram Singha precious elephants and horses, and a sword named Khanjar whose price amounted to 25,000 rupees. Nawab Shaista Khan then imparted the following instructions to Ram Singha:

> "Act in a way that you may remain in the good graces of the emperor. Aurangzeb Badshah is a shrewd diplomat. Shujangar (Hajo in Assam ?) is an unhealthy place; its hills are covered with forests, and poisonous waters flow in its streams during the two months Baisak and Jaistha. The air that blows is also infected with poison. For this reason our men die there in numbers, and you should live very carefully. Do not drink any water but that of the Louhitya or Brahmaputra. Do not admit the women of that place into your mahal; they are wicked and treacherous."

The nawab further advised:

> "Please write to me when you fall short of food-stuff, war provisions or money; I will send them to you, looking upon you as one of mine."

Ram Singha became extremely delighted with the reception given to him, and said to the nawab:

> "The advice which you have given to me is generally imparted by father to his son."

The raja then took leave of the nawab whose sons saluted Ram Singha by touching his feet, and escorted him to a considerable distance. Ram Singha then arrived with his army at Shujanagar.

Reference

1. This story is applicable to Raja Karan Bhurtiyat of Bikanir against whom Jai Singha was sent. Tao Karna himself joined Jai Singha's campaign against Shivaji. *Manucci*, II, pp. 22-23.

Chapter - 12

Subjugation of Eastern India

Jahangir Badshah of Delhi had three sons, Shah Alagzaha, Sultan Khurram and Muhammad Jahan. Sultan Khurram became the Badshah of Delhi by killing two of his brothers by a stratagem. Muhammad Jahan fled in the guise of a *faquir*, and on the death of the Turki Badshah in an island, he married the widowed queen and became Badshah of that kingdom. Turki ponies breed in the kingdom of the Turki Badshah.

Sultan Khurram sat on the throne of Delhi by the name of Shah Jahan. Once a slave of Nawab Saadulla Khan, named Muhammad Sayid, visited the Badshah's court as an attendant of the Nawab. The slave possessed marks of a future Badshah, which were noticed by the Emperor, who said to the Nawab, Give me your slave Muhammad Sayid, and I will give you two slaves in return. To this the Nawab replied, I am a slave of your majesty; what objection can a slave have ?

The Nawab returned to his residence with the slave to whom he said, the Badshah wants you as you are endowed with the marks of a sovereign. He will kill you. Make good your escape by some means or other. The slave said, "If I flee, the Emperor may cause you some harm." The Nawab replied, "Whatever may befall me, you should save yourself anyhow." The slave fled accordingly and took shelter with Shah Bhramara, literally the Prince of Vagrants.

Shah Bhramara said, "Who are you ? Why have you come here?" The slave replied, "Shah Jahan intends to put me to death as I have the marks of a sovereign. So I have fled and sought your protection." The faquir said, " I will give you three crores of rupees. Go and become a Badshah." The slave, with the help of this money, raised and maintained an army, and encountered Shah Jahan

Badshah in a terrible contest. Shah Jahan, being defeated, escaped to Rum and took shelter with the Badshah of that kingdom.

When Muhammad Sayid Gholam ascended the throne, Shah Bhramara conferred on him the name of Shah Muhammad. The faquir said that the new monarch had only three years more to live and not an hour more. Having heard this prophecy of the faquir, the usurper wrote to Shah Jahan Badshah at Rum:

> "Come back and become Badshah. I am renouncing the throne."

The Badshah of Rum gave to Shah Jahan a number of soldiers and attendants who reinstalled him on the throne. The slave of the Nawab, after renouncing the throne, said with prayers and apologies,

> "I am a slave of your slave. I fled in fear of you, and became eventually the Badshah. The enjoyment of a Badshahship is not meant for me; the Badshahship of your kingdom befits you alone."

Shah Jahan Badshah came back to Delhi. The slave of the Nawab died, and the Emperor appointed his son a commander of 5,000

Shah Jahan's Visit to Jai Singha's Capital Amber

Seeing the influence and power of Raja Jai Singha, the Emperor Shah Jahan thought within himself. How shall I kill Jai Singha ? If I can get rid of him the Kingdom of Amber will fall into my hands, and my sovereignty will also be free from danger. Otherwise he may do me mischief some day. So let me visit his State and examine its strength and resources. Thus, thinking, the Emperor said to the Raja one day at *Am-khas*:

> "Well, let me confer on you the honour of a visit to your State."
> The Raja replied, "Grant me leave for a week."
> The Badshah said, "Yes, all right, you may go."

The Raja then proceeded to his capital and conferred with his ministers and relatives, saying, the Badshah, intending to invade and occupy our kingdom, is coming to examine its resources on the pretext of conferring a favour. The Rajput counsellors replied:

> "Let the Badshah come, we shall seize his person and imprison him, and all the Rajput chiefs united will appoint you Badshah instead."

Jai Singh said:

> "It was never done by our family. Though the Badshah may do us wrong, being misguided, we should never act in a hostile manner as proposed. We have never been unfaithful to the *Badshahs* of Delhi."

The Raja then made arrangements for numerous varieties of food for the Emperor, and created a raised platform for the Badshah, befitting the Emperor's position and dignity. The Raja then informed the Emperor of his readiness to receive him, and Shah Jahan went to Amber as promised before.

Raja Jai Singha posted at regular intervals along the routes extending over a distance of eight *prahars* journey, lengthwise and breadth wise as far as the eyes could see, soldiers attired in uniforms and ornaments of gold and silver and equipped with the five weapons, spears, swords and shields, Jamdar, guns and arrows and bows, as well as horses and elephants harnessed with saddles and ornaments of gold and silver.

The roofs and walls of the houses situated in the city and the market-place were covered with trappings of gold and silver, giving the appearance of continuous relays of ants. Along the route, at the interval of a distance of one *danda*, were established outposts with elephants, horses and sepoys and the Raja commanded that at every such station soldiers should be posted on the advent of the Emperor, as he in his travels was accompanied only by a limited number of soldiers.

On the approach of the Badshah, men were placed at the *chowkis* or stations. The Emperor was dismayed at the sight of the splendour and pomp of arms and weapons, of elephants, horses and sepoys.

On reaching Amber, the Badshah turned back and saw that men were being posted at the Chowkis or outposts. Wherever he turned his eyes he saw only spears and weapons.[1] The Emperor was seized with fear and said to the wazir. The Rajputs have by stratagem managed to capture me, and there is no remedy. Besides they have placed soldiers at the *chowkis*.

The Raja received the Badshah with great hospitality, and pleased him with the presents of precious articles. The Emperor returned, having pleased all the nobles of the Raja by making gifts of numerous presents.

Jai Singha Deputed to Eastern India

During the confusion that followed the flight of Shah Jahan Badshah, and the occupation of the throne of Delhi by the Nawab's bondsman, there was anarchy in Bengal. The Raja of Orissa occupied the imperial fort by ousting therefrom the Mogul Nawab. The fort of Rajmahal was attacked and captured by Raja Chandrabhal. The Rajas of Morung seized the fort and established his independence at Morung.

Cooch-Behar also asserted its independence, and the Rajas of Dacca, Chittagong, Sylhet, Gauhati and Arrakan committed ravages in the country and ruled in their own names. On receiving reports of the above, Shah Jahan said to Jai Singha:

> "Bengal has always been subdued by your family. So you should proceed there."

The Raja said:

> "All right, I will go. Please issue orders for supplying me nine Nawabs, five of our Rajput Rajas, and few cannon."

The Raja was given what he wanted, and despatched to Bengal.

Cooch-Behar's Contribution to Nao-Raja Expenses

Jai Singha halted at Patna, and sent messengers to the rulers of the nine principalities, Dacca, etc., with letters to the following effect, Have you heard of the might of the Emperor Shah Jahan ? Have you also heard the rattling of my invincible sword as well as that of Mandhata? If you have, then come promptly and become friends with us, or otherwise be prepared for war.

On receiving this message the Raja of Cooch-Behar brought valuable presents to the Emperor and Jai Singha, and Nawab Galir Beg was despatched to settle the boundaries of Bengal and Cooch-Behar.

The river Ghaghat was fixed as the boundary between the two territories. Rangpur became the *thana* of Cooch-Behar on this side of the river, and the imperial outpost was established at Tajhat on the other bank and placed in charge of Nawab Galir Beg. An ambassador of Cooch-Behar was to remain at Dacca, and it was stipulated that he should hand over to the Nawab of Dacca one lakh of rupees as *selami* for presentation to the Badshah during the *Nao-roz* festival.

Nao-roza Festivities

What is Nao-roza? The Badshah amuses himself for nine days, from the seventh day of the white moon to the full moon day in the month of Kartick. The wives of the Nawabs, and Mansabdars, the begums of the merchant-princes, as well as of other commercial magnates, are to go to the inner apartments of the Badshah's palace. In the interior, a place is nicely constructed with marble stones.

There are tanks, each of which is covered on all its four sides with flowers of all hues and colours, crimson, yellow, white and black, including the lotus and the lily, and on the water float ducks, herons, water-crows, chakra-vakasor ruddy sheldrakes, all made artificially of the eight metals. The birds are tied to strings by which their movements are regulated. Crackers, rockets, squibs, and scintillators all made of explosives, are placed in a gala fashion on the site near about the water. Rose-water, *attar* and *argaza* waters are sprinkled on the decorated floor.

The ladies attractively decorate the stalls where they display their articles for sale. Gorgeous white canopies are pitched at intervals. Mainas, parrots, bulbuls, shrikers, magpies, swallow-tails, all tamed at home, pour forth their melodious strain. The stall-owners and shopkeepers as well as the wives of the merchant-princes, all dressed in their finest apparel and ornaments, display their wares consisting of diamonds, pearls, topazes, rubies, coral, beads and other articles of gold and silver. The ladies of the Badshah's Begum-Mahal and other ladies of the palace, as well as the wives of the Nawabs and Mansabdars in their gorgeous dresses and ornaments, purchase articles offered for sale.

The Emperor accompanied by music flowing from rubab, tambourines, syrangis, flutes, timbals, brazen pipes, setaras, violins, trumpets, and other instruments proceeds to the place where the wives of the nobles and merchants are selling their articles. The Emperor indulges in mirthful laughter and jokes when he haggles about the price of the articles he intends to purchase. The articles are to be purchased at the price demanded by the amiable sellers. No man is admitted into the place; of men only the Badshah has access.

In this way the sales and purchases continue for nine days. The Badshah spends nine lakhs of rupees during the Nao-roz. The stipulation with Cooch-Behar was to the effect that it would contribute a sum of rupees one lakh every year towards the expenses of the Nao-roz. Masim Khan of Bengal came and offered his submission of his own accord.

Subjugation of Morung

The Raja of Morung and other chieftains prepared themselves for war. Raja Jai Singha, being indignant, deputed Nawab Kilis Khan with seven thousand soldiers against Morung. The war with the Raja of Morung continued for three months. The Raja could not stand in the fight and he offered his submission. Hawks and kuhis are found in Morung in abundance.

The Raja presented to the Badshah ten kuhis, ten hawks and ten murchulis[2] or peacocks' tails; Raja Jai Singha was also given five specimens of each of the above birds as well as other precious articles. Nawab Kilis Khan remained in charge of the fort of Morung.

Subjugation of Nepal

The Raja of Nepal surrendered voluntarily. Copper is found in abundance in his territories. The Raja presented to the Badshah ten big caldrons of copper, each capable of holding rice for one hundred men, and one hundred small pitchers; to Jai Singha were given four caldrons and forty small pitchers and other articles. With this the Raja offered his submission.

Subjugation of other Territories

Nawab Adam Khan was placed in charge of Jahangirnagar, while Nawab Zahid Beg and Nawab Uzbeg remained at the Chatgaon thana. Hostilities ensued with the Maghs. The insurgents were defeated, and some Maghs with their wives and children were removed to Dacca and made to settle there.

There is still a place at Dacca called Maghar-bazaar. Chilim Khan was sent to the thana at Sylhet, who occupied the place, and captured some Feringhis who were subsequently taken to Dacca, which has got a section still known as Feringhee bazaar. Raja Naranarayan[3] of Cooch-Behar was at that time the monarch of Kamrupa. He continued to live in friendly terms with Raja Jai Singha. Raja Jai Singha remained at Patna for some time. Having subdued all the Rajas of the place, he left Nawabs in charge of the various thanas, after which he proceeded to bathe in the Ganges.

Chandrabhal, the Raja of Rajmahal, came and offered his submission of his own accord, and Jai Singha pardoned him after extracting from him one lakh of rupees. He then distributed large charities in adoration to the Ganges, and constructed a tower at the Mana-Mardana bathing ghat with stone and brick.

Subjugation of Orissa

Jai Singha despatched Jabardust Khan against Oresha or Orissa. He failed to capture the fortress, though the hostilities continued for a length of time. In connection with this affair, and with the object of paying a visit to Jagannath, Jai Singha proceeded to Orissa. Raja Subal Singha of the line of Raja Indradyumma, was the king of Orissa. On Jai Singha's reaching Orissa Subal Singha died as fate would have it, in his bed while asleep. His son Siva Singha succeeded his father.

Raja Jai Singha deputed a wakil to Siva Singha with the message, a princess of your family was married to our house some time ago. You are my nephew according to the relationship thus established. Both the families have been enjoying mutual friendship and affection to a very great extent. I have come here under the orders of the very powerful sovereign Shah Jahan Badshah.

After subduing Bengal I have come to see Jagannath. so you should arrange for my adoration of the Thakur or image and thus afford an opportunity of knowing each other. If not, be prepared for war. You have done wrong by attacking the imperial thanas, which has made the Badshah highly indignant towards you. Having heard this from the wakil, Siva Singha thought within himself:

> "My father is dead and my reign has not been properly consolidated. Besides, there exists an old relationship between the family of Jai Singha and ours. Jai Singha is a veteran warrior and he has subdued the whole of Bengal. I do not think I shall be able to successfully oppose him in strength. Under these circumstances submission will be the better course."

Thus thinking, Siva Singha marched with his troops to welcome Jai Singha from a distance. He also offered hospitality to the soldiers and followers. Jai Singha worshipped at the shrine of Jagannath. He presented to the image a diamond of the value of one lakh of rupees, a cloth valued at one thousand rupees for fastening on to the standard, and an annual grant of twenty maunds of ghee for burning lamps; he also arranged for the payment of a monthly salary to the man entrusted with the charge of lighting the lamps daily.

The Title of Mirza-Raja Conferred on Jai Singha

After establishing friendly terms with the Raja of Orissa, Jai Singha appointed Jabardust Khan Subha of that place. He then halted at Rajmahal from where he submitted a despatch to the Badshah stating all the particulars about Bengal, and the names of the Nawabs posted at the various thanas. The articles presented by the Rajas were also sent to the Emperor.

The Badshah became extremely delighted, and sent some presents to Jai Singha and conferred on him the title of Mirza-Raja. Similarly, presents and titles were also conferred on the other Rajas, Nawabs and Mansabdars. The Badshah wrote to Jai Singha:

> "The Rajas and Zemindars of Bengal and Orissa are rebelious in their disposition. You should remain at Patna until the thanas are well consolidated or until I summon you to my presence."

Jai Singha Deputed against Kashmir

Jai Singha had a *bag* or estate at Patna yielding an income of one lakh of rupees per year, where he constructed a magnificent residence. He also repaired the entrances of the fort of Muger, and established a market-place named Jai-Singha-pur.

After this the province of Kashmir became rebellious. Jai Singha was summoned from Patna and despatched against Kashmir. These are the details of the events.

Shah Jahan's Longing to See his Peer

Sitting at the Roz-dewan, Shah Jahan once said to his *wazir*, the Almighty God has blessed me with the Badshahship of Delhi, and has bestowed on me all the things necessary for the pleasure and enjoyment of a mortal. He has not withdrawn from me any favour. Yet my heart longs for seeing a man who is as great as I am, or is greater than myself. The men whom I see around me are all inferior to me in position and power. So you should make an attempt to find out my peer. Being thus commanded by the Emperor, the wazir, Asaf Khan Khan-Khana Sipah-salar said:

> "With regard to the enquiry made by the Badshah-Hazarat, I am not in a position to give a reply at once. Give me time to investigate into past accounts, and I will place the information in time at the feet of the Emperor."

Search for Equal Sovereigns

Saying so, the wazir consulted the records deposited in the archives of the Badshah, the wazir and the Kazi, and gathered the following facts and communicated them to the Emperor, "From the time of the Hindu King Judhisthira to Bahram Shah Badshah, which covered a period of 2954 years, there were 58 sovereigns on the throne of Delhi

During this period we come across synchronous sovereigns of equal strength and position From the time of the Hindu King Samudrapal to Pithor Raja, covering a period of 1122 years, 1 month and 28 days, there were 62 sovereigns.

From the reign of the first Musalman Badshah to that of Jahangir, during the period of 769 years, 4 months and 15 days, there were 51 sovereigns. The total number of Rajas and Badshahs thus comes up to 113, covering a total period of 1891 years, 6 months and 13 days. During this period we do not meet any two contemporary Rajas or Badshahs of equal strength and power.

Raja Prithivi Shah of Kandor

With regard to the enquiries whether there is any great monarch whose kingdom is conterminous to that of the Badshah of Delhi, the wazir consulted the ancient records and ascertained the following facts:

> "The kingdom of Prithivi Shah, son of Chandra Raja of Kandor, to the south of Delhi, is contiguous to the kingdom of the Mogul Badshah. His men are more warlike than those of the Delhi Badshah; they are also of a superior *dil* or heart. The rulers of his family eat the powdered grains of burnt pearls. The distance between Delhi and the junction of the two States represents a journey of 35 days, and that between the capital of Prithivi Shah to the same boundary

> can be covered by a journey of 37 days; and it is very convenient to go there as there are villages and rivers on the way.''

The wazir submitted the above details to the Badshah in response to the enquiry lodged by his Majesty some time before.

Shah Jahan Desires to See Prithivi Shah

The Badshah then said to the wazir, arrange to despatch an intelligent wakil of ours to visit the court of Prithivi Shah Raja with costly presents. Let him say to the Raja, Shah Jahan Badshah desires to have an interview with you. If you also participate in the same desire then send men to fit up a place at the junction of the two territories. The messenger of Shah Jahan communicated to Prithivi Raja the intention of the Badshah. Prithivi Shah then replied:

> ''Shah Jahan Badshah of Delhi has expressed his desire to see me; similarly, I also cherish the desire of seeing him.''

Having said so he deputed a clever wakil to Shah Jahan Badshah with the following message:

> ''When we see each other I will address him as Shah Jahan Badshah, my younger brother, and he, in his turn should address me as `Prithivi Shah, his elder brother.''

If he agrees to this proposal, his men as well as mine will come and prepare a place on the boundaries of the two kingdoms. Both of us shall be accompanied by a numerous train. A clever man should be entrusted with the task of preparing the venue of our interview so that there may not be any hitch on the occasion.

Meeting of the Badshah and the Raja

The two wakils informed Shah Jahan Badshah. The Badshah said:

> ''I bind myself to the proposal of Prithivi Shah Raja. I will address him as my elder brother. Asaf Khan Wazir will proceed to prepare the camping ground. The Raja will also send a competent man for the same purpose.''

Thus saying he despatched a wakil with precious presents who communicated to Prithivi Shah what Shah Jahan had said. The Raja deputed an efficient Patra or noble to prepare the place.

The Patra and the Wazir proceeded to the junction of the two territories. A camp was constructed for Prithivi Shah at a distance of one *prahar*'s journey from the boundary the Wazir also prepared a place for Shah Jahan at the same distance. There was a distance of two *prahars* on the east as well as on the west. The hollows and pools were filled up. A ditch was excavated at the boundary which resembled a half-moon. On the actual site of meeting between the Raja and the Badshah ditches were constructed at a distance of twenty cubits.

Prithivi Shah and Shah Jahan moved in the month of Agrahayan and saw each other in Phalgun. Shah Jahan had marched facing the south, and Prithivi Shah facing the north. Thus coming from both sides the two sovereigns met at the point where the ditch was the narrowest.

Exchange of Royal Greetings

> On seeing Shah Jahan, Prithivi Shah said: "I have received the highest pleasure possible for a mortal body."
> On seeing Prithivi Shah, Shah Jahan said: "I have been blessed with the sight of a great man and the desire of the human body has been fulfilled."
> Prithivi Shah replied: "Does my younger brother Shah Jahan Badshah of Delhi enjoy happiness of heart in all ways?"
> Shah Jahan made the reply: "My elder brother Prithivi Shah, Allah, the great God, has made me Badshah of Delhi; can anything be more gratifying to the heart than this, except the limitations springing from my birth and race ?
> Prithivi Shah said: "You have said well by acknowledging that nothing is more glorious than the Badshahship of Delhi. You should not remember at all the limitation of your birth."
> Shah Jahan said: "By seeing and talking with you all the uncleanliness of my heart has been removed."
> Prithivi Shah said: "The discrepancy which existed before between my eyes and ears has now disappeared after having a sight of the Badshah of Delhi attended by his army."
> Shah Jahan said: "My eyes have been blessed with a great fortune by seeing Prithivi Shah with his men."

Duel between two Rajput Warriors

By seeing each other the two sovereigns feasted their eyes to the fill, and it knew no abatement. Just at that moment a Rajput Raja of Prithivi Shah rushed forward with shield and sword, and he was faced by another Rajput Prince of the camp of Shah Jahan. The two warriors then stated their cause to their respective lords, A Raja and a Badshah are here. We have cherished the desire of attaining paradise by dying in a face-to-face combat. Our pious resolve can be accomplished only if the two sovereigns be pleased to accord the necessary permission. The two monarchs then permitted them, saying, 'May your cherished wish be fulfilled.'

On obtaining the permission solicited the two warriors, armed with shield and sword, rushed to the presence of the sovereigns and their followers. Uttering the name Narayana, they at the same time inflicted blows on each other with their swords, and the bodies of each fell simultaneously severed into two equal pieces. A piece of fleece-white cloud descended from heaven and covered the lifeless remains of the combatants. After a while the cloud disappeared; and nothing else was visible; but the sound of tinkling bells could only be heard. The people assembled uttered shouts of praise and glory.

Exchange of Presents between the Sovereigns

Prithivi Shah presented to Shah Jahan 1500 horses all, including four Iraki, eight Arbi and twelve Sujarnis ponies. He also presented precious cloths and pearls and diamonds as well as other articles worthy of a monarch, amounting to six crores of rupees, besides five crores presented to the Badshah's train.

The Badshah presented to Prithivi Shah four hundred elephants and five hundred horses, and other precious articles amounting to a total of five crores of rupees, in addition to another four crores presented to the members of the Raja's retinue. The two sovereigns then took leave of each other after offering assurance of mutual friendship.

The Patra gave to the wazir, horses including one Iraki pony, and two Arbi, and articles to the value of one crore and a half of rupees. The wazir gave to the Patra, eighty elephants and articles of the value of one and a half crores of rupees. The other people in the retinue of the two sovereigns also exchanged presents. The Patra and the wazir were praised by all for controlling the functions without any hitch or misunderstanding though the soldiers and retainers of the two camps were as large as the sea. Here is finished what was said by Gakulpuri.[4]

Proposals to Conquer Kandahar

On the death of Jahangir Badshah, his son Shah Jahan became Badshah, and sat on the *takht* or throne at an auspicious moment. The events which took place during the first eight years of his reign are recorded in other books; only the events which took place after the lapse of eight years of his reign will be found in this book.

One day, sitting in his court at *Dewani-aam* surrounded by his ministers and counsellors. Shah Jahan Badshah put the following question to his wazir relating to the strength of the Badshah of Khandar or Kandahar, "How powerful is that Badshah ? What is the strength of his army ? How invincible is his fortress ?"The wazir replied, " The fortress of the Badshah of Khandar is highly impregnable, his soldiers innumerable, and the splendour of his elephants and horses unlimited. But who can be greater than Your Majesty ? You can easily attack and conquer the country."

Prince Shuja's Expedition against Kandahar

According to the decision of the court, one Galiz Khan, an omrao commanding 7,000, was despatched as Subha to Khandar with Muhammad Khan and Zalandar Khan. Galiz Khan proceeded to the spot, and witnessing the impregnable character of the fortress sent a written communication to the emperor.

The Badshah deputed his son Shah Shuja to Khandar at the head of an army of 20,000 sepoys commanded by ten haft-hazari, char-hazari and panch-hazari omraos, including Raja Jai Singha. The prince received instructions as follows:

> "If Shah Safi,[5] the Badshah of Khandar, takes the battle against you personally, then you should proceed to the battle yourself. But if he sends another man in his place, you should not go. In the latter case you should despatch Galiz Khan with soldiers, and halt yourself at the *thana* of Kabul."

With these instructions Shuja was given leave to depart; he was also presented with rich gifts. The following command was issued to the nawabs in charge of the imperial thanas in the neighbourhood of Khandar:

> "You should send to the fort of Khandar rice, pulse, radish,

> ghee, sugar and other necessaries, to feed the soldiers to enable them to engage themselves in war.''

Shah Shuja, the son of the Emperor, went accordingly to Khandar in the company of a large army. The prince was preceded by an omrao at a distance of one *prahar*'s journey while another followed up in the rear at the same distance, while one nawab accompanied him on the right and another on the left.

In this array did the Badshahzada march to Khandar. When the prince was within a distance of three days' journey, the commander in charge of the advance line of fortifications sent a written report to Shah Safi Badshah about the approach of Prince Shuja.

Shah Safi Prepares for War

Shah Safi wrote back to the commander of the fort, You should remain in readiness with soldiers, arms and munitions, and despatch six thousand troops and fall upon the invaders. The commander remained ready for action with his soldiers as instructed by Shah Safi, and deputed six thousand soldiers to attack the imperialists. The soldiers thus despatched were dismayed at the sight of the magnificence of Shuja's army, and came back without any action.

The commander of the fort of Khandar sent information to Shah Safi on the war array of Prince Shuja, on which Shah Safi thundered at Shah Jahan Badshah. He summoned his counsellors and said:

> ''If Shah Jahan, the Badshah of Delhi, had taken the field in person, I would have gone to the battle myself. It will be unbecoming on my part to fight with his son.''

Thus saying, he despatched to the fort skilful warriors, sirdars, elephants, horses, arms, munitions and other war materials. The two armies stood ready for action near the four fortresses of Khandar.

The Imperialists Occupy Kandahar Fort

From his spies Prince Shuja received intelligence of the resolution of Shah Safi not to take the field in person and acting according to the instructions of his father, the prince made presents to Galiz Khan and appointed him commander in chief of the whole army, and gave him assurance of reinforcement when necessary. The prince remained at the fort of Kabul, ready for action. There was severe fighting between the two armies lasting for one day and one night and two *prahars*. The imperial troops could not in any way capture the fort. The Khandar army fought from within the fort, for which they did not sustain heavy casualties on their side, whereas Galiz Khan lost as many as 20,000 soldiers.

Galiz Khan then adopted a novel device. He excavated a big tank at a distance of one *prahar*'s journey from the fort. A tunnel was dug up connecting the tank with the dike encircling the fort. The moat-water was thus drawn through the tunnel towards the tank, resulting in the drying up of the moat, and the filling up of the tank. Galiz Khan then said to his soldiers:

> "I will pay at the rate of rupees ten to an old man, eight to a boy, and five to a young man. The ditch should be filled up by each of you throwing one basketful of earth."

Being thus commanded, the soldiers threw earth into the ditch and filled it up. Galiz Khan spent twenty lakhs of rupees in carrying out this measure.

Then Khaosar Khan, commander of the Khandar fort seeing that the moat had been filled up with earth, adopted a counter-device in his turn. He sewed up big cases of rhinoceros skin, stuffed them with powder, placed them in a row on the ditch and then set fire to them . The fire burnt up the ditch which resumed its previous shape. The earth thrown in by the imperialists was blown off to unknown quarters.

Being unsuccessful in capturing the fort by any means Galiz Khan reported the matter to the Badshah of Delhi. On the receipt of this intelligence the Badshah expressed his admiration for Galiz Khan saying:

> "The method adopted by Galiz Khan was excellent; but the one adopted by Khasar Khan was superior of the two. Praised be the counsellor! Praised be the commander!"

The Badshah thus showered heaps of praises upon Khosar Khan.

The emperor advised Galiz Khan to capture the fort by whatever contrivance he might adopt under the circumstances. Galiz Khan then adopted a fresh method, the moat was filled up once more by throwing in plantain trees and the bodies of elephants, horses, camels and buffaloes killed specially for that purpose. Seeing this, Khaosar Khan as before, stuffed skin bags with powder and set fire to them. What effect could the fire produce on objects which were so damp ? The fire only touched the surface and merely scalded them.

With this trick Galiz Khan conquered the fort. After the reduction of the fort, the commander attacked the Badshahi fort, where he fought for a long time without any success. At length an underground passage was dug up as far as the fort, and it was filled with loads of powder. On setting fire to the mines the fort was burnt down; and earth, elephants, horses, soldiers were all blown up. The imperial troops advanced along the path thus cleared and captured the fortress. Seeing the fall of the two advance forts, the commander offered his submission to Galiz Khan, who rewarded him with presents. The contest was now transferred to another Badshahi fort. Being unable to capture the same, Galiz Khan excavated a ditch which could be crossed by soldiers on horseback.

The imperial troops marched along the ditch and reached the precincts of the fort. The soldiers on horseback stormed the fort and occupied it after an engagement. The booty obtained at the four forts, consisting of elephants, horses, men, cows and other articles were sent to the Badshah at Delhi. Having received the intelligence of victory Shah Jahan despatched rewards of mansabs and presents.

On the receipt of the presents from the Badshah, Galiz Khan placed four nawabs in charge of the four forts of Khandar, and proceeded to meet Shah Shuja. The Prince honoured Galiz Khan with numerous presents and appointed him Subha of Khandar. He then returned to the presence of the Badshah at Delhi. This is how the fort of Khandahar was reduced.

Jahangir's Letter to his Rebellious Son Prince Khurram

Emperor Jahangir wrote the following letter to his son Sultan Khurram, afterwards Shah Jahan, when he, having quarrelled with his brothers Parvez and Khausru, wandered about raising the standard of revolt against the authority of his father and emperor, "Sultan Khurram, the captivator of the mind, like an idol of the eyes, son of an emperor who is the receptacle of good luck and who always treads on the spiritual path, you should note carefully, being anxious for the favour and blessing of the emperor as a token of his affection. Let shame be heaped upon that son who, deviating from the reverence shown by all good sons, stood aloof from the attitude of submission, by assuming hostility and declaring a revolt in the capital against his emperor and father. Has any son in this family attempted war against his father in the past ? If our son, endowed with luck and wealth, desires to wield his sword and conquer new territories, it is well and good, and who can object to such a course ? All right, he should now return to our presence and accompanied by the omraos, who are our well-wishers and benefactors, he should undertake a war expedition against the Badshahs of Irak and Abbas. They have dishonoured your father's coins, and your duty lies in dishonouring their coins in return.

On the other hand, is it proper on the part of dutiful sons to fight against their fathers for the sceptre, the umbrella and the throne ? Still more, the acquisition of the umbrella and the chamar does not rest with oneself. They are enjoyed by him alone upon whom God confers them. If the prince comes to the presence of the Emperor with a scarf round his neck and explains his condition, he may be again an object of our affectionate glance. What more can be written? One seeking his welfare will not long remain carefree.

Sultan Khurram's Reply

Sultan Khurram sent to Emperor Jahangir the following reply to the above letter ; when the emperor's letter reached the hands of Khurram he kissed and lifted it to his eyes and head; and while reading the same he bowed down at every letter, after which he penned the following note with due submission:

> "He, who is the pillar of the most excellent empire will, out of the abundance of his own love and affection, make my prayer fruitful. There is no one except Your Majesty to forgive the transgressions of my ignorant self, however unpardonable they might be. I have been a victim of shame and repentance since I took up an offensive and disloyal attitude towards you. Your feet alone can offer salvation to the sinful one. You have spoken of my displaying feelings of hostility and disaffection against my father and emperor. It is very astonishing that such an idea which was foreign to my heart has been attributed to me, ill-fated as I am."

As long as the Badshah enjoys bliss and happiness, nothing untoward and improper will spring from me. Did Sulaiman Paygambar suffer imprisonment in the hands of the ants in days of yore ? So, what power have I to quarrel with the emperor. As to the imputation that I am anxious for the throne, I want to say that I pray, may the emperor remain effulgent over my head by illuminating the umbrella and the throne as long as the moon and the sun exist, so that I may remain without any anxiety under the shadow of his umbrella-like feet. The Badshah may be pleased, as a token of his own magnanimity, to forgive whatever offence I might have committed. I have ventured to entertain such hopes at the two feet of the emperor.

You have said that a thing is enjoyed by one upon whom God confers it. To this I would say that if God has conferred the emperorship on Parvez, I have also been provided with my blood-drinking sword. Parvez has obtained the Badshahship from the emperor, while I have been subjected to false scandal and disgrace. If my sword, like a blood-sucking tiger, becomes appeased after tasting the blood of Khusru, then I shall not entertain any apprehension regarding Parvez. When Parvez has intended my ruin, it is not proper that I should remain inactive and careless. So I have come away being afraid of insult and humiliation.

In course of time it becomes necessary, I will certainly renounce my hostility; if, on the other hand hostility is intended, I will take it up without delay. Competent persons, after having served me, are offering their services at the two feet of the Badshah. Is all this proper ? As long as I do not become Badshah, I am at least under his authority and power.

> ''I have been asked to take up arms against Irak and Abbas. If under the command of the emperor, I, a Badshahzada wield the sword in a battle-field, I will not dread even mighty Badshahs. If all the duties and operations were entrusted to me at that time, the fort of Kandahar would not have fallen into the hands of the Badshah of Abbas from within a distance of eleven cubits. When the Deccanites rebelled, Parvez was in his mother's with extreme hardship and at the imminent risk of my life. How I captured the fort of Kankara, and how I converted to Islam the formidable enemies living in the recesses of hills and forests which had never before been subjugated by any one, is still talked of in Hindusthan and is also known at the two feet of the Badshah-Hazarat. If it is desired, the fort of Kandahar

resembling a mountain of rocky stones, will be destroyed immediately on my arrival. As long as I have the sword of Jahangir Badshah in my hands, I will not seek anybody's aid for the key to open the door of my prosperity."

The prince wrote in explanation of his intention after which he sounded a note of humiliation:

"Wandering on the whirlpool of life I have not been able to attain success in my enterprises, whether at the beginning or at the end. People living under my shelter have been protected and maintained in the past, while others have fled for their lives eluding the search of their pursuers. I am the most abominable slave of His Majesty; it is surprising that the Badshah has been affected by the revolt of such a negligible person. Just as the most powerful and princely falcons, which are a dread to all the birds, are captured in the net of the cruel hunter, I, a slave, wherever I may be, am in the sheath of Your Majesty. Regarding his desire to reinstate me in his special favour I beg to say that as I have been deprived of the opportunity of personally offering my obeisance to the Badshah, I only pray that the emperor may show me a great favour by desisting from pursuing my footsteps. What more punishment is necessary for me ? This has proved sufficient: what shall I write more? I pray that the Badshah will not take any umbrage against this mad one."

Shah Jahan's Letter to the Adil Shahi Sultan

During the reign of Emperor Jahangir the Adil Shahi sultans of the Deccan used to send annual presents and wakils with letters to the Mogul court. As they ceased to do so subsequently Shah Jahan Badshah despatched the following letter to the Adil Shahi ruler:

"Glory to the Almighty God, the fulfiller of all prayers, supplications and desires, who as a token of His extensive powers, has placed me in the exalted office of an emperor, out of a drop of water as it were."

It is extremely improper that the rulers of the dominions of Bijapur, Golconda and Bhagnagar, situated on the sea, have been circulating gajmohurs or independent coins in their realms, and looking upon one another as Badshahs like the bird Hud-hud. They should even now pay heed to my command. They could circulate Shah Jahani gajmohurs if they desire to save their necks; otherwise I will let loose all the swiftfooted and powerful kites of the world, the exterminators of the royal falcons, skilled in the extraction of skins and flesh with their sharp and pointed talons and beaks.

They should carefully give ear to the warning. They should not remain inactive like the hare, deer and *randra.* For this we have sent Muddhamatta (Muhammad) Khan accustomed to bring us glory (the chief among the omraos intelligent and efficient in action, who is near us in our confidential deliberations and) the disgracer of our enemies If you seek your welfare, you should carry out our wishes to the best of your ability. What shall I write more ? May your heart be gratified

Reply of the Adil Shahi Sultan

The Adil Shahi Badshah sent the following reply to the Emperor Shah Jahan:

> ''The only receptacle of adoration and praise is the fear-scaring feet of the Almighty God. All promises pertaining to one's duties should be made to Him alone, Who looks upon as dust all those who instal themselves on the pinnacle of the mountain of pride.''

On hearing and reading your message, unapproved by the wise and indicative of your self-esteem, laughter has been caused here in all quarters.

Besides, you have cited the instance of the kite and the Hud-hud. The story is as blatant as the sun and the moon. In the beginning of creation the bird Hud-hud was endowed with a variegated covering, and it was also made the lord of all with a crown on its head. This supremacy of the bird has prevailed automatically for many long ages. Though Mehtar Paygambar (God) conferred sovereignty on the kite for a couple of days, yet during the continuance of the order and rank fixed by the Ordainer of all things, can the kite, raised to eminence only recently, ever strike the Hud-hud with its claws?

In these circumstances, how can a new order of things supersede time-worn ordinances? Yes, the hare sleeps peacefully but it subsequently inflicts upon the pursuer considerable strain and disappointment. Hence, to those who have the welfare of their subjects always in their mind, the attempt.

The Nawabs of Dacca

Here follows an account of the Nawabs who ruled at Dhaka. Raja Mandhata, father of Raja Jai Singha who was the father of Raja Ram Singha, subdued Gaur at the instance of Jahangir Badshah, after which he proceeded to Dhaka and changed its name to Jahangirnagar. He remained there for some time, after which he went to the presence of the Badshah at Delhi, leaving Mus-haf Khan, a commander of 4,000 in charge of Dacca.

Having heard that Mus-haf Khan, a junior Umrao was placed in charge of Jahangirnagar, Emperor Jahangir asked the Wazir Mahmad Khan, "A junior Nawab like Mus-haf Khan is not fit to hold charge of Jahangirnagar. Bengal is a country so large that it deserves administration by a Badshah. The rajas and zemindars of that country are great *haramzadas* or scoundrels. So, you should arrange to send a commander of 6,000 to that place. One Burham Khan, a Dargahi and a commander of 6,000 who was the son of the nurse who had brought up the Emperor's son, was despatched as Governor. The son of a nurse is called Koka. This Burham Khan Koka came and stayed at Jahangirnagar. After this Jahangir died, and was succeeded by Shah Jahan, who deputed Nawab Islam Khan. The latter was subsequently removed and Ajan Khan appointed instead. When Shuja came to Rajmahal, Azam Khan's daughter became the chief begum of the Prince. Ajam Khan remained at Jahangirnagar.

Shaista Khan's Commercial Enterprises

On Aurangzeb's accession to the throne, Nawab Shaista Khan came to Jahangirnagar with his five sons, two sons-in-law, Nawab Nurulla Khan, Muhammad Maqim, Zohag Beg, and other mansabdars. He lived there for some years. Shaista Khan used to import by ship salt, supari or arecanuts and other articles, and sold them in Bengal on profitable terms. Besides, he accumulated seventeen crores of rupees by procuring two or three tolas of gold for one gold mohur. He also sold salt and supari to the merchants and traders in the city of Dacca. The latter were thus debarred from making purchases and sales on their own account.

Manowar Khan,[5] son of Masim Khan, Zemindar of Bengal, was despatched to the Badshah at Delhi as a prisoner chained in iron shackles with the charge that the administration of Bengal could not be carried on smoothly owing to his obstructive acts. The merchants and traders complained to the Badshah at Delhi regarding Shaista Khan's acts of injustice. Manowar Khan added to the allegations by saying:

> "O Padhsha-Hazrat, Shaista Khan has contrived to be as great as you are. He has become the Badshah of Bengal."

The Emperor became indignant and sent Manowar Khan as a prisoner to Gwalior saying:

> "However wealthy and prosperous Shaista Khan may be, he is still a subject of mine. He ventures to place Shaista Khan on the same level with me."

This incensed the Emperor, for which he sent Manowar Khan to Gwalior, which is a place where rebels are detained in custody.

The Badshah asked the Wazir as to the advisability of recalling Shaista Khan from Jahangirnagar. The Wazir, Amanat Khan, said,

> "It is not desirable that Shaista Khan should be withdrawn by levelling charges against him, as he is a benefactor of yours. You should call him back in a friendly way."

The Emperor wrote accordingly to Shaista Khan:

> "I am now old and so are you. Our days should be spent in devotion to God. Besides, you are a man of intelligence, and I desire to be absent from Delhi in order to subdue a few more Badshahs as I have a mind to die in the battle-field, leaving my eldest son Sultan Muhammad and yourself in charge of the affairs here. You should come back with all your relations."

Having received this *farman* or command Shaista Khan came back with his whole family. One Fede Khan Koka, son of Aurangzeb's nurse and a commander of 6,000 came to Jahangirnagar in place of Shaista Khan.

Sultan Azamtara at Dacca

Sultan Azamtara, son of Aurangzeb, received report from men that Bengal was an excellent place for hunting fish and deer; it also produced musk, agar and other precious articles. He said to his father that he wanted to go to Bengal, adding that Sultan Shuja had ruled there before. Prince Azamtara, accordingly came to Bengal in place of Fede-Khan Koka. He destroyed the quarters of Shaista Khan and erected his own residence at the same site.

There was an extensive marsh over which a river had flowed before. It was filled up with bamboos and woods which were purchased at a cost of 80,000 rupees; a market-place was constructed there with bricks and stones for the convenience of shopkeepers and tradeswomen. There were emporiums of salt worth 152,000 rupees at several places on the bank of the Bangsha river, which Shaista Khan could not transport. They were left in charge of one of his Mansabdar Khans who happened to be near. The Kotwal reported to the Emperor's son about this salt:

> "I want to deposit the salt at the sarkar or royal store-house. The place will be cleared as the salt depots have occupied a large area of land. We shall then get ample spaces for establishing markets and shops."

To this Azamtara replied:

> " Shaista Khan is a subject of ours. It will look odd if we appropriate his goods, and people will condemn this action of ours. To transact business with his commodity by sale or distribution befits a mean person. So, you should destroy the depots and pour down the salt into the river."

The Kotwal demolished the stores and threw the salt into the Bangsha river, and erected markets and shops in the place.

Sultan Azamtara, a Hunter

The Badshahzada appointed Mir Maulla his Dewan; and handed over the duties of the state to the Dewan and the Hazurnavis, Malukchand, and passed his days in hunting on horseback. Besides, he confiscated the household belongings of one Muhammad Maqim, a mansabdar in command of 700, on the pretext of an offence, and degraded him to the position of a mansabdar of 200. In this way he lived at Dacca for one year. The Barphukan[6] of Gauhati sent the following message to Mansur Khan and Baduli Phukan:

> "I am ready to surrender the fort (of Gauhati). Let Mansur Khan come."

This message was communicated to the Badshahzada, who summoned Mansur Khan overnight to his presence, and asked him to go to Gauhati. Mansur Khan replied:

> "I, an old subject of yours, intend to die on the battle-field. I am prepared to go to Gauhati if you send me there in the same rank and magnificence in which had proceeded Mirza Jahina, Majum Khan and Raja Ram Singha. Or if you send me alone, I am prepared to go in that manner. What objection could I have?"

The Badshahzada promised to confer on him the rank and precedence formerly allotted to Ram Singha, and asked him to go. Shahji and other mansabdars were despatched in the company of Mansur Khan who now came to Gauhati and took possession of the garrison which had already been evacuated by the Barphukan.

Prince Azamtara's Misrule in Bengal

Prince Azamtara had once gone out a-hunting. Alone he pursued a deer on horseback. He wended his steps homeward singly, being unattended by his follows, after bagging several deer and other animals. He had on his head an aigrette worth one lakh of rupees which fell somewhere in the jungle and was lost. On meeting the Prince the Dewan asked him where he had left the jewel. Azamtara felt his head and, not finding the jewel there, returned home.

The prince sent for the Zemindar in whose jurisdiction the jewel was lost, and asked him to recover it. The Zemindar sought for it without any success. The Prince extorted from the Zemindar one lakh of rupees as the price of the aigrette. One of the retainers of the Zemindar came upon the jewel and fled with it to Gujrat. On receiving this news, the Zemindar pursued the absconder and ultimately succeeded in recovering the gem from him. The jewel was returned by the Zemindar to the Badshahzada, who retained the jewel, but did not return the money.

Thus did Azamtara rule in Bengal. He neglected the duties entrusted to him by the emperor; he simply roamed about hunting on horseback. The loss of a jewel is highly inauspicious and objectionable. The waqayanavis wrote a detailed account of the incident to the Emperor at Delhi: and Aurangzeb being furiously annoyed recalled Prince Azamtara from Jahangirnagar. The Prince had offered to the newswriter a pony, with saddlery and harness worth one thousand rupees, requesting him not to communicate anything to the Emperor that would place the Prince in bad odour with his father; but the waqayanavis replied, "I can never be untrue to the salt of the Badshah;" and he sent his report to Delhi.

Shaista Khan again at Dacca

Shaista Khan was once informed by his Khezmatgar that Azamtara had thrown into the river all the salt that was stocked in the Nawab's emporium at Dacca, estimated at a value of 15,000 rupees. The Khazmatgar asked the Nawab to report the matter to the Emperor, at which Shaista Khan said:

> "Is the loss so significant that I should inform the Emperor about it? If I do so, it will not be safe for my children in future, as Azamtara may some day become the Badshah."

Shaista Khan then sought the mediation of the chief Begum and the Wazir, and he himself said to the Badshah:

> "I am now far advanced in years, and cannot even remain erect before His Majesty. Besides, I have constructed a tomb at Dacca with care for burying my remains. So I want to pass the few days of my life at Dacca."

Shaista Khan, accordingly came back to Dacca in place of Sultan Azamtara.

Distances from Delhi to other Important Places

Here follows a statement of the distances from Delhi to other places having thanas[7]

To Rasatpur	..	3 days,		0 *prahars*	and	4 *dandas*.	
" Agara	..	2	"	3	"	0	"
" Gulbah	..	0	"	0	"	5	"
" Ahmedabad	..	2	"	2	"	0	"
" Malpur	..	11	"	0	"	0	"
" Itlast	..	1	"	3	"	0	"
" Hariduwar	..	2	"	3	"	0	"
" Gharath	..	10	"	0	"	0	"
" Kanauj	..	5	"	2	"	5	"
" Hasana Abdal	..	11	"	0	"	0	"
" Karnat	..	1	"	2	"	4	"
" Bahrambad from Karnat		1	"			-	
" Garirdwar from Bahramabad		1	"	1		-	
" Kashmir from Delhi		12	"	2		-	
" Khayerabad or Naukhas		7	"	1	"	-	
" Hayedarabad		23	"	0	"	6	"
" Lakhirabad-thana		28	"	30	"	0	"

	to Samarkand							
"	Rohtap	..	6	"	3	"	0	"
"	Mathura	..	8	"	1	"	0	"
"	Bijaypur	..	22	"	1	"	4	"
"	Khangraka	..	23	"	0	"	0	"
	bilerbandar							
"	Dhameli	..	8	"	1	"	0	"
"	Marahat	..	7	"	3	"	0	"
"	Tajgaru	..	8	"	1	"	0	"
"	Muhmedabad	..	15	"	1	"	0	"
"	Sitabpur	..	2	"	1	"	0	"
"	Ajmer	..	5	"	0	"	2	"
"	Gujrat	..	16	"	0	"	2	"
"	Illahabad	..	8	"	2	"	..	
"	Nurnagar	..	2	"	3	"	..	
"	Sarat-bandar	..	19	"	2	"	0	"
"	Khidrabad	..	3	"	2	"	4	"
"	Laganpur	..	8	"	1	"	2	"
"	Ahal-Nagar	..	3	"	0	"	6	
"	Ilampur	..	..	"	7	"		
"	Lahore	..	6	"	2	"	4	"
"	Lahore (South City)	..	3	"	1	"	4	"

Distances from Agra to other Important Places

From Agara to Rabija	..	1	days	1	prahar	4	dandas
Do Gogarnagar	..	1	"	0	"	0	"
Do Ajmer	..	5	"	1	"	0	"
Do Raitap	..	0	"	2	"	4	"
From Agara to							
Do Saratpur-Sikeli	..	0	"	2	"	0	"
Do Islampur	..	1	"	2	"	0	"
Do Muhammadabad	2	"	"	..			
Do Ujjalpur	..	7	"	3	"	4	"
Do Amber	..	10	"	0	"	10	"
Delhi to	..	13	"	0	"	6	"
Agara to Prayag	..	6	"	0	"	0	"
Do Patna	..	2	"	2	"	0	"

Do	Burhanpur..	9	"	2	"	0	"
Do	Gwalior ..	2	"	0	"	0	"

Distances between other Places

	From Gwalior to Paradiksha	..	3	days	3	prahars	0	dandas.
"	Paradiksha to Barbara		2	"	2	"	0	"
"	Barbara to Burhanpur	..	2	"	2	"		
"	Kanauj to itast	..	1	"	1	"	0	"
"	Itast to Nadiya-tatu	..	1	"	0	"	0	"
"	Nadiya-tatu to Lahore	..	1	"	0	"	4	"
"	Aurangabad to Hasan Abdal		2	"	0	"	10	"
"	Kabirband-mahda		6	"	2	"	2	"
"	Gulasabad	..	4	"	0	"	0	"
"	Baraksal	..	28	"	0	"	0	"
"	Surbidpur	..	2	"	2	"	0	"
"	Kashmir and Bharatpur	..	4	"	0	"	0	"

Rajas and Zemindars who helped Jai Singha II

There is a leaf missing here, which would have given us a few more names of Rajas and Zemindars. The page begins by saying, ''500 horses and 500 camels, ''Which must be the equipment of some Raja mentioned in the missing leaf (Translator).

1 Raja Raorup Sing lived at patnagram at a distance of 9 days' journey, with 2,000 soldiers, 2 elephants, 250 horses and 300 camels.

2. Raja Gopal Sing lived at Karauligram at a distance of 20 days' journey, with 2,000 soldiers, 20 elephants, 300 horses and 2,000 camels.

3. Raja Rao-Kusal Sing lived at Zilagram at a distance of 12 days' journey, with 5,000 soldiers, 5 elephants, 250 horses and 200 camels.

4. Raja Dip Sing lived at Bhararigram at a distance of 4 days' journey, with 2,000 soldiers, 1 elephant, 200 horses and 300 camels.

5. Nawab Wajit Khan lived at Gosawaligram at a distance of 10 days' journey, with 5,000 soldiers, 5 elephants, 400 horses and 500 camels

6. Raja Gad Sing lived at Jauligram at a distance of 8 days' journey, with 2,000 soldiers, 1 elephant, 500 horses and 250

camels.

7. Raja Krishna Sing lived at Kutgram at a distance of 15 days' journey, with 2,000 soldiers, 2 elephants, 100 horses and 200 camels.
8. Raja Jalum Sing lived at Rajgargram at a distance of one month's journey, with 2 elephants, 500 horses and 250 camels.
9. Raja Bud Sing lived at Budigram at a distance of one months's journey, with 10,000 soldiers, 40 elephants, 200 horses and 1,000 camels.
10. Raja Indar Sing lived at Champargram at a distance of 9 days' journey, with 1,500 soldiers, 1 elephant, 200 horses and 210 camels.
11. Raja Bhawar Sing lived at Pehelegram at a distance of 20 days' journey, with 2,000 soldiers, 2 elephants, 300 horses and 210 camels.
12. Raja Badan Sing lived at Diggram at a distance of 25 days' journey, with 1,200 soldiers, 40 elephants, 1,000 horses and 10,000 camels.
13. Raja Suryyamal lived at Pratapgarh-gram at a distance of 25 days' journey, with 14,000 soldiers, 60 elephants, 2,000 horses and 250 camels.
14. Raja Pratap Sing lived at Bharathpurgram at a distance of 25 days' journey, with 5,000 soldiers, 15 elephants, 1,000 horses and 500 camels.
15. Raja Prataprai lived at Unaragram at a distance of 9 days' journey with 5,000 soldiers, 2 elephants, 500 horses and 300 camels.
16. Raja Syam Sing lived at Bachuagram at a distance of 3 days' journey, with 15,000 soldiers, 5 elephants, 500 horses and 1,000 camels.
17. Raja Bakat Sing lived at Ekbarpurgram at a distance of 4 days' journey, with 2,000 soldiers, 2 elephants, 200 horses, and 500 camels.
18. Raja Bano Sing lived at Bichangram at a distance of 2 days' journey, with 5,000 soldiers, 2 elephants, 1,000 horses and 2,000 camels.
19. Raja Pratap sing lived at Babaligram at a distance of 4 days' journey, with 2,000 soldiers, 1 elephant, 1,000 horses and 500 camels.

20. Raja Lal Sing lived at Antaragram at a distance of 5 days' journey, with 1,000 soldiers, 2 elephants, 1,000 horses and 800 camels.
21. Raja Jut Sing lived at Barialgram at a distance of 6 days' journey, with 3,000 soldiers, 2 elephants, 1,000 horses and 500 camels.
22. Raja Smram Sing lived at Atergram at a distance of 1 month's journey, with 1,200 soldiers, 40 elephants, 1,000 horses and 250 camels.
23. Raja Syam Sing lived at Majpurgram at a distance of 7 days' journey, with 2,000 soldiers, 1 elephant, 500 horses and 200 camels.
24. Raja Krit Sing lived at Kambangram at a distance of 29 days' journey, with 1,200 soldiers, 20 elephants, 1,000 horses and 1,000 horses and 1,500 camels.
25. Raja Baloram Sing lived at Bangargram at a distance of 1 month's journey, with 1,500 soldiers, 20 elephants, 1,000 horses and 1,000 camels.
26. Raja Bahadur Sing lived at Ghachieagram at a distance of 15 days' journey, with 5,000 soldiers, 15 elephants, 1000 horses and 1,400 camels.
27. Rao Guzarmal lived at Rewaligram at a distance of 20 days' journey, with 11,000 soldiers, 20 elephants, 500 horses and 2,000 camels.
28. Rao Brindaban Sing lived at Manoharpurgram at a distance of 2 days' journey, with 12,000 soldiers, 10 elephants, 1,000 horses and 1,500 camels.
29. Raja Kisor Sing lived at Marachgram at a distance of 2 days' journey, with 15,000 soldiers, 49 elephants, 2,000 horses and 6,000 camels.
30. Raja Eklakpa lived at Jarpurgram at a distance of 9 days' journey, with 7,000 soldiers, 5 elephants, 1,000 horses and 600 camels.
31. Raja Mirzabeg lived at Narnau at a distance of 3 days' journey, with 12,000 soldiers, 5 elephants, 1,000 horses and 1,000 camels.
32. Raja Jadu Sing lived at Terogram at a distance of 10 days' journey, with 12,000 soldiers, 5 elephants, 500 horses and 1,500 camels.
33. Rao Pheriram lived at Chatasgram at a distance of 2 days' journey, with 5,000 soldiers, 5 elephants, 500 horses and

1,000 camels.

34. Raja Malohar lived at Ramporagram at a distance of 2 months' journey, with 80,000 soldiers, 80 elephants, 500 horses and 8,000 camels.

The above Rajas gave their support to Sewai Jai Singh.

Legendary Kings of Kamarupa

Kamapristha extends from the Dui-muni-sila to the Manas river including the river Sonkosh in Kamapristha. The territory lying between the Bar-Sonkosh to the two extremities of Morung is known as Ratnapristha, while Bhadrapristha extends from the Kalong river to the Kailas river flowing in Kariabari. The region between the Dekkaravahini and the Dui-munisila is known as Saumarpristha. Mairanga Danava, son of Brahma, was the first ruler of these four pristhas. Mairanga Danava's son was Hatakasur, Hatakas' son Sambarasur Sambara's son Raktasur. Then ruled Narakasur of a different dynasty; he was succeeded by his son Bhagadatta whose son was Dharmapal, his son Karmapal, his son Prithvipal, his son Suvahu. The last ruled in an impolitic and unjust way at which Kamakhya became angry and drove him to Kailas.

Raja Dharmapal

One Dharmapal, a Khetri, came from Gauda and became King of Kamarupa. He erected his palace on the Godanda-parvat, and imported Brahmans, Kayasthas and Kalitas from the following six places, Gauda, Kanauj, Mandartala, Jabai-sahan, Tirhut and Baraka. With the above people he established a council of Pandits and continued to govern the country.

Kendu-Kalai Bapu

One Kendu-kalai Bapu used to offer worship to Kamakhya by singing devotional songs, at which the goddess became pleased and danced in utter nudity. Hearing this, the Raja begged the Brahman to show him the dance of Kamakhya. The Brahman promised to show him the dance and directed him to peep through a chink hole. Kendu-kali with other devotees clapped their hands and sang songs, and the goddess danced as usual. But, having caught a glimpse of the Raja through the hole, she was seized with shame, and fell flat on the ground, with her face downwards, bereft of her habiliments. She became wroth and cursed the King saying that any member of his family having a sight of her would perish instantaneously; she also cursed Kendu kalai, saying his line would be extinct.

Pratap Singha and Chandraprabha

Dharmapal's son was Raktapal, his son Somapal. His son Pratap Singha, who erected his capital at Kanyakagram. He subjugated the Bhuyans of Upper Assam, and became a great king by bringing them under his suzerainty. His son was Arimatta. One day Pratap Singh bathed in the Brahmaputra with his wife. At night Brahmaputra caused him to see a dream to the effect that the King should deliver his consort Chandraprabha to the river, threatening to destroy his kingdom by bringing in a deluge over his villages and towns in the event of non-compliance.

The nobles and ministers advised the King to renounce his affection for his consort, as it was for a wife of his that the country was on the verge of destruction. The King delivered the queen to the Brahmaputra, having put on her complete set of ornaments . After some time the Brahmaputra threw her on the bank at Amarajuri near Nilachal. A Brahman took the queen to his house and maintained her as his own daughter.

Arimatta Commits Patricide

Some time after the queen gave birth to a son. A serpent covered the new-born baby with its hood like an umbrella. The Brahman who had given shelter to the queen saw a dream prophesying that her son would become King of Kamarup. The prince's face and head looked like those of an *ari* fish for which he was named Arimatta.

After becoming King, Arimatta subdued the people around him and fought against his father Pratap Singha who was then reigning in Upper Assam, without knowing that his antagonist was his own father. Pratap Singha fell in the battle. On his return Arimatta communicated the intelligence of Pratap Singha's death to his mother, who having received the news, began to wail and narrated to her son the old story of the Brahmaputra. The son replied, 'It was unjust on his part to deliver you to Brahmaputra, and for this sin he has died unknown at my hands.'

Chandraprabha followed her husband on the funeral pyre, and Arimatta performed the expiation ceremony for killing his father unawares, as well as the funeral obsequies of Pratap Singha. He then became King of Kamarupa.

Construction of the Rampart Vaidyargarh

The he began to construct a rampart, having employed each of his subjects for one *prahar* by rotation. During the construction of the fort, poisonous insects and snakes used to kill the workers. A *vaidya* or physician exercised his virtues and said:

> "The snakes and insects will cease to kill men if they utter the name *vaidya*."

At this the body of workers shouted *Vaidya, Vaidya*, and thus escaped from death. So the rampart became known as *Vaidyar-garh*. Six scores of tanks were excavated within the walls of the fort.

Phingua's Conquest of Kamarupa

One Phingua Raja of the family of the Kings of Kamata, having subdued the territories commencing from Bihar , threw up stockades at several places in Dakhinkul. He erected a fort in the village Sonkuriha within the jurisdiction of Barbhag and waged a severe battle with Arimatta, Raja at Vaidyar-garh. Being unable to defeat Arimatta, Phingua negotiated with Arimatta's wife Raktamala who said:

> "He should fight when I send information after having rubbed my husband's bow strings with *Khar*, (an alkaline substance). Victory will then be achieved."

This was done, and then ensued the battle. The arrow would not shoot itself from the bow strings on account of the latters' oily character. Phingua won the day. Arimatta dived into the river and disappeared. Phingua then fetched Arimatta's wife Raktamala and killed her saying :

> " She has betrayed her own husband and how can we expect her to be faithful to us?"

Arimatta's son, Raktasingha, ascended the throne after having killed Phingua. The new king carried on a liaison with a Brahaman woman and consequently lost his kingdom on the curse of the Brahman who was thus wronged.

Revival of the Bara-Bhuyan's Supremacy

The Bara-Bhuyans then asserted their supremacy. They subdued the house of the Swarga-Maharaja and the Sandikais, and erected a fortress at Hathisal in Karaibari. They also subjugated Ghila Bijaypur and constructed roads and tanks in the vicinity of the Karatoya-Gangna.

After this one Masalanda Gazi of Bengal ruled here for some years. Then came Husain Shah Badshah's son Sultan Gayasuddin who died at Gadurachal. The Bhuyans attained suzerain power once again.

Rival Cooch Princes at the Mogul Court

Prince Cilarai or Sukladwaja, brother of Maharaja Naranarayan of Cooch Bihar died leaving a son named Raghudevnarayan. Naranarayan shifted his capital, as the Raja of Morung threatened an invasion of Bihar. Raghudev was with his uncle. Cilarai had the following Baras and Baruks or officers Kabindra Patra, Yudhisthir Bhandar Kayastha, Sri-rai Laskar, Kaipur Giri, Sonabar, Rupabar, Sardar Kabiraj, Gopal Chaulia, Gadai Barkayastha, Gadadhar Chaulia, Purandar Laskar as well as other.

They now said to Raghudev Patkowar or the heir apparent; If you remain like this you will always be subservient to the king Maharaja Biswa Singha at the time of his death had bestowed Bihar up to the Bar-Sonkos river upon Naranarayan, and the eastern portion of his kingdom upon Cilarai Diwan. We now propose to make you a Raja at Ghila so that you may become an independent monarch. Get possession by some means of your father's elephants horses and other provisions, and then come out on the pretext of a travelling excursion.

> Raghudev accordingly said to the Raja, "f your Majesty permits I intend to go out on a travelling expedition."
> The King replied, "I love you more than a son, so I have appointed you my heir apparent Do as you like."
> Raghudev said , "I want to take with me the officers, elephants horses and provisions belonging to my father."
> The King replied, "All that is mine is also yours, Take with you whatever you choose."

The Prince took with him his father's accoutrements and property, and after travelling for some time crossed the Sonkos river, and seeing that snakes were being eaten up by frogs he established his headquarter at Ghila. Naranarayan continued to remain at Bihar. In the meantime a son was born to Raja Naranarayan, and he was named Lakhshminarayan. Raghudev then deputed two Baras to Naranarayan with the following message:

> "The Maharaja has now been blessed with a son,. Nothing untoward will happen during the life time of the Maharaja; but after his demise things may not go so smoothly with his son. Two tigers cannot live in the same den. If the king approves of my leaving Bihar for good, he should appoint me king over the territory belonging to my father, according to the partition of the kingdom made by my grandfather. Then we shall all remain in peace and happiness ."

The King became pleased with this proposal, and said "my nephew has thought well. It is an excellent proposal." The King offered the royal sceptre, umbrella and throne to Raghudev and made him Raja with his headquarters at Ghila. There was no man so handsome and virtuous as Maharaja Raghudevnarayan and he ruled for thirty two years.

Hostility between Raghudev and Lakshminarayan

As Maharaja Naranarayan demanded tribute from Raghudev there was a war between the two, but it occurred only once. After the death of Naranarayan, Raghudev fought with his son Lakshminarayan. Raja Raghudev was defeated, and he returned to his territory, leaving behind his royal umbrella at Bihar. Lakshminarayan detained this insignia of royalty as a souvenir of his victory over Raghudev.

The defeated prince now conferred with his men, Sil Khan, Fateh Khan the King's son in law Purandar Laskar, Nitai Chandra Nazir, Thakur Panchananda, Kabindra Patra, Gadahdar Barua and other Baras and Buruks, as a result of which he made preparations for invading Bihar. Hearing this Lakshminarayan marched towards Ghila. Raghudev came out victorious and Lakshminarayan took to his heels after being repulsed. Raghudev Raja did not lose any of his Baras and Buruks.

Raghudevnarayan had the following sons: Parikshit, Indranarayan, Jadurai, Bhawa Singha, Mukundadev, Balinarayan, Man Singha, Maḥindra Singha, Gohain-Magal, Gohain-Raichanda, Sundarnarayan, Gohain-Maidan, Gohain Mehnarayan, Madhunarayan, Brishaketu, Ananta-narayan, Pratapnarayan and

Bijoy Singha. Maharaja Raghudevnarayan breathed his last on a full moon day in the month of Agrahayan.

Bilinarayan's Death

At the instigation of Parikshit, a Mech murdered Indranarayan by twisting his neck. Parikshit then ascended the throne. Hearing of this disturbance, Lakshminarayan entered Ghila by the gate of Kamakhya-guri. There followed a terrible battle, wherein Balinarayan, brother of Lakshminarayan, was transfixed by a spear at dusk by Parikshitnarayan's *dhali* or shieldsman Rupabar through ignorance, being taken for some unknown sardar. Then Rupabar came to know that it was no other than Balinarayan he unsheathed his sword and laid it before the prince, saying:

> "You are the brother of the King, and I, a *paik* or subject of yours, have wounded you. so you should cut me down with your own hand, by which my sin will be expiated."

To this Balinarayan replied:

> "What shall I gain by killing you? Besides, it will not be easy to save my life. You are permitted to commit even an act of unrighteousness if commanded to do so by the person whose salt you eat. More especially, you have slain me through ignorance, and so you are exempted from all guilt."

Saying this, Balinarayan breathed his last. Parikshit then removed the body of Balinarayan and cremated it with agar chandan according to the custom of the country. His bones were sent to Bihar. Twelve Karzis[8] including Para Karzi were captured in that battle.

Parikshit and the Karzis of Cooch Bihar

Parikshit's elephant named Mahindra-singha demolished the camp of Lakshminarayan. Parikshit also captured two elephants belonging to Lakshminarayan, who fled with his *mahadoi* or queen-consort. A Pathan of the camp of Parikshit intended to capture Lakshminarayan, but he was dissuaded by his master from doing so, who said:

> "My aunt is with the fugitive. I shall be reprimanded by people if I capture him at this stage."

Lakshminarayan, being thus defeated, returned to Bihar. The captive Karzis bowed down to Parikshit. But Para Karzi refused to do so. Parikshit said to Para Karzi:

> "All other Karzis have paid their obeisance to me. But you have not done so. What is the reason?"

To this Para Karzi replied:

> "With this head I have bowed down to Maharaja Lakshminarayan, and I cannot bow down to you."

The Raja became indignant, and ten stripes were inflicted on the Karzi daily. Still he did not pay his obeisance. Lakshminarayan then sent his Katakis or messengers to Parikshit, asking for the release of the Karzis. Parikshit demanded in turn his father's umbrella left behind at Bihar. Lakshminarayan returned the umbrella, and Parikshit made presents to the Karzis and gave them leave to depart. Para Karzi now bowed down to Parikshit, who said:

> "You did not bow down before. Why have you done so now?"

The Karzi replied,

> "To me you are the same as Maharaja Lakshminarayan. If I had bowed to you before, you would have attributed it to my fear for my life."

The Karzis then departed for their country.

Mukarram Khan's Expedition against Parikshit

Parikshit used to conduct a pillaging expedition to Bihar every year. Being unable to tolerate these oppressions, Lakshminarayan presented his daughter,[9] and offered his allegiance to the Badshah, with the complaint that he could not peacefully govern his kingdom on account of Parikshit. The Badshah despatched Nawab Mukarram Khan and twenty-two Omraos with Lakshminarayan, charging them to bring Parikshit as prisoner without taking his life.

During Mukarram Khan's march, the Raja of Susanga, Raghunath Rai, also complained [10] to him regarding Parikshit's frequent depredations. Mukarram Khan gave assurance to the Raja, who placed a contingent of his army under the command of the Nawab. Lakshminarayan also handed over his army and officer to Mukarram Khan and proceeded in advance to Bihar fearing that the city would be pillaged during his absence, as it was then empty.

War between Parikshit and Mukarram Khan

Mukarram Khan encamped at Dhubri. Parikshit despatched Fateh Khan of Phulaguri at the head of his troops and officers. There ensued a terrible battle with Mukarram Khan, in which the

Phulaguria Fateh Khan was captured. One Paramananda Doloi, who was on a war- elephant, died in the engagement. The elephant demolished a large number of camps, but it was subsequently captured.

Fighting on land remaining indecisive, there ensued a naval engagement. Purandar Laskar had a hard fight with Kuber Khan of the Bangals. Kuber Khan perished in the fight and Purandar destroyed a large number of the hostile camp. Then followed a battle with the son of Purandar fell in the battle.

After the death of Purandar, the Raja spent some time in negotiating through wakils, after which he retreated from the fight, crossed the Manah, and halted at a stockade erected at Sola. The Bangals also pursued the fugitive, and halted on the other side of the river.

Parikshit and Lakshminarayan before the Badshah

The nobles and ministers of Parikshit held a conference among themselves, at which they came to the following decision:

> "If the Raja surrenders to the Bangals, and govern the country as independent chiefs." With this intent they said to the Raja, "Save your Raj by offering submission, as we fear we shall not be able to oppose the Bangals in strength."

Wakils were despatched to Mukarram Khan with the message:

> "I promise to deliver to the Badshah an annual tribute consisting of 2 maunds of agar or lignum aloes, 100 elephants, 200 tangon ghoras or ponies, 500 *thungas* and *kamalis* or blankets, ,usks, and 400 yak- tails. I will give half of the obover presents to Mukarram Khan. I hope he will retire from the place."

To this Mukarram Khan replied:

> " It is not proper that I should do haram or injustice to the salt of the Badshah, and so I will not retire from here. All right, let the Raja himself come. There will be peace and concert if the Raja bows down to the Padshan. I also promise to the King, I will put forward my life first, irrespective of what may befall the Raja afterwards. The Badshah simply wants to see the Raja, having heard his name for a long time."

Then Parikshit, accompanied by his nobles and ministers, offered his submission to Mukarram Khan, who received the Raja with great honour, presented to him clothes and ornaments, and took him to the Badshah. On this side, Nawab Sayid Babakar or Abu Bakar remained at Hajo. Mukarram Khan took with him Lakshminarayan also, who offered his allegiance to the Emperor. The Badshah said to Lakshminarayan and Parikshit:

> ''You should both carry on your kingship being friends with one another. And Parikshit, Lakshminarayan is your *chacha* or uncle: bow down to him by touching his feet.''

To this Parikshit replied:

> ''What you have said is just and proper. An infuriated lion kills elephants as he chooses and eats them.''

Sometimes he desists from slaughter at the intercession of the female ones. The great ocean attains increase or decrease at the stipulated period. But men and animals are not subjected to increase or decrease through us. You are in that position too. There exists a feeling of animosity between himself and me. I will never lower my head to him not even at the cost of my life. The Badshah being indignant seized Parikshit and detained him.

The Cooch Bihar Princes Leave the Mogul Court

The Badshah gave leave to Lakshminarayan and said, You should ask me for things which are not available in your kingdom.'' The Raja replied, I have all things in my country, except *purud*, *kale* and *tarowal* or sword, and Iraki ponies. He was given leave to depart after being presented with horses and swords.

Mukarram Khan, interceding on behalf of Parikshit, procured his leave as well. The Badshah requested the Raja to ask for articles not found in his territory. Parikshit said:

> ''Everything is found in my kingdom. I would request the Badshah to give me a picture of His Majesty so that I may always salute it.''

The Badshah replied:

> ' We do not give our pictures to anybody and everybody. I give one to you on the understanding that you will refrain from any hostility to our family. If, on the contrary, you become unfriendly to us, you will be destroyed."

The Raja took leave and departed with due humility.

Parikshit Sent again to Delhi

Having heard of Parikshit's departure from the presence of the Badshah, the Baras and Baruks of Kamarupa wrote to Islam Khan, Nawab of Dacca, that they would flee from the kingdom if Parikshit returned. The Nawab also received intimation to that effect from the imperial court. When Parikshit reached Dacca, the Nawab said:

> "I hear Parikshit has brought a picture of the Badshah. When he comes to see me he should leave behind the picture as in the event of the picture being brought to the court, I shall have to leave my seat and bow down to it."

Parikshit did not pay heed to this advice, and he went to the presence of the Nawab with the picture, seeing whether the Nawab advanced from his seat and saluted it.

The Nawab flew into a rage, and wrote to the Badshah, and sent also the letter of the Baras and Baruks of Kamarup in which Parikshit was described as a *haramzada* . The Nawab also reported about Parikshit's harassing of the Rajas and Zemindars living in the neighbourhood of his territories adding:

> "These are the misdeeds of Parikshit. The Badshah has released a tiger of the woods after having captured him once. When he returns to the forest, the country is not to subsist."

The Badshah wrote to the Nawab asking him to send Parikshit again to His Majesty's Presence. The Nawab accordingly sent Parikshit to Delhi.

Parikshit dies at Tribeni

The Raja reached the pilgrimage of Tribeni, where he asked the Brahmans as to the resultant merits of a visit to that sacred place. The Brahmans replied, "Whatever desire a man cherishes here before death is attained. No sin accrues from suicide if committed in this place by him.' Having heard this the Raja said:

"No one gets an opportunity of visiting the pilgrimage, and how long does one's life exist ?"

With this vow he distributed charities and renounced his body. Kabi-sekhar, son of Kabindra Patra, Sriram Laskar and other companions of the Raja then went to the presence of the Badshah. The office of *Kanungui* of the vilayat Cooch Hajo was conferred on Kabi-sekhar. The Nawab gave leave to the other companions of the

Raja some of whom were appointed as Chaudhuris, some as Patwaris, and others as Laskars.

Cooch Hajo Under the Mughals

Sayyid Babakar pursued (the Assamese) from Hajo to Chamdhara. The soldiers of the Swarga Maharaja captured him at the latter place. Mirza Baqi then came to Hajo and stayed there for some time. He was turned out from the place, and Bahram Beg remained at Hajo. The latter was also removed, and Nawab 'Abdullah Islam remained at Hajo. Then Momai Tamuli an officer of the Swarga-Maharaja proceeded with Raja Dharmanarayan, and captured ' Abdullah Islam, who was sent to Garagram. The Dhekeri territory or Western Assam was given to Raja Dharmanarayan.

Ibrahim Karori Organises the Perganas

The Baruas and Baruks headed by Kabi-sekhar had taken leave of the Badshah and returned to their own country. They were accompanied by Sheikh Ibrahim Karori who came to reorganise the administration of the country.

During the Raja's reign, there were only *gaons* or villages, and no perganas, Sheikh Ibrahim introduced the pergana system. The whole area was designated Ullayat Cooch Hajo, which was divided into four sarkars - Sarkar Kamrup Sarkar Dhekeri, Sarkar Dakhinkul and Sarkar Bangalbhum.

Perganas of Sarkar Kamrup

The following were under Sarkar Kamsup Pergana Kowarbhag, Pergana Patidarang, Peergana Benbhag, Pergana Basa amalgamated with Banbhag, Pergana Bardarang, Pergana Bahabari, Pergana Satrajia, Pergana Chaurahi-khata, Pergana Kasimpur, Pergana Barbhag, Pergana Dehor, Pergana Khetribhag, Pergana Bajali, Pergana Bahukhata amalgamated with Bajali, Pergana Bausi, Pergana Barangar, Pergana Petkata amalgamated with Barnagar, Pergana Barpeta, Pergana Bejini, Pergana Phulaguri amalgamated with Bejini, Pergana Baska, Pergana Digjal, Kasbe Jajo Kasbe Gauhati, Rikab Mahal, Peshkosh Pandari or Barag mahal, Pumba-mahal, Gudara umananda, Hema-mahal, Maki-mahal, Chetal baxi Phara where elephants are captured by Khedda operations, Agadhubis, Nikathi-mahal, Paikan-mahal, Chutia-mahal Karkhana. There are altogether 41 mahals.

Perganas of Sarkar Dhekeri

The following perganas were in the jurisdiction of Sarkar Dhekeri;- Pergana Khutaghat, Pergana Guma, Pergana Parbatjowarm Pergana Kasbe Dhubri, Pergana Jamira, Pergana Taria, Pergana Ghurla, Pergana Jalkar-mahal, Pergana Kasbe Ghila, Pergana Chapgar, Pergana Resham-tati, Pergana Koknar, Pergana Khumar, Pergana Kath mahal, Pergana Kotwali, Perganna Dimyali-mahal, Pergana Dhamadi-mahal, Pergana Chulhat, Pergana Destalk-mahal. Altogether 10 mahals.

Perganas of Sarkar Dakhinkul

The following perganas were under Sarkar Dakhinkul: Pergana Sambhor, which had 5 *tapas* - Tape Bagaribari, Tape Samaria, Tape Bekeli, Tape Haljal Oza Kheli and Tape Tisimpur; Peragana pandu had 7 tapas, Tape Bangeswar, Tape Majhiali, Tape Chayania, Tape Beltola, Tape Bharuakata, Pergana Dumuria, Pergana Baranti, Pergana Mechipara, Pergana Kalmaluapara, Pergana Karaibari, Pergana Pumba Pergana Garo-mahal and Pergana Gorkati.

Perganas of Sarkar Bangalbhum

The following Perganas were under Sarkar Bangalbhum :- Pergana Baherbandh, Pergana Bhitarbandh, Pergana Gaybari, Pergana Choki- Baretala Chandiani. There are 75 mahals in the four sarkars mentioned above.

A Glossary of the names of Perganas

Sheik Ibrahim, coming from the imperial presence, reorganised the country by dividing it into perganas.

Bahbari -- There was in this pergana a clump of red bamboos with five or six joints at intervals of one cubit, watched by the Raja's officers, hence the pergana is called Bahabari or orchard of bamboos.

Darang --The expenses incurred in connection with the amusements of the country (were met from here), hence it is called Dar-rang literally, Price of amusements.

Kowarbhag. -- This place was governed by princes hence it is called Kowarbhag or princes' portion.

The Darang -- Pergana was made by combining a couple of villages from other perganas, and a few from Darrang.

Kachari-mahal -- It was so called because it was inhabited by the Kacharis.

Chutiya-mahal -- It was so called because it was inhabited by the Chutias.

Barbhag -- This was governed by princes who were labourers, hence it is called Ban bhag, or the portion of labour.

Dehor is so called because there were many devalayas or temples here. Khetri bhag is so called because it was inhabited by the Khetri -sepoys serving under the Raja.

Bajali is so called because it was enjoyed by one Bajalia(?) prince.

Baher-Khata was the pergana where the Khats or estates of princes and princesses were situated.

Phulaguri literally flower-land, is so called because there was a Kanakchampa plant here. An officer in charge of the royal revenue was stationed here.

Bausi was enjoyed by a queen mother, hence it is so called.

Bijini, literally a barber woman is so called as it was inhabited by the queen's barber woman who used to trim her finger-nails.

After this Raja Dharmanarayan governed the country. Mirza Jahina, Subha of Bengal, fought at Bare- Pointa. The Bangals and the Dhekeris lost a large number of their soldiers, and Mirza Jahina pursued his foes as far as Chamdhara but he had to come back to Gauhati being unable to stand against the forces of the Swarga-Maharaja. He hailed down to Bengal, having appointed Allah Yar Khan a Nawab.

References

1. Mannucci relates a similar experience of Shah Jahan when he proposed to payRaja Chattrasal Rae a visit to his country. *Irvine* II, p. 432.
2. Murchilli, see *Hobson-Jobson*, p. 586.
3. Naranarayan, King of Cooch-Behar, was a contemporary of Akbar and he died about 1584. It is not unusual to attribute the name of a famous king to his descendants as well. See my note on Hussain Shah, *Islamic Culture,* January 1929, page 29.
4. For Gakulpuri, see I.C., for October 1928, pp. 547-8.
5. Shah Safi or Safavi II was King of Persia, 1929-42; vide *Bernerl's Travels,* O. U. Press, II, p. 6. About Prince Shuja's expedition against Shah Safi, see *Maasir-ul-Umara,* Beveridge, p. 233.
6. Manowar Khan was the great-grandson of Ise Khan. He was a

Zemindar and an owner of numerous war boats, and was commonly known as the cruising admiral. He was attached to Mir Juma's expedition to Assam, and held change of the Mogul fleet at lakhangarh. A bazar near the Dacca railway station is known as Manowar Khan's Bazar.

7. This Barphukan was Laluk Sola, who surrendered Gauhati to Mansur Khan without fighting in lieu of a promise that Azmatara should make him king of Assam. Baduli Phukan was Mir Jumla's chief ally. He went to Bengal along with Mir Jumla and became the medium of all treasonable correspondence which Assamese officers had with Nawabs of Dacca.
8. This table can be compared with "Tables of distances in Hindustan" in British miles, from Agra, Delhi, Hyderabad, etc., in Rennell's "*Memoir of a Map of Hindustan*," See VII.
9. Viswa Singha, the founder of the Cooch Bihar dynasty, on ascending the throne in 1527 A.D. appointed his twelve principal followers as Karzis-Bhakura Karzi, Paro K., Nichila K., Churchal K., Satananda K., Megha K., Purandra K., Bhota K., Biru K., Sharanamk., Harish Chandra K., and Ripunjoy Karz. Their descendants also enjoyed the kerziship.
10. In *Ain-i-Akbari*, Blochman, Lakshmi Narayan gave his daughter to Man Singha, vol. I. 340. also J.A.S.B. 1872, p. 53.
11. For Parikshit's imprisonment of the family of Raghunath and the latter's complaint, see, *Padishah-nama*, quoted in J.A.S.B. 1872 p. 53.
12. According to the *Padishah-namah*, the articles offered by Parikshit to Mukarram Khan were 100 elephants, 100 tanghans (ponies) *J.A.S.B.* 1872, p. 54.
13. Koch Hajo almost coincides with the modern district of Gwalpara, Lower Assam, extending from above Hatisalah in the Karibari Hills and Pergana, on the left side of the Brahmaputra, along the bend of the river to Gwalpara.On the right side, it commenced north of the pargana of Bhitaraband and contained the district along the angle of the river as far as Parganah Khoon-taghas inclusively, with the towns of Dhubri and Rangamati. On the east Koch Hajo bordered on Kamrup, or that part of Assam which lies between Gawlpara and Guhati on both sides on the Brahmaputa." *J.A.S.B.* 1872, p. 50. But from the text it appears that from the time of Ibrhmin Karori, Koch Hajo included Kamrup which formed a separate sarkar. Sarkar Dakhinkul also included several parganas of Kamrup, Koch hajo was beself of Kamrup when the latter was governed by Raja Dharmanarayan or when it was conquered by the Ahoms, and thus it fell outside the hegemony of Moguldominion.

Bibliography

Primary Sources

Abbas Khan Sarwani, *Tuhfa-i Akbar Shahi,* Dacca, 1964.

Abdu'i-Baqi Nihawandi Khwaja, *Ma'asir-i Rahimi,* Calcutta, 1910-1931.

Abdu'i-Hamid Lahori, *Padshah-nama,* Calcutta, 1866-72.

Abdu'i-Karim Khwaja, *Bayan-i Waqi',* Lahore, 1970.

Abdu'i-Latif, *Ahmad-nama*, I.O., 1964.

Abdu'i-Qadir Bada'uni, *Muntakhab u't-tawarikh*, Calcutta, 1864-69; Vol. I, (English tr.) G.S.A. Ranking, Calcutta, 1895-99; Vol. II, W.H. Lowe, Calcutta, 1884-98; Vol. III, T.W. Haig, Calcutta, 1899-1925.

Abdu'i-Qadir Khan, Ja'isi, *Tarikh Imad al-Mulk,* Vol. VIII, Bankipur, 615.

Abdu'r-Razzaq Ishaq Samarqandi, *Matla'i sa 'dain wa-majma'-i, Baharin,* Ivanow, 1981.

Oriental College Magazine, Lahore, 1933.

Abdu'i-Fazi 'Allami, Shaikh, *Akbar-nama,* Calcutta, 1873-87. English tr. by H. Beveridge, Calcutta, 1897-1921.

A'in-i-Akbari, Lucknow, 1892 (English tr.), Vol. I, H. Blochmann, (2nd rev. edn.) D.C. Phillot, Calcutta, 1939; Vols. II and III (tr.), H.S. Jarrett and (revised) J.N. Sarkar, Calcutta, 1948.

Muktabat-i' Allami, Delhi, 1846.

Abdu's-Sattar B. Qasim Lahori, *Samratu'i-Falasifa,* Rampur MS.

Abu Nu'aim al-Isfahani, *Hilyat al-awliya',* 10 vols., Cairo, 1351-57/1932-38.

Abu Talib al-Makki, *Qut al-Qulab,* 2 vol., Cairo, 1306/1888-89.

Abu'i-Faiz Kamalu'd-Din Muhammad Ihsan, *Rauztu'i-Qayyumiyya,* Ivanow, Curzon, 82.

Ahmad, B. Muhammad Baqir al-Isfahani, *Mir'at al-ahwal-i-Jahan-nama,* Rieu, I, 385a.

Ahmad Tattavi, *Tarikh-i-Alfi,* Rieu, I, 199a, Ethe, 110.

Akhtar Wahid, Khwaja Mir Dard, *Tasawwufaursha'iri,* Aligarh, 1971.

Ali Muhammad Khan, *Mir'at-i Ahmadi,* Baroda, 1927-28, 1930.

Amin Ahmad Razi, *Haft Iqlim,* Tehran, n.d.

Amir, Shah Khan, *Amirui-Rawayat*, Saharanpur, n.d.

Amir Khwurd, *Siyar al-Auliya Fimahabbat u'i-Haqq jall wa'ala,* 1302/1885.

Anonymous, *A'ina-i Haqq-nama,* India Office, D.P., 259b.

Ansari, Muhammad Riza, *Bani-i dars-i Nizami,* Lucknow, 1973.

Aqil Khan Razi, *Waqi'at-i Alamgiri,* Aligarh, 1946.

Arif Qandahari, Muhammad, *Tarikh-i Akbari,* Rampur, 1962.

Asad Beg Qazwini, *Halat-i Asad Beg,* Rieu, III, 979b.

Aurangzib, *Adabi-i' Alamgiri*, Lahore, 1972.

Ruqa'at, Kanpur, 1879.

'Kalimat-i Tayyibat', *Bibilotheque Nationale,* Paris.

Azad, Mir Ghulam Ali, *Yad-ibayza',* Bankipur, VIII, 691.

Sarw-i Azad, Lahore, 1913.

Khizana-a'Amira, Kanpur, 1900.

Ma'asiru'i-Kiram, Lahore, 1971.

Subhat'u i-Marjan, Bombay, 1903.

Azad, Mawlana Abu'i-Kalam, *Tazkira,* Lahore, n.d.

Azar, Hajji Lutf Ali Beg, *Atash-Kada,* Bombay, 1277/1860.

Aziau'r-Rahman, Mawlana Mufti, *Tazkira-i Masha' ik-i Deoband,* Bijnor, 1950.

Babur, Zahiru'd-Din Muhammad, *Babur-nama*, Turkish Text, Leiden and London 1905, (English tr.), A.S. Beveridge, London, 1921, (reprint), Delhi, 1972.

Badakhshi, Hajji Muhammad Amin, *Manoqib-i Hazrat,* Author's Personal Collection.

Barnawi, 'Ala'u'd-Din Muhammad Chishti, *Chishtiyya-i bihishtiyya or Firdawsiyya-if Qudsiyya,* Punjab University, Lahore MS.

Bashiru'd-Din Ahmad, *Waqi-at-i daru'i Hukumat-i-Dihli,* Delhi, 1337/1918-1919.

Waqo'at-i Mumlikat-i Bijapur, Agra, 1915.

Faramini-i Salatin, Delhi 1944.

Bayazid Biyat, *Tazkira-i Humayuna wa Akbar,* Calcutta, 1941.

Bhim Sen, *Dilkusha,* Rieu, I, 271a.

Bhupat Ray, *Insha'-i Roshan-Kalam,* Aligarh MS.

Chand, Shaikh, *Sawda,* Delhi. 1940.

Chandrabhan Barahman, *Char Chaman-i Barahaman,* Rieu 838b.
Munsh'at, Lucknow, 1885.

Chaturman Kayath Sakesena, Ray, *Chahar-Gulshan or Akhbar Chawadir,* Bodleian, 264, (English tr. of Topographical and Statistical Portions) Jadunath Sarkar, Calcutta, 1901.

Chekhovich, O.D., *Samarqand Documents,* Moscow, 1974.

Danishmand Khan, Ni'mat Khan-i 'Ali, *Ruz-nama-i Waqa't' ayyamidarjuljihad,* Hydarabad, Kanpur, 1901.
Jang-nama, Kanpur, 1279/1862-62.
Bahadur-Shah-nama, Rieu, II, 745a.
Ni'mat-i'Uzma, Ivanow, Curzon, 337.

Farid, B. Shaikh Ma'ruf Bhakkari, *Zakhiratu'l-Khawanin,* 3 vols., Karachi, 1961-74.

Fazlu'llah al-Amin B. Ruzbihan, *Sulukue-muluk,* Tahskent MS. (English tr.), M. Aslam, Islamabad, 1976.
Milliman-nama-i Bukhara, Tehran, n.d.

Fayzi Sirhindi, Shaikh Ilahbad, *Akbar-nama,* Ethe, 289.

Firishta, M. Qasim Hindu-Shah Astarabadi, *Gulshan-i Ibrahimi,* Lucknow, n.d.

Gardizi, Fath 'Ali Hussaini, *Tajkira-i 'Ali-i Hussaini Gardizi,* Aurangabad, n.d.

Ghaziu'd Din Khan Firuz-jang, *'Imadud-Mulk, Manaqib-i Fakhriyya,* I.O. D.P., 728, Delhi, 1315/1897.

Ghulam Husain B. Hidayat 'Ali Khan, *Tarikh-i Muhammad-Shahi,* Asafiya MS.

Ghulam Husain Khan Jawhar, *Gulzar-i Asafiya,* Bombay, 1308/1891.
Tarikh-i Dil afruz, Asafiya MS.

Ghulam Husain Khan Tabataba'i, *Siyar al-muta' Ahkirin,* Lucknow, 1282/1866.

Ghulam Murtaza, *Basatinu'i-Salatin,* Hyderabad, Deccan, 1310/1892-1893.

Ghulam Sharafu'd-Din, *Ganj-i Fayyazi,* Cambridge University MS.

Gilani, Manazir Ahsan, *Tazkira-i Hazrat Shah Waliu'llah,* Hyderabad, Deccan, 1946.

Gulbadan Begam, *Humayun-nama,* London, 1902.

Hasan Beg Rumlu, *Ahsanu't-tawarikh,* Baroda, 1931.

Haydar, Sayyid Kamalu'd-Din, *Tarikh-i Awadh,* Rieu, III, 962b.

Haydar Malik, *Tarikh-i Kashmir,* Ethe, 2846.

Ibn Jubayr, *Rihla, Beirut,* 1389/1959.

Ikram, Shaikh Muhammad, *Ab-i Kawsar,* Lahore, 1975.
Rud-i Kawsar, Lahore, 1975.

Mauj-i Kawsar, Lahore, 1975.
Ishwar Das Nagar, *Futuhat-i' Alamgiri,* Rieu, I, 269a.
Iskandar Beg Munshi, *Tarikhi-i 'Alam-aray-i 'Abbasi,* Tehran, 1350/1971.
Jahangir, the Emperor , *Tuzuk-i Jahangiri,* Ghazipur and Aligarh, 1863-64, (English tr.) A. Rogers, (ed.) H. Beveridge, London 1909-14, (reprinted), New Delhi, 1978.
Jawhar Aftabchi, *Tazkiratu'i-Waqi'at,* Rieu, I, 246a.
Jur'at, Mir Hashim Musawi Khan, *Munshat-i Musawi Khan,* State Archives, Hyderabad, Deccan, MS.
Karl Jahn, Rashid u'd-Din's, *History of India,* the Hague, 1965.
Kashifi, Husain B. 'Ali Wa'iz, *Rawzat ush-shuhada*, Kanpur, 1891.
Mawahib-i 'Aliya, Lucknow, 1888.
Khafi Khan, Muhammad Hashim, *Muntakhabu'l-lubab,* Calcutta, 1850-1874.
Khaliq, Anjum, *Mirza Muhammad Rafi Sauda,* Aligarh, 1966.
Mirza Jan-i-Janan ke Khutut, Delhi, 1962.
Khwaja M. A'zam Dida-mari, *Woqi'at-Kashmir,* Lahore, 1303/1885-1986.
Khwurshah, B. Qubad al-Husaini, *Tarikhi-i Ilchi-i Nizam-Shah,* Rieu, Suppl., 32.
Lal Ram, *Tuhfatu'i-Hind,* Rieu, I, 236a.
Lutf, 'Ali Mirza, *Gulshan-i Hind*, Delhi, 1960.
Mir, Alam Abu'l-Qasim, B. Raziu'd-Din al-Musawi, *Hadiqatu'i-Alam,* Ethe, 465.
Mir, M. Amin Bukhari, *Ubaydullah-nama,* Tashkent MS.
Mir, Sayyid Muhammad Sha'ir, *Tabsirata'i-nazirin,* Rieu, III, 963b.
Mirza, Haydar Dughlat, *Tarikh-i Rashidi,* Rieu, I, 164b, English tr. by E. Denison Ross, London, 1898.
Mirza, Muhammad B. Mu'tamad Khan, *Tarikh-i Muhammadi,* Rampur MS.
Muhammad Aslam, *Farhtu'i-Nazirin,* John Ryland Library, Manchester MS.
Muhammad Baga, *Shaikh, Mir'atu'i-'Alam* Rieu, I, 1256.
Mir'at-i-Jahan-Nama, Rampur MS.
Muhammad Kazim Munishi, *Alamgir-Nama,* Calcutta, 1865-73.
Muhammad Murad, B. Shaikh Shihabud-Din, *A history of Aurangzeb's Successors,* Bodleian, 262.
Muhammad Sadiq Khan and Abu'i-Fazl Ma'muri, *Shahjahan-nama,* Rieu, I, 262.
Muhammad Salih Manbo Lahori, *'Amal-i Salikh,* Calcutta, 1912-36.

Murtaza Husain, *Hadiqat al-Aqalim,* Lucknow, 1881.

Mushtaqi Shaikh Rizaqullah, *Waqi'at-i Mushtaqi,* Rieu, II, 820b.

Musta'id Khan, Muhammad Sharif B. Dust M., *Iqbal-nama-i Jahan-giri,* III, Lucknow, 1870, Allahabad, 1931.

Mawdudi, Mawlans Abu'l-'Ala', *Tajdid wa Ihya'i-Din,* Lahore, 1953.

Mazhar Baqa, *Usul-i Fiqh aur Shah Waliu'llah,* Islamabad, 1973.

Mihr, Ghulam Rasul, *Saiyid Ahmad Shahid,* Lahore, n.d.

Mirza' Ali Lutf, *Gulshan-i Hind,* Hyderabad-Deccan, 1906.

Mufti Muhammad Ghulam Sarwar, *Hadiqatu'i-Auliya',* (2nd edn.),1976.

Muhammad Ihsanu'llah Gorakhpuri, *Sawanih 'Umri Hazrat Mujaddid Alf-i Sani,* Rampur, 1926.

Muhammad Iqbal Mujaddidi, *Ahwal wa Asar-i 'Abdu'llah Khweshgi Qasuri,* Lahore, 1972.

Muhammad Latif, *Auliya'-i Lahore,* Lahore, 1962.

Muhammad Miyan, *Ulama-i Hind ka Shandar Mazi,* 4 vols., Delhi, 1957-60.

Muhammad Qasim, Nanawtawi, *Qibla-nama',* Deoband, 1969.

Muhammad Tayyib, *Daru'i-'Ulu Deoband,* Karachi, 1972.

Mujibu'i-Hassan, *Sufiyya-i Wududi,* Delhi, 1366/1946.

Nami, Mir M. Ma'sum, *Tarikh-i Sind,* Poona, 1938.

Nadwi, Saiyid Abu'i-Hassan 'Ali, *Sirat Saiyid Ahmad Shahid,* Karachi, 1974-75.

Naqwi, Sayyid Ghulam 'Ali Khan, *'Imadus-sa'adat,* Lucknow, 1864.

Nawwab Dargah Quli Khan Salarjang, *Muraqqa'i Delhi,* Hyderabad-Deccan, n.d.

Ni'matullah B. Habibullah al-Harawi, *Tarikh-i Khan-Jahani wa Makhzan-i Afghani,* Decca, 1960.

Nisyani, Mir Tahir Muhammad, *Tarikh-i Tahiri,* Hyderabad, Sind, 1964.

Nizami, K.A., *Shah Waliu'llah ke Siyasi Maktubat,* Aligarh, 1950.

Hayat-i Shaikh 'Abdu'l-Haqq Muhuddis Dihlawi, Delhi, 1953.

Tarikh-i Masha-ikh-i Chishti, Delhi, 1953.

Nizamu'd-Din Ahmad, Khwaja, *Tabaqat-i Akbar Shahi,* Calcutta, 1913, 1927, 1931.

Nizamu'i-Mulk Tusi, *Siyasat-nama,* Tehran 1320/1920-3, (English tr.) H. Darke, The Book of Government, London, 1960.

Nu'mani, Muhammad Manzur al-Furqan, *Mujaddid-i Alf-i Sani Nambar,* Bareilly, 1357/1937.

Tazkira-i Imam-i Rabbani Mujaddid-i Alf-i Sani, Lucknow, n.d.

Nur Ahmad, Chishti, *Tahqiqat-i Chishti,* Lahore, 1964.
Yadgar-i Chishti, Lahore, 1975.

Nuru'i-Haqq al-Mashriqi al-Dihlawi al-Bukhari, *Zubadatu't-tawarikh,* Rieu, I, 224b.

Qalqashandi, *Subhu'l-A'sha,* 14 Vols., Cairo, 1914-28.

Qazi, Jawid, *Afkar-i Shah Waliu'llah,* Lahore, 1977.
Barr-i Saghir men Muslim Fikr ka Irtiqa', Lahore, 1977.

Qazwini, Mirza Muhammad Amin, *Badshah-nama,* Rieu, I, 258b.

Quddusi, Fijazu'-Haqq, *Tazkira-i Sufiya'i-Sind,* Karachi, 1959.
Tazkira-i Sufiya'-i Panjab, Karachi, 1962.
Tazkira-i Sufiya'- i Bangal, Lahore, 1965.
Tazakira-i Sufiya'-i Sarhad, Lahore, 1966.

Quraishi, 'Abdu'l-Razzaq, *Mirza Mazhar Jan-i Janan aur unka Kalam,* Bombay, 1961.
Makatib-i Mirza Mazhar, Bombay, 1966.

Rafi'u'd-Din Ibrahim Shirazi, *Tazkiratu'l-Muluk,* Rieu, I, 316a.

Rahim Bakksh Dihlawi, *Hayat-i W'ali,* 2nd edn., Lahore, 1972.
Hayat-i Tayyiba, Lahore, 1976.

Rashidu'd-Din Fazlu'llah, *Jamit'u't-tawarikh,* Tehran, 1338/1970, English tr. by J.E. Boyle, New York and London, 1971.

Sadiq Sadiqi, Mirza Muhammad, *Subh-i Sadiq,* VI, Bankipur, 471-74.

Shah-Nawaz Khan, Nawwab 'Abd al-Rahman, *Mir'at-i Aftab-nama,* Aligarh, MS.

Shahid, Muhammad Isma'il, *Taqwiyat al-Iman wa Tazkirat al-Ikhwan.*
Kalam-i Shah Isma'il Shahid, Lalitpur, 1974.

Shakir Khan, *Tarikh-i Shakir-Khani,* Rieu, I, 279b.

Shamsu'r-Rahman, *Shah Waliu'llah ke 'Umarani Nazariye,* Lahore, 1968.

Shirani, Mazhar Mahmud ed., *Maqalat-i Hafiz Mohmud Shirani,* 6 Vols., Lahore, 1966-72.

Sikandar, B.M. Manjhu, *Mir'at-i Sikandari,* Bombay 1890.

Sujan Ray Bhandari, Munshi, *Khulasatu't Tawarikh,* Delhi, 1918.

Syed Ahmad Khan, Sir, *Tazkira-i Ahl-i Delhi,* Karachi, 1955.

Tahmas Khan, *Tahmas-nama,* Rieu, III, 980b.

Talish, Shihabu'd-Din Ahmad, *Fathiya-i 'Ibriya,* Bodleian, 240.

Thaneswari, Muhammad Ja'far, *Hayat-i Saiyid Ahmad Shahid,* Karachi, 1968.

Maktubat-i Saiyid Ahmad Shahid, Lahore, 1969.

Tattawi, Mir 'Ali Sher Qani, *'Tuhfatu'l-Kiram,* Hyderabad, Sind, 1971.

Ubaydu'llah Sindhi, *Shah Waliu'llah aur unka Falsafa,* 3rd edn., Lahore, 1946.

Shah Waliu'llah aur unki Siyasi Tahrik, 2nd edn., Lahore, 1945.

Tasawwuf ke Adab wa Ashghal Lahore, 1946.

Wali, Mir Abu Turab, *Tarikh-Gujarat,* Calcutta, 1909.

Wali'ullah Dihlawi, Shah, *Tafhimat-i Ilahiyya,* Hyderabad, Sind, 1970.

Iqd al-jidd fi Bayan Ahkam al-ijtihad Wa't-taqlid, Delhi, 1310/1892.

Sarf-i Mir, Delhi, n.d.

Al-musaffa, Delhi, n.d.

Al-insaf fi bayan -i Sabab al-ikhtalaf, Delhi, 1935.

Sharh Tarajama Ba'z abwab Bukhari, Hyderabad-Deccan, 1949.

Risala-i Danishmandi, Lucknow, 1894, at the margin of the *Wasiyatnama.*

Husn u'l-'aquida, Delhi, n.d.

Maktubat, ma' Manaqib-i Bukhari wa Fazilat-i Ibu Taymiyya, Delhi, n.d.

Al-Muqaddimt al-swnniya fi'l-intisar li-i firaqa al-Sanniya, Asafiya MS.

Al-durr al-samin, Delhi, n.d.

Al-irshad ila muhimumat 'ilm al-isnad, Lahore, n.d. *Muktubat,* Rampur MS.

Warid, Muhammad Shafi, *Mir'at -i-Waridat,* Bodleian, 424.

Tarikh-i Chaghatay, Rieu, III, 924b.

Yusuf Mirak B. Amir Abu' i-Qasim Namkin in Bhakkari, *Mazhar-i Shahjahani,* Hyderabad, Sind, 1962.

Yusuf Salim Chishti, *Anwar-i Mujaddidi,* Lahore, 1961.

Zahiru'd-Din, Saiyid Ahmad, *Kamalat-i 'Azizi,* Karachi, 1972.

Zaidpuri, Ghulam Husain Khan Salim, *Riyazu's -Salatin,* Calcutta, 1902-1904.

Zawwar Husain Shah, Saiyid, *Hazrat Mujaddidi Alf-i Sani,* Karach, 1972.

Zubaidi, Sayyid Murtaza, *Ithaf al-Sadat at-Muttaqin,* 10 vols., Cairo, 1311/1893-94.

Secondary Sources

Afifi Abu'l-' Ala, *The Mystical Philosophy of Muhiy'd-Din Ibnu'l 'Arabi,* Cambridge, 1939.

Ahmad, Aziz, *Studies in Islamic Culture in the Indian Environment,* Oxford 1964.

Alger, *Religion and State,* nd.

Anawati, G.C. and Louis Gardet, *Mystique Musulmane,* Paris, 1961.

Ansterdam, D., *Historical Atlas of the Muslim People,* Amesterdam, 1957.

Arberry, A.J., *The Docrines of the Sufis,*(tr., of Kalabadhi's Kitab alta Aruf), Cambridge, 1935.

An Introduction to the History of Sufism, London, 1942.

Pages from the Kitab al-luma, London, 1947.

Sufism: An Account of the Mystics of Islam, London, 1950

(ed.), *The Mystical poems of Ibn at-Farid,* Dublin, 1956.

Classical Persian Literature, London, 1958.

The Ruba'iyat of Jalalu'd-Din Rumi, London, 1959

(tr.), *Discourses of Rumi,* London, 1961.

Tales from the Matnawi, London, 1963.

Mare Tales from the Mathnawi, London, 1963.

Muslim Saints and Mystics, London 1964.

Aspects of Islamic Civilization, Ann Arbor, 1963.

Mystical Poems of Rumi, Chicago, 1968.

(ed.), *Religion in the Middle East,* 2 vols., Cambridge, 1969.

A Sufi Martyr, London, 1969.

Arnold, Sir Thomas, *The Preaching of Islam,* (reprint), Lahore, 1956.

The Calilhate, (rev. edn.), London, 1965.

Athar 'Ali, *Mughal Nobility under Aurangzeb,* Bombay, 1968.

Bagley, R.R.C. (tr.), *Ghazali's Book of Counself for Kings,* Oxford, 1964.

Basham, A. L. (ed.), *A Cultural History of India,* Oxford, 1975.

Boyle, J.A. (ed.), *The Cambridge History of Iran,* Cambridge, 1968.

Browne, E.G., *A Literary History of Persia*, 4 vols., (reprint), Cambridge, 1957.

Burton, Sir Richard, *Sind and Races that Inhabit the Valley of the Indus,* London, 1851.

Calverley, Edwin Elliot, *Worship in Islam* (being a translation with Commentary and introduction of al-Ghazzali's book the *Ihya'on the Worship,* Madras, 1925.

Corbin, H, *Avicenna and the Visionary Recital,* (tr.), W. Trash,New York and London, 1960.

Confessions Extatiques de Mir Damad, Melanges Louis Massing non, I, France 1965, pp. 331-78.

Imagination Creatrice Et priere Ereatrice dans le Soufisme di'ibn 'Arabi', Eranos Jahrbuch, XXV, 1956, pp. 122-240.

Divine Epiphany and Spiritual Rebirth in Ismaliian Gnosis', Man and Transformation, New York and London, 1964, pp. 69-160.

Etude preliminaire pour le'Livre reunissant les deux sagesses', de Nasir-e Khosraw, Tehran and Paris, 1953.

L'ismaelisme et le symbole de la Croix', La Table Ronde, Paris, December, 1957, pp. 122-34.

Les Motifis Zoroastriens dans la philosophie de Sohrawardi, Tehran, 1946.

Recherches sur l' hermeneutique lutherienne' in Annuairde l'Ecole des Hautes Etudfs Section des Sciences Religieuses, Paris, 1939, pp. 99-102.

Terre celeste et Corpus de resurrection: de l'Iran mazdeen a l'Iran Shi'ite, Paris, 1961.

Histoire de la Philosophie islamique, Paris, 1964.

(ed.), *Opera Metaphysica et Mystica,* vol. I. Istanbul, 1945, Vol. II, Tehran, 1952.

Czaplicka, M.A., *The Turks of Central Asia in History and the Present Day*, (Reprint), Amsterdam, 1973.

Dawud, Rahbar, *God of Justice,* Leiden, 1960.

De Laet, *Description of India and Fragtment of Indian History,* (tr.), J.S. Hoyland and (annotated) S.N., *The Political Systems of Empire,* New York, 1963.

Faris, Nabith A., *The Book of Knowledge*, (tr., of a chapter of Chazali's Ihya'), Lahore, 1962.

The Foundations of the Articles of Faith, (tr., of a chapter of Ghazali's Ihya'), Lahore, 1963.

The Mysteries of Alms, (tr., of a chapter of Ghazali's Ihya'), Beirut, 1966.

Faruqi, Bhrhan Ahmad, *The Mujaddid's Conception of Tauhid,* Lahore, 1940.

Faruqi, Ziya'u-i Hasan *The Deoband School and the Demand for Pakistan,* Bombay, 1963.

Field, Cland H., *Al-Ghazali: The Alchemy of Happiness,* London, 1910.

Mystics and Saints of Islam, London, 1910.

Foster, W., *The English Factories in India,* 13 Vols., Oxford, 1906-27.

Flynn, *V*.J.A., *Fathpur-Sikri,* Bombay, 1975.

Francois Bernier, *Travels in the Mogul Empire,* 1656-58 (tr.), *A. Constable* (ed.), V.A. Smith, London, 1916.

Friedmann, Johanan, *Shaykh Ahmad Sirhindi: An outline of his thought and a study of his image in the eyes of posterity,* Montreal, 1971.

Frykenberg, R.E. (ed.), *Land Control and Social Structure in Indian History,* Wisconsin, 1969.

Gairdner, W.H. Temple, *Al-Ghazzali's Mishkatu'l-Anwar, The niche for lights,* London, 1915.

Gibb, H.A.R, *Islamic Society and the West*, London, 1960.

Gilsenan, Mechael, *Saint and Sufi in Modern Egypt: An Essay in the Sociology of Religion,* Oxford, 1973.

Gullaume, A., *The Legacy of Islam*, London, 1952.

Halepota, A.J., *Philosophy of Shah Waliu'llah,* Lahore, n.d.

Haq. M. Anwaru'l *The Faith Movement of Mawlana Muhammad Ilyas,* London. 1972.

Haqq, En'amul, *Muslim Bengali Literature,* Karachi, 1957.

Hasan, Ibn, *The Central Structure of the Mughal Empire* (reprint), New Delhi, 1980.

Hasrat, B.J., *Dara Shikuh: Life and Works* (reprinted), New Delhi, 1982.

Hodgson, G.S., *The Order of Assassin,* The Hague, 1955.

Holt, P.M., Lambton, A.K.S. and Lewis, B., *The Cambridge History of Islam,* Cambridge, 1970.

Husaini, S.A.Q., *The Pantheistic Monism of Ibn al-' Arabi,* Lahore, 1970.

Ikbal 'Ali Shah, Sardar, *Islamic Sufism,* London, 1933.

Ikram, S.M., *Muslim Civilization in India,* New York.

The Cultural Heritage of Pakistan, Karachi, 1955.

Iqbal, Sir Muhammad, *The Development of Metaphysics in Persia* (reprint), Lahore, 1964.

Six Lectures on the Reconstruction of Religious Thought in Islam, Lahore, 1930.

Irfan Habib, *The Agrarian System of Mughal India,* Bombay, 1963.

Irvin, W., *Later Mughals* (reprint), New Delhi, 1971.

Izutsu, Toshihido, *A Comprehensive Study of the Key Philosophical Concepts of Sufism and Taoism,* Tokyo, 1966-67.

Ethico-religious Concepts in the Quran, McGill, 1966.

Ja'far Sharif, *Islam in India, or the Qamun-i Islam,* (tr.), G.A. Herklots (ed.), W. Crooke, Oxford, 1921 (reprinted), New Delhi, 1972.

Jalbani, G.N., *Teachings of Shah Waliyullah of Delhi* (2nd edn.), Lahore, 1973.

Khaja Khan, *Studies in Tasawwuf,* Madras, 1923.

Khuda Buksh, S., *The Orient under the Caliph,* Delhi, nd.

Khushwant Singh, *A History of the Sikhs,* Vol., 1469-1839, Princeton, 1963.

Leake, W.M., *Journal of Tour in Asia Minor,* London, 1824.

Lewis, Bernard, *Islam,* New York, 1974.

Landau, R., *The Philosophy of the Ibn'Arabi,* London, 1959.

Lings, Martin, *A Sufi Saint of the Twentieth Century* (2nd edn.), London, 1971.

Lkram, S.M., *Muslim Civilization in India,* London, 1964.

McCarthy, R.J., *The Theology of al-Ash'ari,* Beirut, 1953.

MacDonald, D.B., *The Religious Attitude and Life in Islam,* Beirut, 1965.

Manucci, N., *Storia do Mogor,* 1653-1708 (tr.), W. Irvine, London, 1907-8 (reprint), New Delhi, 1980.

Massignon, L., *La passion d'al-husayn Ibn Mansour al-Hallaj,* 2 vols., Paris, 1922.

Essai sur les origines de lexique technique de la mystique musulmane, Paris, 1928.

Mayne, P., *Saints of Sind,* London, 1965.

Meer Hassan Ali, *Observations on the Musulmans of India,* 2 vols., London, 1832.

Mir Valiuddin, *Love of God,* Hyderabad-Deccan, 1968.

Mohaghegh, Mahdi and Landolt, *Collected Papers on Islamic Philosophy and Mysticism,* Tehran, 1971.

Mohan Singh Diwana, *An Introduction to Punjabi Literature,* Amritsar, 1951.

Shikh Mysticism, Amritsar, 1964.

Mohiuddin Ahmad, *Saiyid Ahmad Shahid,* Lucknow, 1975.

Mole Marigan, *Les Mystiques Musulmans*, Paris, 1965.

Monserrate, Fr. A., *Commentary* (tr.), J.S. Holyland and (annotated),

S.N. Banerjee, Cuttack, 1922.

Moreland, W.H., *India at the Death of Akbar*, London, 1920.

From Akbar to Aurangzeb, London, 1923 (reprint), New Delhi, 1972.

Mujeeb, M., *The Indian Muslims,* London, 1969.

Nageeb al-Attas, Syed, *The Mysticism of Hazmali Fansuri,* Kualalumpur, 1970.

Raniri and the Wajudiyyah of 17th Century Acheh, Singapore, 1966.

Some Aspects of Sufism as Understood and Practised among the Malays (ed.), S. Gordon, Singapore, 1963.

Preliminary Statement on a General theory of the Islamization of the Malay-Indonesian Archipelago, Kualalumpur, 1969.

The Origin of Malay Sha'ir, Kualalumpur, 1968.

Concluding Postscript to the Origin of the Malay Sha'ir, Kualalampur, 1971.

Nasr, Seyyed H., *Three Muslim Sages,* Cambridge, Mass., 1964.

An Introduction to Islamic Cosmological Doctrines, Cambridge, Mass., 1964.

Science and Civilization in Islam, Cambridge, Mass., 1966.

Ideas and Realities of Islam, London, 1966.

Sufi Essays, London, 1972 (ed.), *Isma'ili Contributions to Islamic Culture,* Tehran, 1977.

Nicholson, R.A., *The Mysteries of Islam,* London, 1914.

Studies in Islamic Mysticism, 1921, (reprint), Cambridge, 1967.

The Idea of Personality in Sufism, Cambridge, 1923.

A Literary History of the Arabs, Cambridge, 1930.

Tales of Mystic Meaning, London, 1931.

A Persian Forerunner of Dante, Tocoyn-on-Sea, 1944.

Rumi, Poet and Mystic, London, 1950 (ed.), and (tr.) *Selected Poems from the Divan-i Shams-i Tabriz,* 1898 (reprinted), Cambridge, 1961.

Nyberg, H.S., *Kleinere Schrifteu des Iban 'Arabi*, Leiden, 1919.

Padwick, C.E., *Muslim Devotions,* London, 1960.

Palamer, E.H., *Oriental Mysticism: A treatise on the Sufistic and Unitaian Theosophy of the Persians*, 1867 (reprint), London, 1969.

Petersen, E.L., *Ali and Mu'awiya in early Arabic Traditions,* Copenhagen, 1964.

Philips, E.C. (ed.), *Politics and Society in India,* London 1963.

Qanungo, K.R., *Dara Shikoh,* Calcutta, 1935.

Qureshi, I.H., *The Administration of the Sultanate of Delhi,* Karachi, 1944 (reprinted), New Delhi, 1971.

The Muslim Community of the Indo-Pakistan Subcontinent, The Hague, 1962.

The Administration of the Mughul Empire, Karachi, 1966.

Rafiqi, A.Q., *Sufism in Kashmir,* Delhi, 1977.

Raverty, H.G., *Selections from the Poetry of the Afghans,* London 1862.

Richards, J.F., *Mughal Administration in Golkonda,* Oxford, 1975.

Riazu'l Islam, *Indo-Persian Relations,* Tehran/Lahore, 1970.

Rizvi, S.A.A., *Muslim Revivalist Movements in Northern Indian in the Sixteenth and Seventeenth Centuries,* Agra, 1965.

Religious and Intellectual History of the Muslims in Akbar's Reign, Delhi, 1975.

A History of Sufism in India, Vol. I, Delhi, 1978.

Shah Wali Allah and His Times, Canberra, 1980.

Shah 'Abd al-Aziz, Canberra, 1982.

Rosenthal, E.I.J., *Political Thought in Medieval Islam* (reprint), Cambridge, 1962.

Russel, Ralph and Khurshidu'l Islam, *There Mughal Poets,* Cambridge, Mass., 1968.

Sadarangani, H.I., *Persian Poets of Sind,* Karachi, 1956.

Sadiq, M., *A History of Urdu Poetry,* London, 1964.

Saksena, B.P., *History of Shahjahan of Dihli,* Allahabad, 1958.

Saksena, R.B., *A History of Urdu Literature,* Allahabad, 1927.

Saran, P., *Provincial Government of the Mughals,* Allahabad, 1941.

Studies in Medieval Indian History, Delhi, 1952.

Schacht, J., *The Origin of Muhammadan Jurisprudence,* Oxford, 1950.

Schimmel, A., *Islamic Literatures of India, Sindhi Literature, Classical Urdu Literature, in J. Gonda, History of Indian Literature,* Wiesbaden, 1973-75.

Gobriel's Wing, Leiden, 1963.

Mystical Dimensions of Islam, Chape Hill, 1975.

Pain and Grace, Leiden, 1976.

The Triumphal, Sum, London, 1978.

Sharif, M.M., *A History of Muslim Philosophy,* 2 vols., Wlesbaden.

Sharma, R.S. and Jha, V. (Ed.), *Indian Society: Historical Probings,* Delhi, 1974.

Sharma, S.R., *Mughal Government and Administration*, Bombay, 1951.
The Religious Policy of the Mughal Emperors, (2nd edn.), London, 1962.

Shehadi, F., *Ghazali's Unique Unknowable God*, Leiden, 1964.

Shejwalker, T.S., *Panipat: 1761*, Poona, 1946.

Shemesh, A.B., *Taxation in Islam* , Leiden, 1958, 1965.

Sherwani, H.K., *The Bahmanis of the Deccan*, Hyderabad-Deccan, 1953.
Muhammad Quli Qutb Shah, Bombay, 1968.
Cultural Trends in Medieval India, Bombay, 1968.

Siddiqi, M.Z., *Hadith Literature*, Calcutta, 1961.

Smith, M. Rabi'a, *The Mystic and her Fellow Saints in Islam*, Cambridge, 1929.
An early Mystic of Baghdad, Cambridge, 1920.
Studies in early Mysticism in the Near and Middle East, London, 1931.
Al-Ghazali: the Mysic; London, 1944.
The Sufi Path of Love, London, 1954.
Readings from the Mystics of Islam, London, 1950.

Soerly, H.T., *Shah 'Abdu' i Latif of Bhit: His Poetry, Life and Times*, 1940, (reprint), Oxford, 1966.

Spear, P., *Twilight of the Mughals*, (2nd edn.), Cambridge, 1969 (reprint), New Delhi, 1970.

Storey, C.A., *Persian Literature: A Bibliographical Survey*, London, 1927-58.

Subhan, J.A., *Sufism: Its Saints and Shrines*, 2nd edn., Lucknow, 1960.

Sufi, G.M.D., *Kashmir*, Lahore, 1940-49.

Tarachand, *Influence of Islam on Indian Culture* (2nd edn.), Allahabad, 1963.
Society and State in the Mughal Period. Delhi, 1961.

Tavernier, Jean-Baptiste, *Travels in India*, 1640-67 (tr.), V. Ball (ed. and revised), W. Crooke, London, 1925, (reprinted), New Delhi, 1977.

Temple, R.C., *Legends of the Punjab*, London, 1893-1901.

Thevenot, Jean de., *Relation dei'Indostan*, 1666-67 (tr.), Lovell (edn.), S.N. Sen, *The Indian Travels of Thevenat and Careri*, New Delhi, 1949.

Thomas, R.C., *Legends of the Punjab*, London 1893-1901.

Thomas, W.F., *Mutual Influence of Muhammedans and Hindus in India,* Cambridge, 1892.

Titus, M., *Indian Islam,* Milford, 1930 (reprinted), New Delhi, 1979.

Tod, J., *Annals and Antiquities of Rajashtan,* Oxford, 1920.

Trimingham. J.S., *The Sufi Orders in Islam,* Oxford, 1971.

Tripathi, R.P., *Some aspects of Muslim Administration* (2nd edn.), Allahabad, 1959.

Tritton, A.S., *The Caliphs and their non-Muslim Subjects,* Oxford, 1930.

Underhill, E., *Mysticism: A Study in the Nature and Development of Man's Spiritual Consciousness,* Paperback, New York, 1956.

Vaudeville, Charlotte, *Kabir,* Vol. I., Oxford, 1974.

Wahed Husain, *Administration of Justice during the Muslim Rule in India* (reprint), Delhi, 1977.

Waheed Mirza, *The Life and Works of Amir Khusrau,* Calcutta, 1935.

Walker, B., *Hindu World,* London, 1968.

Wang Gungwu (ed.), *Self and Biography,* Sydney, 1974.

Watanmal, L., *The Life of Shah'Abdul Latif,* Hyderabad, Sind, 1889.

Watt, M., *The Faith and Practice of Al-Ghazali,* London, 1953.

Muslim Intellectual: A Study of al-Ghazali, Edinburgh, 1963.

Wensinck, A.J., *The Muslim Creed,* Cambridge, 1922.

Whitting, C.E.J., *Al-Fakhri,* London, 1947.

Wolfson, H.A., *The Philosophy of the Kalam,* London, 1976.

Yusuf Hussain, *L'Inde Mystique au Moyen Age,* Paris, 1929.

Glimpses of Medieval Indian Culture (2nd edn.), Bombay, 1959.

Yusuf Iblish and Peter Lambron Wilson, *Traditional Modes of Contemplation and Action*, Tehran, 1977.

Zaehner, R.C., *Hindu and Muslim Mysticism,* London, 1960.

Ziadah, N.A., *Sanusiyah: A Study of a Revivalist Movement in Islam,* Leiden, 1958.

Zubaid Ahmad, *The Contribution of Indo-Pakistan to Arabi Literature* (2nd edn.), Lahore, 1968.

Index